Qualities of food

C000097221

Published in our
centenary year
∽ **2004** ∾
MANCHESTER
UNIVERSITY
PRESS

New Dynamics of Innovation and Competition

The series New Dynamics of Innovation and Competition, published in association with the ESRC Centre for Research in Innovation and Competition at the University of Manchester and UMIST emanates from an engagement of the Centre's research agenda with a wide range of internationally renowned scholars in the field. The series casts new light on the significance of demand and consumption, markets and competition, and the complex inter-organisational basis for innovation processes. The volumes are multi-disciplinary and comparative in perspective.

Series editor:
Mark Harvey, Senior Research Fellow at CRIC

Qualities of food

edited by
Mark Harvey
Andrew McMeekin
Alan Warde

Manchester University Press
Manchester and New York

distributed exclusively in the USA by Palgrave

Published by Manchester University Press
Oxford Road, Manchester M13 9NR, UK
and Room 400, 175 Fifth Avenue, New York, NY 10010, USA
www.manchesteruniversitypress.co.uk

Distributed in the United States exclusively by
Palgrave Macmillan, 175 Fifth Avenue,
New York, NY 10010, USA

Distributed in Canada exclusively by
UBC Press, University of British Columbia, 2029 West Mall,
Vancouver, BC, Canada V6T 1Z2

British Library Cataloguing-in-Publication Data is available

Library of Congress Cataloging-in-Publication Data is available

ISBN 978 0 7190 6855 3 paperback

First published by Manchester University Press in hardback 2004

This paperback edition first published 2013

Printed by Lightning Source

Contents

List of tables and figures   *page* vi

Series foreword   vii

List of contributors   viii

Preface   ix

Introduction   *Mark Harvey, Andrew McMeekin and
Alan Warde*   1

1 Discovering quality or performing taste? A sociology of
   the amateur   *Geneviève Teil and Antoine Hennion*   19

2 Standards of taste and varieties of goodness: the
   (un)predictability of modern consumption   *Jukka Gronow*   38

3 Quality in economics: a cognitive perspective   *Gilles Allaire*   61

4 Social definitions of *halal* quality: the case of Maghrebi
   Muslims in France   *Florence Bergeaud-Blackler*   94

5 Food agencies as an institutional response to policy failure
   by the UK and the EU   *David Barling*   108

6 Theorising food quality: some key issues in understanding its
   competitive production and regulation   *Terry Marsden*   129

7 A new aesthetic of food? Relational reflexivity in the 'alternative'
   food movement   *Jonathan Murdoch and Mara Miele*   156

8 The political morality of food: discourses, contestation and
   alternative consumption   *Roberta Sassatelli*   176

Conclusion: quality and processes of qualification
Mark Harvey, Andrew McMeekin and Alan Warde   192

Index   209

Tables and figures

Tables

6.1 Estimated incidence of Sass in seven European countries
(1998) *page* 140
6.2 Socio-economic impact levels of SFSCs in seven European
countries (1998) 142
6.3 Hierarchies in the regulation of food quality 152

Figures

6.1 Different mechanisms for extending SFSCs in time and space 133
6.2 Different quality definitions employed within SFSCs 135
6.3 Opening up the quality food spectrum: the SFSC battleground 137
8.1 The domain of alternative consumption 187

Series foreword

The CRIC–MUP series New Dynamics of Innovation and Competition is designed to make an important contribution to this continually expanding field of research and scholarship. As a series of edited volumes, it combines approaches and perspectives developed by CRIC's own research agenda with those of a wide range of internationally renowned scholars. A distinctive emphasis on processes of economic and social transformation frames the CRIC research programme. Research on the significance of demand and consumption, on the empirical and theoretical understanding of competition and markets, and on the complex inter-organisational basis of innovation processes provides the thematic linkage between the successive volumes of the series. At the interface between the different disciplines of economics, sociology, management studies and geography, the development of economic sociology lends a unifying methodological approach. Strong comparative and historical dimensions to the variety of innovation processes in different capitalist economies and societies are supported by the international character of the contributions.

The series is based on international workshops hosted by CRIC which have encouraged debate and diversity at the leading edge of innovation studies.

CRIC is an ESRC-funded research centre based in the University of Manchester and UMIST.

Contributors

Gilles Allaire Unité d'Economie et Sociologie Rurales, Institut National de la Recherche Agronomique, Paris

David Barling Department of Health Management and Food Policy, City University, London

Florence Bergeaud-Blackler ESRC Centre for Research on Innovation and Competition, University of Manchester

Jukka Gronow Department of Sociology, Uppsala University, Sweden

Mark Harvey ESRC Centre for Research on Innovation and Competition, University of Manchester

Antoine Hennion Centre for the Sociology of Innovation, Ecole des Mines de Paris

Terry Marsden School of City and Regional Planning, Cardiff University and Centre for Business Relationships, Accountability, Sustainability and Society (BRASS)

Andrew McMeekin ESRC Centre for Research on Innovation and Competition, University of Manchester

Mara Miele School of City and Regional Planning, University of Cardiff and Department of Agronomy and Agro-ecosystem Management, University of Pisa

Jonathan Murdoch School of City and Regional Planning, Cardiff University

Roberta Sassatelli School of Economic and Social Studies, University of East Anglia and Dipartimento di Discipline della Comunicazione, Universita of Bologna

Geneviève Teil Systemes Agraires et Developpement – Attitides, Produits, Territoires, Institut National de la Recherche Agronomique, Paris

Alan Warde Department of Sociology and ESRC Centre for Research on Innovation and Competition, University of Manchester

Preface

This book arises from the proceedings of one of a continuing series of international workshops organised by the UK Economic and Social Research Council-funded Centre for Research on Innovation and Competition. Principal themes of CRIC's research programme include markets and competition, consumption practices and the development of the service economy; the workshop, which was held in January 2002, was mounted to promote discussion of those topics in the field of food, and focused on various aspects of production and consumption.

We express our thanks to the authors who contribute to this book. We thank also other participants of the workshop whose comments have been incorporated in the text during the revision of the preliminary papers. Our gratitude goes to Sharon Hammond and Deborah Woodman for the vital part they played in organising the workshop, to Philippa Grand who prepared the typescript for the publisher and to the staff at Manchester University Press who processed the book.

Introduction

Mark Harvey, Andrew McMeekin and Alan Warde

Food and quality

Food in late modern societies is marked by controversy. It was never a matter of indifference, of course, in other times and places. Yet, with the food supply secured in the western world against the seasons, pestilence and drought, with most foods wholesome, and mostly available at affordable prices, its significance as a topic of political argument must appear somewhat surprising. Subject to enormous scrutiny – in the media, through political disputation and by cultural evaluation, as well as in everyday conversation – it is a field of contrary opinions.

The unifying theme of this book is a highly contentious issue, that of the use of the intriguing concept of *quality*. 'Quality' is one of those words with unfailingly positive connotations. True, it may be prefixed by terms like 'poor', 'bad' or 'inferior', but in the absence of such qualification the intimation is wholly positive. To say that something 'has quality' is almost always to recommend it. As an abstract noun the capacity of 'quality' for recommendation is blanket, yet implicitly there is always contained a reference to some particular attribute or attributes. A 'quality steak' is one which is, let us say, tasty, tender, or both. Having the quality 'fresh' precludes the quality frozen, but says nothing about the qualities of, for example, safeness or toxicity, or whether it is factory-made or home-made. Most foodstuffs have several relevant quality attributes.

In many contexts there is advantage to be had, for food producers or advocates, in concentrating attention on just one attribute, or, in some instances – if one can make the argument stick – on none at all. One example discussed in the book is the notion of 'quality chains', a label that small farmers have deployed as part of a strategy to sell products with comparatively high value-added, but one which is substantively empty without specification of the attributes to which reference is being made. Being locally produced, from an identifiable source and involving face-to-face contact between producer and retailer are the presumed relevant attributes. Acceptance of the claim entails acquiescing in the judgement that such produce is in some way better than produce accessed in other ways. But the making of that judgment is potentially obscured, and the claim might easily be accepted without reflection. In other words, the term 'quality' is one which enmeshes tightly, though not inextricably, the empirical and the normative: it refers to particular attributes (qualities) of a product and at the same time makes a presumptive judgement that is positive. This is precisely the type of concept that social scientists must handle with care. One danger is actually accepting uncritically the normative claim. Another is underestimating the importance of examining the means by which such claims are generated, established and defended. It is this second task which provides the central connecting theme of this book.

Because it is about judgement in contexts where there is no final and definitive arbiter of the most relevant quality or the absolute standard whereby better or worse can be identified, the concept of quality performs some of the functions – and poses some of the problems – associated with *taste*, a concept which has received a great deal of attention over the past 250 years. Indeed, several of the chapters in the book focus directly on taste. Debates about taste are about standards of judgement, mostly of an aesthetic nature, and concern ways in which to validate a claim that one thing is more worthy or more beautiful than another. The advent of postmodernism made answering that question even more difficult than it had been, by challenging the basis of an established cultural hierarchy, whereby, as Bourdieu might put it, the preferences of the powerful were canonised as good taste. Certainly it is no longer easy to accept older conceptions of good taste which, Gronow (1997) reminds us, was portrayed as ineffable, indivisible, unquestionable, embodied by persons who somehow inherited impeccable judgement and whose judgements were therefore not open to dissection into component parts which might be scrutinised forensically and held up to challenge. Instead, to look more closely for the grounds on which aesthetic judgements are routinely made suggests a route forward.

Quality is, arguably, a more useful term than taste because it is much easier to see that judging X to be of good quality refers to one or, usually, more *qualities* in which X excels. Moreover those qualities are not just aesthetic, for the term also applies to effective social performances of several kinds, including fitness for purpose. When a producer refers to the quality of a product, it is as likely that the reference is to one 'well-made' or functionally appropriate as it is to its taste. In relation to food, this draws our attention to the various qualities, or dimensions of quality, which may be the basis of recommendation. We can easily recognise that any item may be good with respect to one quality and bad with respect to another. Foods which are tasty but unhealthful provide a common example. It is also easy to be alert to the fact that a producer is likely to draw the public's attention to the first property, while the nutritionist will highlight the second. Public health and economic competitiveness thus partly revolve around persuading people to prioritise one quality over another. That still, however, leaves open the difficulty of determining whether in respect of any one quality an item is excellent, mediocre or poor. Who shall say? What criteria shall we use?

Chapters in the book offer various answers to these questions, answers dependent partly on theoretical and disciplinary traditions, partly on the techniques of investigation selected.

It is the normative, or evaluative, sense of the term 'quality' that inspires popular and public debate. Its increasing use might be understood in terms of crises of confidence in the food supply. The term has come to refer to foods, or processes of production and distribution of foods, which operate beyond or alongside of the industrialised system of large-scale production, preparation through manufacturing, and distribution through large super-market chains. The term 'quality chain' implicitly attributes high quality to locally produced and marketed food, a strategy of small producers according to Marsden (chapter 6). In this context the idea of quality plays mostly on a contrast with the orientations of the mainstream industrialised food system towards low cost, convenience, consistency, reliability and predictability. Yet a moment's reflection suggests that these, too, are 'qualities', and indeed ones with positive valence. Quality is, thus, to be associated not only with an authentifiable place of origin, knowable and traceable sources of supply, and exceptional flavour and texture, but with guarantees regarding safety, nutri-tiousness and accessibility. It might be more appropriate, unless we can demonstrate that some qualities are more valuable than others, to say simply that the industrial food chain is directed towards different aspects of quality. Certainly, at the outset, we should be cautious lest we slip unawares between the descriptive and the normative registers of the concept, thereby implying that those things not labelled of quality are inferior or defective.

The crisis of confidence in the food industries of Europe is remarkable. The population of western Europe is probably better fed now than ever before: the supply chain is reliable, secure and capable of furnishing widely diverse foodstuffs in support of many different diets and culinary prefer-ences. Yet there is widespread popular mistrust of the food supply which finds expression most obviously over matters of safety, where BSE, foot and mouth disease, chemical contamination, E-coli, dioxins, Salmonella, etc., pose direct threats to human health. This might imply that we should think of food as a very special case of consumption because of the obvious threat to health arising either from being without food or from food being adulter-ated. One can starve or be poisoned. But this in no measure accounts for the level of concern shown regarding food provision. Arguably the field of food provision has become one of the most controversial in the political arena and at the level of everyday life. But that this can be attributed primarily to crises and scandals regarding safety is a moot point. Though several papers attrib-ute considerable importance to highly publicised episodes like BSE, none presumes that this is a sufficient basis for the current attention to food. For many other changes in the organisation of the food system have occurred independently. Some are to be found in the upper reaches of the food supply chain, a result of globalisation of sourcing, transformation in the agro-food industry, concentration of food manufacturers and distributors, and the like.

Others appear as paradoxes of behaviour in everyday life. People in Britain watch many more cookery programmes and buy more cookery books, but they cook less than do their fellow Europeans. They have access to a better regulated and much more varied supply of food, yet are more likely to suffer from food disorders like obesity and anorexia, and to adopt highly specialised diets. And, important to this book, they are prepared to engage in public and collective action to express their discontent with existing provision and to advocate alternative modes of food supply. In the latter regard, we can see changed behaviour on the part of ordinary people: perhaps the emergence of a degree of critical reflexivity on the part of many citizens, from mothers to gourmets; new forms of informal collective organisation claiming to act in the interests of the consumer (not just the consumer associations, but also the Slow Food and Fair Trade movements, etc.). A vocal minority devotes considerable energy to bringing to light the deficiencies of the agencies involved farther up in the food chain, making their voice heard in political circles and media debates, and changing their personal eating habits and diets. Food is not a matter of indifference to the public. People are concerned about food – though that concern is not necessarily expressed in the stereotypical economics model of the consumer – and are constantly involved in evaluating it.

As the chapters of the book indicate, there are many dimensions of concern besides that of safety. The predicted epidemic of obesity means that the consequences for nutrition and health of eating currently available food are deeply problematical. Other people worry about the culinary and aesthetic value of foodstuffs. And there are movements for animal welfare which raise ethical questions about the propriety of the practices of major actors in the food chain. Then there is the environmental damage that modern large-scale farming techniques bring. All these exist on top of more mainstream concerns with the price of food, with the level of profit and the degree of oligopoly in the various markets which constitute the food chain. Food has many qualities which attract public attention.

The issue of food quality is widely construed as closely involving the consumer. The problem that has arisen from food crises is described as the decline of consumer trust or confidence. And it is at the points of transfer to and use by consumers that the issue of quality actually bites. New strategies for developing trust, from European Commission (EC) policies designed to increase the openness and transparency of the food chain to attempts to reduce the distance and number of steps between farm and fork – described in chapter 6 as the spread of short supply chains – apparently give great priority to consumers' concerns and interests. (The extent to which this is a matter more of rhetoric than of substance is, of course, much debated.) Thus the analysis of quality cannot be far separated from the analyses of consumers and consumption. Indeed, each chapter of the book makes extensive reference to consumption, conceived either as purchase or use of commodities. Several of the authors take it almost for granted that understanding food preferences is just a particular case of the more general question 'How do people come to select what to consume?' Answering that question has, however, proved notoriously difficult. The approaches of such disciplines as psychology, economics and sociology have traditionally been very different (see Miller 1995). And the more the consumer becomes a focus of political discourse, the greater the apparent confusion.

Arguably western Europe has seen recently a blurring of the boundaries between politics and shopping. The distinction between exit and voice as alternative strategies for the discontented (Hirschman 1982) used to be applied without hesitation to contrast two different circumstances, between withdrawing one's custom in a market relationship (exit) and vocally expressing one's opposition in a political relationship (voice). That separation is now much harder to achieve. There are two opposing views of how demands might be made for improvements in particular quality dimensions. First, some activists and analysts think that there is a role for highly active consumers to make personal everyday purchasing decisions which would express political convictions. The attempts to persuade people to become 'green consumers' was based on just such a model. On the other hand, rather than trying to politicise purchasing decisions, there are attempts to make political action more like the process of purchasing. In addressing citizens, political parties and governments have tried to draw them into politics as if they were consumers. Burgess (2001) makes a good case that governments are increasingly speaking as representative of 'the consumer' – rather than the nation or its social classes – a tendency which addresses citizens as individuals rather than as members of social groups and categories. They are also increasingly designing policies to model public service delivery on market discipline. Thus the boundary between public and private becomes less clear.

In the understanding of 'the consumer' that lies at the core of official recognition and policy formulation in this field there is an associated problem. The dominant view of consumer freedom and consumers' interest as the right to purchase whatever they please in a free market, a view overwhelmingly dominant in the USA (Cohen 2000; Cross 2000) and increasingly so in Europe, is predicated on the tenets of orthodox neo-classical economics. Consumption is seen as a realm of individual autonomy, and one where it is to be expected than rational individuals will act in accordance with what they take to be their personal self-interest. Consumption involves disparate individuals making decisions in the light of their personal preferences. But while this may be a model of action necessary for purposes of neo-classical macroeconomic analysis, it is a very strange representation of what most people do most of the time when going to market. That this model is at all plausible seems to be a matter of temporal and spatial circumstances of contemporary western economies. There are other ways of thinking about consumption.

For instance, historians have recently been making a major contribution to the understanding of the construction of the consumer (for a review see Trentmann forthcoming). They show the elimination of alternative ways to understand the role of consumers and how that has made for a particular form of contemporary consumer politics. Cohen (2000: 204) makes a rather ungainly distinction, but one which is very effective, between citizen–consumers and customer–consumers: the former are

> consumers who take on the political responsibility we usually associate with citizens to consider the general good of the nation through their consumption, and the latter . . . consumers who seek primarily to maximise their personal economic interests in the market place.

The move in the mid-1980s to appeal to the consumer in public service delivery is the latest stage in the shift from consumption as a citizenship issue to one of mere customer concern.

The dominant understanding of consumer behaviour in both the economic sphere and in political circles rests on presuppositions which all our authors contest in one way or another. It follows that the chapters in this book also demonstrate little sympathy with the principal mode of understanding food crises. Both nation states and the EC operate on the assumption that restoring trust in food is a matter of altering popular perceptions of risk, and of setting up organisations and procedures to manage risk. This is best achieved by greater openness and transparency along the food chain which will, through devices like labelling, provide consumers with sufficient information on the basis of which they feel confident to exercise informed personal choice. This conclusion is not one arrived at in the chapters of this book, largely because it offers an inadequate understanding of the processes of consumption.

This suggests that we might usefully deploy theories of consumption to clarify more of the contentious issues surrounding food, particularly since, by the admission of most authorities, the theoretical basis of the social science of food consumption is comparatively weak (e.g. Mennell et al. 1992; Wood 1995; Warde 1997). Reviews of theoretical approaches have contrasted developmental, structuralist and functionalist accounts (Mennell et al. 1992). Others have identified cultural and systems approaches, with, for instance, Atkins and Bowler (2001) distinguishing within systems approaches between theories of the commodity chain, of networks and of systems of provision. Such contrasts between theories have been made at only the very highest levels of abstraction, and even then they are not highly distinct. Arguably, middle-range theoretical concepts, those that can be applied in the analysis of particular episodes or with respect to particular products or practices, are the more useful. This volume makes some progress by taking theoretically contrasting approaches and applying them to explain particular aspects of behaviour and institutions. The chapters start from a desire to explore new applications of established theories or to adapt theoretical approaches in order to illuminate behaviour in the field of food. They focus particularly on social processes at the downstream end of the food chain, processes of distribution and consumption. This reflects our conviction that these are stages in the food chain which are insufficiently examined. It is perhaps particularly the processes mediating the space between market demand and final consumption which require most attention (see Harvey et al. 2001).

We are interested in agents, their strategies and the associated social processes through which reputations of things good to eat are constructed and justified. Such a concern directs attention to advocacy of different and often competing systems for the delivery of food (organics or biotech, for instance), to new procedures for determining and guaranteeing food standards, to the variety of objectives involved in the selection of foods (safety, taste, identity) and to processes of the social judgement of taste. The determination of what is 'good' food involves, *inter alia*, state regulation, pressure from consumer movements, popular and media discourses, promotional campaigns by producers and tourist boards, the social practices of households and the creation of new markets for food products. The very breadth of the processes and the institutions involved suggests the possibility of applying many different theories and analytical approaches, and our authors use variously conventions theory, social movement theory, ethnomethodology, social worlds theory, regulation theory, cultural sociology and anthropology, actor-network theory, as well as the more established developmental, structural and systems theories. There is an equally diverse range of distinct qualities that form the basis for contributions in this book, with attention drawn to economic, social, aesthetic, symbolic, biological, religious, geographical and technological attributes.

The themes

The chapters are ordered to best display their collective theoretical and conceptual contributions. Genevieve Teil and Antoine Hennion set the scene in the first part of their chapter with a brief review of existing disciplinary approaches to understanding judgements about taste. Their empirical examples concern music and wine, raising thus a major and intriguing question about whether there is anything unique or special about food when it comes to developing a general theory of taste. They contest the applicability of the understandings which various scientific disciplines (psychology, sociology, biology, engineering) bring to the analysis of taste. All, with their established approaches to the issue of taste, are partial and limited, their analytic foci serving to obscure the reality of taste.

Their own account of taste draws on the ethnomethodological perspective. Ethnomethodology – a tradition of analysis which was at its height in the 1970s and 1980s – defined itself initially primarily in opposition to the dominant version of sociology of the 1960s, the normative functionalism associated with Talcott Parsons. It insisted on recognising that people were highly skilled, knowledgeable, reflexive agents who made and reproduced the social world to which they belonged in the performances of their ordinary practices. People did not simply learn and abide by the rules of behaviour associated with particular social roles, but improvised continually as they sought to fit their conduct to the specific situations in which they encountered other actors. Among the other positions adopted by ethnomethodologists was a strong opposition to positivistic approaches to social science, both to the search for laws and probabilities, and to attempts to analyse social conduct from a vantage point outside of the experience and understanding of ordinary competent actors. The point rather was to identify the theoretical understandings of the actors; there was no theory beyond that already accessible to actors.

For Hennion and Teil, taste is the product of performing the activity of tasting. That is a complex activity which involves individual cognisant subjects, operating in social collectivities, using mechanical devices and processed through the body. They present these four elements as an heuristic device for describing how people with a level of interest in wine and music undertake the process of making judgements about taste. Such people they call 'amateurs', to distinguish them from experts in the various competing scientific disciplines who seek to pronounce on the sources and standards of taste. The competences of amateurs range from passing interest to connoisseurship. Other sociologists might describe such people as 'enthusiasts' or participants in a social world.

The result is a strong reminder of the foibles and selectivity of academic disciplines, registering less a call for inter-disciplinarity than for a return to careful description of how people go about their daily lives, thereby avoiding the necessity of abstracting partially from their practices or subjecting people to a puzzled condescension, or rather the condescension associated with imagining that people do not themselves know the real basis of their actions and their judgements (and that the academic who knows better can therefore inform them). It is indeed a major point of their argument that in the course of reflecting on music or wine, afficionados do indeed draw on discourses which are very similar to those formalised in academic analyses, but they move relatively freely between them and see no purpose in trying to engage with any one of them consistently or systematically. In such a view taste becomes a consequence of the practical performance of tasting, and that taste, or what tastes good, is not in any sense given or static. Rather taste is constantly disputed among amateurs, who are obliged to consider the views of others in the community, change their minds, develop their competences, talk about the activity and justify their judgements. The impression is, then, one of considerable uncertainty, much movement and perpetual learning and clarification. Judgements about quality come in the course of performances in particular contexts, and thus appear constantly in flux, constantly in the making.

Chapter 2, by Jukka Gronow, takes a different line, analysing how aggregates of people who do not necessarily interact with one another come to share opinions and valuations. The approach focuses on the social processes that connect them together to account for the existence of groups with shared understandings which provide the foundation for a determinate shared appreciation of the quality of foods. He seeks the social foundations for the existence of associations of tasters (the starting point of Teil and Hennion) and the consequences for establishing the judgements that arise from their mode of organisation. To do this, Gronow explores in a programmatic way the application of another tradition of social theory to judgements about food quality. Written as a sympathetic critique of Schulze's 1992 book *Die Erlebnisgesellschaft: Kultursoziologie der Gegenwart*, Gronow employs the insights of the social worlds approach espoused by the symbolic interactionist tradition in sociology to extend and remedy the apparent defects of Schulze's approach.

Schulze stresses the importance of personal inner experience in contemporary consumption, apparently making taste increasingly individualised, taste being something inseparable from personal satisfaction. The only acknowledged grounds for evaluating the quality of experience are subjective and there is no external or objective criteria for determining whether one should be satisfied. Paradoxically, however, the effect is not to encourage highly individualised behaviour but to increase conformity. With no external criteria for attributing value, both producers and consumers tend to prefer that with which they are familiar and which others around them appreciate. Social approval becomes the main guarantee of acceptable taste and appropriate choices. The consequence, according to Schulze, is a much underestimated conservatism in terms of consumption and taste. Gronow, though sympathetic to the view that most consumption is routine and conventional, finds Schulze's argument inadequate in two main respects. First, it is unable to explain shifts in taste, or purchasing, which are at times radical. Second, it denies any degree of objectivity in determining that some items, products or services are better than others. He contends that theorems adopted from social worlds theory can provide answers to these problems.

The social worlds perspective draws on the ideas of Georg Simmel and his observation that the modern world can be conceptualised as a great number of social circles that overlap only partially. Modern individuals are members of many such circles, and each has its own distinctive etiquettes, rules and standards of value. A social world, by analogy, is one with its own distinctive conventions, created over time by its most committed members. The prototypical example of a social world is a voluntary association of people devoted to a particular recreational activity. Such social worlds are informally constituted, though with the passage of time they are likely to become more regularised in their activities and, indeed, formally organised, as with, for example, sports clubs or dining societies. Social worlds are populated by persons with different levels of commitment, with 'enthusiasts' the most central of their insiders and supported by 'regulars' who show loyalty to the activity and the established manner in which it is conducted. The activity may sometimes be visited by 'tourists' who like to browse, without commitment, but who offer some support. Inevitably there is a fourth class of person, 'strangers', who know and care nothing about a given social world, but whose existence is necessary to the insiders' recognition of their own distinctiveness.

Gronow draws from this a sense that there are groups of people particularly likely to welcome innovative products: enthusiasts for whom the activity is central are particularly likely to experiment with new and different items. Moreover, a social world is one with an established set of – essentially aesthetic – conventions and standards, which, though subject to alteration, make it likely that members of that social world will agree on which products and which performances are to be most valued. This sense of what Gronow refers to as '(semi-)objective' criteria of judgement corresponds to ordinary discussion about products, where there are groups of people who will agree entirely about the superiority of one car over another, one wine over another, one foodstuff over another. The reality of this is attested to partly by the fact that producers constantly appeal to such shared understandings in their advertising and sales' campaigns. At least temporarily and locally, though the actual scale and scope of such shared judgement may be much greater, there are shared standards of excellence. Gronow thus is able to reconcile two apparently contradictory claims:

> that modern consumers make choices on their own, often free from both physical and social constraints, following their personal wishes and whims and, nevertheless, that there are some (semi-)objective, aesthetic schemes, codes or guidelines of taste which help to evaluate and to choose the various objects of consumption. (p. 45)

Applying these concepts to taste in foods Gronow prescribes some lines of investigation – of products, of tools, of literatures, of cuisines – that would reveal the existence of such social worlds in respect of cooking and eating. What is 'good' or 'bad' food is determined within social worlds, of which the most influential are those offering competing accounts of authentic cuisine and those concerned with diets addressed to maintaining health and fitness.

Just as Gronow seeks to develop a particular sociological tradition, Allaire in chapter 3 takes to task economists' approaches to quality and demand with a view to providing a more adequate and persuasive account. Economics has been notoriously unconcerned about accounting for the origin and basis of taste, or preferences, by opting to consider them analytically as given and assumed. But Allaire demonstrates how quality has been a central concern in mainstream economic views of market functioning, reminding us that in speaking of food quality in contemporary societies we are essentially talking about food commodities (products and services) traded in markets. By exposing the weaknesses of mainstream economists' approaches to quality, and in particular, their limited understandings of quality as an aspect of market knowledge, Allaire develops a counter-position that draws substantially on actor-network theory, especially that of Callon, convention theory and evolutionary economics. In so doing, he views quality as the outcome of a 'process of qualification' that amounts to the development of 'cognitive paradigms' shared by networks of products (or 'product networks'), all the main actors of a food provision system, including consumers, and various intermediaries between provisioners and consumers, including amateurs and connoisseurs.

Economists' notions of perfect markets are immediately faced with a dilemma about quality that several different approaches have attempted to resolve. For a good to be a tradable good, a certain homogeneity, measurability and comparability are assumed, and this places quality and quality differentiation at the heart of market operations, otherwise price signals are difficult to link analytically to commodity properties. Establishing norms of measurement, with transparent information, is seen as essential to the rational behaviours of optimising consumers. In this respect, for example, labels which list all the ingredients provide perfect information – assuming that the same list is adhered to by all those providing equivalent homogeneous products at different prices to the market. Quality differentiation, including semiotic and presentational differentiation, however, immediately creates heterogeneity and monopoly market conditions, where informational comparability becomes problematical. This becomes even more so in normative technology approaches, where consumers are faced with a 'make or buy' decision for food services – cooking, presentation, delivery, and so on (Becker 1965; Stigler and Becker 1977).

These approaches share the assumption that self-provisioning and commodity provisioning are comparable under some norms of quality measurement. Allaire argues that these accounts have become more problematical as heterogeneity and globalisation of food markets have increased, and as quality itself has become subject to competing and incompatible norms. Some notions, such as ethical or ecological food, are difficult to place in the same quality space as those that refer to inherent properties of food ingredients. The general thrust of the argument is that the problem of quality cannot be reduced to an information gap between producers and consumers, or between labels and products, which *could* be filled by more or better information.

Another approach of economists has seen reputation – or knowledge and trust of the producer of a good – as a substitute for objective information, so successfully enabling rational, if sub-optimal, market transactions. 'Credence goods' are ubiquitous in food markets – whether in certification of organic, or fair trade goods, or in branding by manufacturers and retailers. But Allaire notes that credence, as a form of market belief, is also fallible, and therefore credence cannot become a viable substitute for information. Once more, heterogeneity and globalisation easily undermine credence, and Allaire gives the example of how the best Bordeaux wines have had to abandon the Bordeaux name as Bordeaux was increasingly mass produced for global markets. Heterogeneity from alternative credence systems – say, concerning the healthfulness of food – also indicates a lack of common frames of reference implied by orthodox economic theory.

The common weakness of these theories – and the real issues they raise for markets for quality – is their impoverished view of knowledge, and this is addressed by Allaire in his development of a view of emergent, relatively stabilised, cognitive paradigms, shared by networks of actors from farm to fork, in which particular products are produced and consumed. But those paradigms are emergent, historical and transitory, involving a process of qualification – or quality making–knowing – shared by a given provisioning–consuming system.

Allaire and Wolf (2004) identify two main contemporary cognitive paradigms, locked in conflict, and producing many 'quality hybrids'. The one follows the logic of decomposition, a kind of Taylorisation of food production and consumption, where each input to food production and consumption is seen as an object of innovation. The other follows the logic of identity, a holistic view of quality that embraces all dimensions of food, aesthetics, ethics, sociality, purity, naturalness, and so on. Allaire introduces this approach into the framework of an evolutionary theory of knowledge and presents quality as cognitive coordination in a product network.

These three theoretically oriented contributions successfully problematise the concept of quality as explicitly or implicitly analysed in economics and sociology, each offering a distinctive new position developed from the application and extension of an existing approach (the use of an ethnomethodology perspective by Teil and Hennion) or by seeking a synthetic development of previously discrete approaches (as with Gronow and Allaire).

In the second half of the book attention turns to a closer examination of the regulation of quality, both formal and informal. It begins with chapter 4, by Florence Bergeaud-Blackler, which shows how complex, and also how almost whimsical, are the social processes involved in convincing people that a product about to be purchased has a particular desired attribute. While all the chapters problematise the notion of quality, none is more intriguing than this. She examines the processes whereby meat comes to be purchased as *halal* by France's Muslim communities from the Magreb. Consumer identification and acceptance of particular items as halal is a function of religious identification. However, the doctrinal foundations of proper behaviour in observance are indeterminate, there being several competing interpretations; religious authorities are not involved, and there is no certification process. Indeed the religious rules governing eating are more ambivalent than are the informal regulations which have emerged regarding the cultural and commercial practices surrounding the marketing of halal meat. The procedures which result in the recognition of meat as halal are even more surprising. The slaughtering process is increasingly the same as that for meats of other provenance. It is the fact that it is sold by Muslims, and butchered and displayed at the retail stage in ways reminiscent of those practised in Morocco, which qualifies the meat to halal status. Thus halal meat displays a symbolic significance often attributed to food – to emphasise belongingness to one ethnic group and resistance to incorporation into another – and it does this irrespective of the production process. Bergeaud-Blackler describes the factors which have influenced the formation of the current system, among which was the adoption of a domestic convention brought to France by wives who, in anticipation of new legislation governing immigration, in the 1970s followed their husbands in substantial numbers. Thus ethnic identification, commercial competition, religious ambivalence and state regulation combine to create the quality halal which is recognised, endorsed and valued socially. Yet, as Bergeaud-Blackler emphasises, there are neither formal regulations nor any aspect of the process of production which distinguish halal from non-halal meat.

Bergeaud-Blackler's study throws light on a number of issues that are germane to an understanding of the symbolic aspects of food, as well as presenting an interesting case of what it means for a food item to have a particular quality. Among the features highlighted is the apparent arbitrariness of the cultural imperative – the indirect connection between religious doctrine and lay practice, the invention of a set of procedures in France that would be unnecessary back in the Maghreb and the adaptation of mores to ways of life in a bureaucratic and industrialised society. Bergeaud-Blackler also underlines the extent to which quality is the outcome of a process of qualification: halal meat is given its special identifying quality as a result of the development and application of collective procedures of manipulation of symbols and cultural recognition. In this instance, the consumers played a particularly important role, both in creating a demand for a special product and, at the same time, becoming coopted into meat purchasing behaviours which result in them being restricted to a limited number of suppliers. Equally important in this were the social demographic determinations which resulted in wives of immigrants who, arriving in substantial numbers at a particular period, recognised in the atmosphere of the halal butcher's shop's comforting cultural signs of home. So, if one wanted a story to indicate that producers have limited control on their own to define the qualities of their products, this is one. It is from the relations between producers, retailers and customers that products come to have their acknowledged properties. Social trends, social groups and social movements have an irreducible and independent contribution to make to the definition of a quality product.

While Bergeaud-Blackler teases out the tangle of informal and local bases for the ascription of quality, David Barling, in chapter 5, attends to formal modes of regulation. He looks in detail at contemporary institutional and organisational change in the UK and the EC. Barling makes clear that food issues are politically very important, both nationally and in the EC, and he examines recent developments in the formal arrangements and regulatory frameworks for ensuring food quality. Once again, the aspect of food quality featured proves to be a function of the type of social actor charged with discerning or guaranteeing quality. In this instance it is departments of state and non-governmental organisations (NGOs). He gives an account of the development of institutional frameworks, especially of NGOs and governmental organisations, for dealing with problems of food and agriculture in the 1990s. His is a description of rapidly changing organisational arrangements for the management of the food chain, particularly with regard to safety in the face of a perceived loss of trust in food.

Barling's institutional approach stresses the path dependent features of development, which complements and provides a backcloth to his analysis of representation of interests and the distribution of power. The British experience is presented through his story of the constitution of the Food Standards Agency, a body whose priorities are seen as protecting public health and reassuring the consumer.

In an evaluation of the success of recent policy, he highlights the problems associated with the distribution of the many and diverse responsibilities arising out of the complexity of the food chain. Problems of coordination – within countries, between countries and the EU – are considerable, the different arrangements made being of some importance in determining outcomes. Among the important factors necessitating division of responsibility is the extension of mixed public and private forms of governance.

Despite the differing priorities among agents in the chain, there is a degree of consensus at governmental level on the importance of safety, as opposed to other qualities. In response to crises, organisational reform, directed towards better risk assessment and management, the re-legitimisation of science, and transparency and openness, are the principal themes of an official discourse in which protection of the interests of the consumer is central to the rhetoric of legitimacy. Policies are, though, set within the parameters of the liberalisation of World Trade Organisation regulations, are conciliatory to industry, and have a narrow and particular view of the consumer presumed to be concerned with prices, hygiene aspects of safety and choice. Labelling and traceability, methods of giving information to consumers, are the principal solutions. Other issues, like nutrition, environment and animal welfare, about which sections of the public clearly have concerns, are much less salient.

Regulation implies exercise of power and, most often, the involvement of authoritative political direction in the setting up and operation of regulatory instruments. Regulation is also a spur for contestation. In contemporary Europe, the fusion of regulation and mobilisation is part of an apparent resituating of food in the economy, culture and politics. The third section of the book is concerned with reactions against the dominant tendencies of the industrial system.

Terry Marsden, in chapter 6, considers a form of challenge, orchestrated primarily by groups of agricultural producers, to the conventional industrial food system. He considers those organisations, essentially small operators, who use the claim to quality as a tool of economic competitiveness. These are businesses engaged in what he calls 'short food supply chains' (SFSCs), those characterised by reduced physical or symbolic distance between producer and consumer. SFSCs include farm gate sales and box schemes, farmers' markets and cooperatives, but also procedures to indicate product origins. These forms of alternative supply typically lay claim to quality either in terms of artisanal specialisation or ecological purity. The claim to quality is generally the basis of a strategy for selling at premium prices comparatively small quantities of particular types of produce which are locally sourced and identified. The chapter offers a typology of SFSCs and examines their distribution through different countries in Europe.

On the basis of an exploratory research project, Marsden debates the long-term future of this alternative system. He explores the dynamics of the conflict and competition between two supply chains, noting the central importance of state policy and regulation in shaping the outcome. He suggests that both protection of small farming businesses and rural development would be better served if the State intervened to support SFSCs, for indeed this is a political matter. In the particular context, in Wales, and also in the rest of the UK, the prices paid by big retailers to primary producers are subjected to much comment, as is the decline of the small rural farming sector and the extent to which the retail food sector is competitive. He argues that the State is less than willing to intervene, partly because of its established relationship with corporate organisations in the food sector. He also notes that the corporate retailers have themselves quickly re-orientated themselves towards this new thrust, themselves using the term 'quality' – and the same suppliers – which serves to maintain their existing power in the marketplace.

The chapter thus emphasises the importance of economic competition and state regulation in the production and legitimation of quality food. Marsden's account is firmly rooted in an analysis of the distribution of power and control across the system of production and distribution. He shows that it is the operation of competition and power which determines what is accepted as 'quality'. He charts the jostling for position among competitors in the various stages of the food chain, and the process whereby the power of different agents in that chain is restructured over time. The actors in SFSCs, consumers included, are part of a struggle against the existing distribution of power in the food supply system, a resistance mobilised behind the slogan 'quality'. Attention to quality as provenance of provision becomes a means to advocate the redistribution of economic value from dominant retailers to small primary producers and processors.

In chapter 7, Murdoch and Miele also examine the emergence of alternatives to the industrial food system. They see the emerging alternatives as an artisanal reaction to an industrial system based on high output and standardisation. The alternatives convey different notions of quality, those which reject dominant economic conventions and replace them with, in particular, aesthetic notions. Here, they make good use of conventions theory to identify incommensurate notions of quality. They make use also of Michel Callon's distinction which posits that foods, like all other products, pass through a series of 'qualification processes' which amalgamate their intrinsic properties and extrinsic attributes, arising from social judgements, in giving items their identity. Such processes result in the quality of an item being essentially fluid, able to be altered through social intervention. Qualification comes from struggles entered into through the economic process by which firms emphasise the positive differentiating features of their own products – though Murdoch and Miele argue that this is difficult because the foods produced in the industrial system are highly uniform.

However, the industrial system, as a result of crises and scandals, has come under increasingly widespread suspicion. Some people have begun to evaluate critically what lies behind the veneer of advertised products. They now increasingly dissociate themselves from industrial products, a detachment achieved through a reflexivity which allows them to calculate and evaluate the associated risks. Subsequently, they find alternative bases for confidence, which they discover in reconnection with nature and tradition. The consequence of crises is thus new assessments and judgements which constitute a 'requalification' of foods.

Murdoch and Miele argue that new social movements have played a key role in this process, and demonstrate the point by looking at three contemporary mobilisations. The Slow Food Movement seeks to resituate eating in cultural and traditional contexts, presenting food consumption as an aesthetic activity. The Soil Association of the UK has changed from a scientific body to an advocate of organic and local foods. The Fair Trade Movement has re-empasised the social impact of the economics of farming, thereby bringing to attention the tendency of globalisation to dissociate totally producers from consumers. These three movements, then, exhibit different perceptions and concerns with regard to quality. Yet, Murdoch and Miele argue, taken together they 'promote a new aesthetic of food' (p. 170), which they see as the main contribution of new social movements (though, in passing, they note that revalorisation is also concerned with conviviality and social justice).

Roberta Sassatelli, in chapter 8, is also concerned with emergent orientations of recent years, but for her it is moral re-evaluation which is central. She argues that consumption has now become a topic of everyday ethical thinking and that we have recently seen a shift in popular concerns away from self-regarding attitudes to consumption. Consumption is posed not as an opportunity for hedonistic and selfish behaviour, nor as the active pursuit of uncontrolled wants. Rather, notions of 'duty' and consideration of the 'public good' are thematised by individuals and groups promoting alternative attitudes to consumption. Offering a variety of messages and justifications, discourses of alternative consumption, as they become more widespread, present a new sense of consumer sovereignty, defined in terms more of the individual's 'duty' than of the individual's 'right'. Sassatelli proposes a classification of alternative consumption activities and concerns, and illustrates them with some examples of recent consumer movements and boycotts.

She shows that quality is multi-dimensional: substantively, it is not a matter just of safety or price; procedurally, it is accorded in a process described by conventions theory, wherein quality is established and attributed in the course of justifications, emerging often from contested episodes. Contestations can result in a change in the register of judgement or the moral valency of particular actions. While these shifts are not yet great in terms of breadth of influence, she argues that they are a reason for optimism about the future. Consumer behaviour certainly can be oriented towards positive moves in the improvement of quality of life and the public good.

Sassatellli notes that the critique of consumption offered in the contemporary alternative movement, unlike some of the precursors, is neither especially ascetic nor anti-hedonistic. It is accepted that consumption is a necessary part of daily life and existence. It is not to be condemned outright; nor, indeed, is the appropriate attitude one of suspicion. Rather it is a matter of consuming in a suitably thoughtful and selective manner.

In the Conclusion we review the alternative approaches set out in the eight chapters to assess progress towards a better developed conceptualisation of food quality and, in particular, of processes of qualification in the realm of food. We then consider areas that require still further treatment, discussing possibilities for further empirical research and theoretical development grouped under the headings 'biology and ecology', 'history and cuisine', 'cooking and eating' and 'innovation and competition'.

References

Atkins, P. and Bowler, I. (2001), *Food in Society: Economy, Culture, Geography*, London, Arnold.

Becker, G. (1965), 'A theory of the allocation of time', *Economic Journal*, 299(74), pp. 493–517.

Burgess, A. (2001), 'Flattering consumption: creating a Europe of the consumer', *Journal of Consumer Culture*, 1(1), pp. 93–118.

Cohen, L. (2000), 'Citizens and consumers in the United States in the century of mass consumption', in Daunton, M. and Hilton, M. (eds), *The Politics of Consumption: Material Culture and Citizenship in Europe and America*, Oxford, Berg.

Cross, G. (2000), 'Corralling consumer culture: shifting rationales for American state intervention in free markets', in Daunton, M. and Hilton, M. (eds), *The Politics of Consumption: Material Culture and Citizenship in Europe and America*, Oxford, Berg.

Gronow, J. (1997), *The Sociology of Taste*, London, Routledge.

Harvey, M., McMeekin, A., Randles, S., Southerton, D., Tether, B. and Warde, A. (2001), 'Between demand and consumption: a framework for research', Discussion Paper No. 40, Manchester, ESRC Centre for Research in Innovation and Competition, University of Manchester.

Hirschman, A. O. (1982), *Shifting Involvements: Private Interest and Public Action*, Princeton, NJ, Princeton University Press.

Mennell, S., Murcott, A. and Otterloo, A. van (1992), *The Sociology of Food: Eating, Diet and Culture*, London, Sage.

Miller, D. (ed.) (1995), *Acknowledging Consumption: A Review of New Studies*, London, Routledge.

Schulze, G. (1992), *Die Erlebnisgesellschaft: Kultursoziologie der Gegenwart*, Frankfurt and Main, Suhrkamp.

Stigler, G. and Becker, G. (1977), 'De gustibus non est disputandum', *American Economic Review*, 67(2), pp. 76–90.

Trentmann, F. (forthcoming), 'Beyond consumerism: new historical perspectives on consumption', *Journal of Contemporary History*.

Warde, A. (1997), *Consumption, Food and Taste: Culinary Antinomies and Commodity Culture*, London, Sage.

Wood, R. (1995). *The Sociology of the Meal*, Edinburgh, Edinburgh University Press.

1

Discovering quality or performing taste?
A sociology of the amateur

Geneviève Teil and Antoine Hennion

This chapter draws on a study of amateurs' – music- and food-lovers' – practices, to show that taste is an *activity* and not a passive or determined state. We use the words 'amateur', 'taste' and 'lover' in their broad senses referring to any form of love or practice, and not only the restrictive cultured sense of a connoisseurship centred on a knowledge of the object itself. Amateurism is contrasted, on the one hand, to the lack of concern of lay-people who pay little attention to what they eat or listen to, and, on the other hand, to the certified expertise of the professional. These three levels differ more as types of engagement than as degrees of intensity. We were especially interested in great amateurs, not because their knowledge of the product is greater, but because their reflexive activity on the object of their passion more clearly reveals the diverse forms and devices, gestures and timings, training and guides, needed for such an involved taste to develop. Throughout the discussion we also examine systematic comparisons between types of attachment, contrasting food with, primarily, music: a historical repertoire and a complex performance, centred on a mysterious state of emotion induced, in the case of music; and, by contrast, a concentrated object, giving immediate physical pleasure or satisfaction and instantly destroyed by its own tasting, in the case of food. The idea was the same: comparison is a good means by which to further our understanding of these diverse forms and media of taste, depending on the products tasted.

Our purpose here is to present and justify a new research programme on food taste. A systematic and critical review of the most prominent research on the subject has revealed that when it comes to the status of products concerned with taste, the various disciplines are divided, unsatisfactorily, along the lines of a nature–culture approach: either food products are just things and their properties are analysed through laboratory tests and measurements; or they are simply signs, the media for various rites and mechanisms of social identity, in which case their physical reality disappears in the analysis. In our opinion, this duality is detrimental in so far as it eliminates the very object of taste, i.e. it obscures the inevitable uncertainty about the effect that arises, about the nature of attachments, on the variable importance of the product tasted, on the circumstances of the tasting and the taster, and, more generally, on the systematic heterogeneity of the elements involved in preferences and habits.

The simple adding of physiological causes and social determinations is not enough to solve the problem. That would overlook the modalities through which amateurs, in a situation, can reach a compromise between diverse or even incompatible criteria of appreciation. Formulated in this way, the problem suggests the solution that we here attempt to formulate, that of reflexivity. Is taste not, above all, a work on what taste is? Instead of seeing amateurs as passive subjects of objectifying (naturalising or sociologising) measurements and analyses, the idea is, on the contrary, to consider them as guides and to observe them as actively seeking the causes and determinations prompting them to make choices, to appreciate and to consume. In short, it is to make their very activity the object of our research.

Taste: a polymorphic concept

A number of sociological and anthropological works offer literature reviews (Goody 1984; Mennell et al. 1992; Beardsworth and Keil 1997; Bell and Valentine 1997; Warde 1997) or compilations of key writings (McIntosh 1996; Couniham and van Esterick 1997; Poulain 2002) on taste. These sometimes very complete books can help to draw up an inventory of the results obtained by various research programmes on food. In this introduction we wish to draw the reader's attention not to those results but rather to the various ways in which different authors address the question of taste. We also wish to point out the difficulties posed by the articulation and synthesis of those diverse approaches, due primarily to the incompatibility of some of the hypotheses mobilised.

This review[1] considers five fairly precise meanings of the word 'taste': taste as a biological need; as social differentiation of attraction towards things; as a relationship of perception between a subject and a product; as the emergence of reflexivity; and, lastly, as the practice of perception. We stress the importance of each of these points of view, as well as their limits, in furthering an understanding of the phenomena of food and, especially, taste. Our aim is to highlight the relevance of a more complete analysis of food, capable of organising the contributions of all these works into a single theoretical framework whose limits can then be transcended.

Inferring tastes from needs

Why do we like what we eat? Biological approaches tend to interpret our preferences as a biological mechanism of adaptation to the range of resources available in each biotope. Our preferences express our needs and, when the environment changes, a process of conditioning through the pleasure derived from a food taste enables us to adjust our consumption to changes of availability. Taste is thus a biological adaptation (Farb and Armelagos 1985) or, more often, a functional adaptation (Harris and Ross 1987). In terms of the former, the Aztecs ate the flesh of their human sacrifices to remedy a deficiency in nutrients from meat. The interpretation of taste as a need tends to see food as a universal diet hidden by a superficial variety of empirical situations.

Inferring food differentiation from socio-cultural differentiation

The critique of functionalism and the substantial corpus of observations showing the immense variety of situations of consumption has led to the opposite hypothesis, i.e. a relativism of tastes and the absence of their determination by any general relationship between the material properties of products and their perception by actors, that might subsequently determine their evaluations, actions or behaviours. Research has therefore turned away from the question of perception and towards that of consumption, which is now acknowledged as giving a clear indication of tastes and preferences. Numerous studies have aimed at describing the homology between food differentiation and social differentiation. Yet it is no longer physiological principles, such as the pleasure experienced, that are taken to be the motivations for individuals to adapt their consumption to their socio-cultural position, but principles of significance (Lévi-Strauss 1964): structural homology between the field of consumption and that of distribution (Bourdieu 1979); the effects of socialisation; cultural skills brought into play in the kitchen; table manners; or, more generally, all operations and practices from food production to the elimination of waste (Goody 1984).

By distinguishing the different parts of a plant or animal and then transforming them through physical and chemical processes, cooking multiplies the possibilities of diversification of foods. Time is another resource for diversification, daily and throughout the year, as are table manners and the various ways and means through which people come into contact with food – the list of the elements of diversification is not closed: the person who provides or who cooks, for example, can add to it. Although these studies have the merit of throwing open the list of elements producing food differentiation, they also highlight the difficulties that can be encountered in closing it. How can we account for the individual and the daily variations in food, for example?

This research has introduced a collective dimension to the question of food: foods in themselves are not nice; rather they are nice for a collective and in a shared context that gives them meaning, e.g. the precise time of a meal, determined by a calendar, by people, etc. But to describe the link established between the two differentiations, the analysis of collective determination of consumption has to consider the product as a container devoid of properties or characteristics. All the differences produced by the social accumulate in this container and are imprinted within it without resistance. On the other hand, the signification inscribed in products constitutes a formal, unequivocal system that is always collectively shared.

The contingency of products and individuals makes food changes strictly dependent on cultural and social changes. This is what Bourdieu suggests when he makes the evolution of taste the result of a movement peculiar to society, independent of individuals and categories of products since the schemas driving *habitus* are the same for a class and for all areas of practice (Bourdieu 1979: 196). By contrast, advocates of material culture defend the irreducible difference between all forms of consumption but fail to show what irreversible trace these differences leave on food and taste.

Taste as a multifactoral relation

Another body of research stemming from the experimental sciences seeks to overcome this difficulty by considering taste as a test of the real based on the product, and by refusing to treat the experience of food globally as an illusion. Instead of contrasting the qualities perceived by actors with an objective quality, some research programmes try to articulate the social and material dimensions of taste (Giachetti 1992 and 1996). An individual's taste is interpreted as a function of the transformation of the taste of foods. Three different types of relationship can be identified. First, perception can be considered as a *juxtaposition* of two determinations: social and material. Second, taste can be analysed as the result of the influence of external factors that act on the sensorial perception of a stimulus from a product or its interpretation. Finally, taste can be studied as the result of an oriented temporal process, shaped by habits, experiences, and socially and culturally constrained or constructed learning.

In each case, it is the incorporation and translation of collective determinations into the physiological perception of the product that are in question. Does the social modify the physiology of perception or simply the interpretation of the stimulus? Is it a process requiring time or is it an immediate influence?

Compared to anthropological and sociological studies, experimental and interdisciplinary research have the merit of considering the body as a central mediator that articulates material individual and collective determinations. But, paradoxically, this body is nothing more than a receptacle shaped entirely by education or by stimuli given out by the product. From that point of view, food is reduced to a juxtaposition of causalities to which individuals are subjected. In particular, it excludes tasting as a questioning of taste by the eater. By placing the accent on experience, on what happens to the eater, the analysis of crossed biological, sociological and psychological influences opens the field of determinations to a vast range of events. But the experience in question here is always passive; its results are always independent of the eater, on whom they are imposed. Tastes and preferences are incorporated by habit, by the conditioning of supply, by social experiences, by the encounters one happens to have. What acts here is not the actor but the factors. But this passivity, which seems necessary for the right conditioning of the body, is paradoxical. Do we get used to something that simply happens to us, unwittingly, by accident, receiving it in our bodies without paying much attention to it? In other words, is the individual totally separate from her or his tastes?

From attraction to desire: reflexive taste

Several 'crises' have recently shaken our food system, triggering particularly rapid changes that are hardly compatible with slow processes of socialisation or cultural habituation. The theories proposed above treat taste as an acquired involuntary attraction to specific products. To account for aversions as sudden as those spawned by the so-called 'mad cow' crisis, two processes have been proposed. The first relates to the structuring anxieties of consumption, due to behavioural alternatives which crises bring to the foreground (Fischler 1990; Beardsworth and Keil 1997) and between which the individual has to make choices postulated as a source of anxiety because linked to her or his survival. The second relates the recent succession of such crises to a social or socio-economic trend that confirms the emergence of a reflexive actor (see Rose and Miller 1990 and 1992; Featherstone 1991; Giddens 1991; Beck et al. 1994).The process of 'commodification' observed in markets is concomitant with a reflexive fragmentation of demand, transforming the taste, from an attraction experienced by the actor into a desire, and thus into active and deliberate consumption.

Irrespective of the position of the authors in this debate, all these works highlight a stronger engagement by actors regarding the variety of available products. Despite the profound divergences sometimes expressed in the debate on food change, they agree that consumers have more interest in what they buy, and that food purchases are subject to more careful attention, consideration and concern. People's reasons for this attentiveness to themselves differ widely, depending on which of these authors is consulted: underlying anxiety; social evolution; or producers' marketing techniques and strategies. But this attention always leads to a doubt and attention to oneself and one's preferences, or to the intermediaries who specify one's needs or the qualities of products. The doubt and attention thus is never directly concerned with the qualities of foods, which remain either external and contingent phenomena or are simply unquestionable. Although reflexively interested in products, in their food, individuals are nevertheless hostages of the social, cultural or economic forces running through them. The fact remains that the conception of taste as desire marks a theoretical turnaround. As soon as the individual engages herself or himself, or undertakes some activity to determine what she or he likes, she or he can no longer be described so easily by the play of determinations.

A collectively produced historical sensitivity

Since Braudel's appeal, many historians have also described the variations of our food, especially through an imposing range of reconstructed consumptions. Studies on the ranking of these consumptions have spawned a new concept of taste: food sensitivity. They have described our food tastes as a historical result often based on practices (see Capatti 1989; Camporesi 1992; Vigarello 1993; Flandrin and Montanari 1996). Like the disciplinary programmes described above, these works try to fit both dimensions – the product and the social – into the analysis of perception. They have thus made it possible to enhance experience of the product with the practices giving it substance. Yet most of them endorse *a priori* either the hypothesis of an illusory quality or taste of products (e.g. Mennell 1985; Camporesi 1989; Terrio 1997), excluding any idea of the product's participation in perception, or the operation of an objective determinant of good taste (see Aron 1989; Pitte 1991; Mintz 1996). Practices thus reduce experience to a social or material determinism, instead of opening it up to the techniques and means of perception. However, some studies (see Bessy and Chateauraynaud 1993 and 1995; Letablier 1997) have avoided this twofold reductionism by taking taste neither as a given nor as a determinant of action, just to be explained from the outside, but as a self-accomplishing result of a practice on the part of an organised group of actors, of gestures, products, etc. They rely on the same theoretical strand as the historians above, but extend it to the ontology of products – as had the analysis by Merleau-Ponty (1964) of perception as a reflexive activity engaging objects and not guided by an essence of objects that only science could reveal in its purity. Here perception is an interaction, a doing that knows it is perceiving – but which is not the revealing of – a given to be perceived.

Finally, the conjunction of all these works highlights a variety of characteristics of the food phenomenon: a physiological phenomenon, engaging a product and a perceiving body; a collective phenomenon, both cultural and social, inscribing perception in a frame that is shared to a greater or lesser degree; and a situated phenomenon, in time and space, engaging practices that shape the perception of an increasingly reflexive being. But unfortunately the compartmentalisation of disciplinary specialities leads to a reduction in the phenomenon observed, producing incompatibility between the hypotheses mobilised. Adaptive devices, or those of biological or social incorporation, can explain the origins of complex determinations that pluridisciplinary programmes have tried to group together in the same theoretical framework. But that framework of determinations is incompatible with the idea of a reflexive taste which is an activity and the result of historically constituted practices – unless it reduces the practices themselves to the transmission of determinations.

The extension of the theoretical framework to these results therefore requires a reconceptualisation and reshaping of the analytical tools used to account for all of these aspects of taste.

Analysing taste as an activity

The main shift in the analytical position we defend, to underscore the crucial limitations of the current works on taste discussed above, relates to the status we give to taste as its own main descriptor, analyst and producer. We do not conceive of our work as a long process of tracking diverse kinds of external determinations that help to explain why different people have differing tastes. Different people in different situations bring into play a collective knowledge, of which taste is a result. In other words, taste is a way of building relationships, with things and with people; it is not simply a property of goods, nor is it a competence of people.

The work presented here is based on comparative ethnographical observations of wine amateurs and gourmets, on the one hand, and music lovers on the other. The comparison of music and wine or food was aimed at providing evidence about the relationship between the amateur and what she or he likes, beyond native self-descriptions that always insist on the radical specificity of each object of love.

One of the crucial challenges, if one wants to respect the variety of amateurs' practices, is to be able to analytically display the modalities of those practices, knowing that they can vary widely inside each form. The main measurable modalities that we first identified empirically, and that we will reformulate below into a more analytical framework, are:

- the degree of involvement (in time, money, personal relations, etc.);
- the central social form that performing the activity requires (collectively or in a solitary way, going out often or mostly practising at home, independently or relying on a network of friends and/or other amateurs);
- the long-term physical training or level of engagement required (for instance, in the case of singing or playing an instrument the level required is very high, and in the case of wine-tasting it is high yet more concentrated, though it may be much more diffused, as in the case of gastronomy; or it can be undertaken mostly collectively in a more or less overt way, as it is for a rock band);
- the physical form taken by the product, which leads to typical amateur practices like collecting old or specific repertoires and/or over-investing in technical knowledge about production (like amateurs who continually tinker with instruments or hi-fi, or wine-lovers who dream about making their own wine). This includes the extent and commercial availability of 'catalogues', giving easy access to the object of passion (a typical case being music, which is recordable), and the existence of a more or less wide range of technical sets and devices considered as the 'equipment' or the 'material' of the activity (like hi-fi for music, or glasses, corkscrews and, of course, the cellar, for wine).

Other modalities can be more or less crucial, depending on the activity, in particular the depth of its tradition, the existence of a specific and elaborated vocabulary, the size and variety of the available 'library' dealing with its various aspects (guides, books, critiques, secondary literature, amateurs' chronicles, novels, etc.), the formalisation of training or education and, more broadly, the level of social recognition, valorisation and institutionalisation.

A matter of method: beyond external accounts or arbitrary outside references

Amateurs are our informants

Based on a method we had already used to analyse the advertising profession and its practical theories about objects and desire (Hennion and Méadel 1989), we focus here on the study of the practices of amateurs – ways of doing things, manners, obsessive procedures, use of books and guides, and so on – and consider them as *our* experts in order to understand how taste works, rather than placing ourselves in the position of experts and theorising on the basis of supposedly tacit understandings and informal knowledge of which they are not themselves aware.

Comparing amateurs in various fields, we discover many different views of what it is to like something, or to be an amateur practitioner, but most of them are reflexively and collectively debated and empirically tested by amateurs themselves. In particular, amateurs seem very good at mobilising, combining or refusing different modes of tasting in practice. Briefly, as we argue below, if we focus on the objects, on the collective, on the self, on conditions and technical devices, we see modes of appreciation that resemble the rival bases on which disciplines and knowledge have built their theoretical models – physics and bio-chemistry, sociology, psychology and sciences of cognition, and technical expertise.

This shift of focus completely changes the nature of our accounts, and the status of major questions about quality. If we consider amateurs as our informants, instead of deciphering them with our theoretical preconceptions, these questions become difficult issues in their debates and experiments, instead of being dogmatic and definitive answers defended by each theory. Does one need others' recommendations to like good products or to be sensitive to high quality? Do tastes depend on objective features or properties of the products, or are they dependent mostly on each person's profound attachments? Must the relationship with the objects be purified and made independent of any circumstances? Or, on the contrary, is the pleasure of things always related to a whole situation, much of the art of tasting being the ability to put oneself into the right conditions? What is predetermined and what is radically unpredictable in the feeling that something is good (whatever definition one gives of that quality of things)?

Amateurs *do* find their own answers, defining what we call diverse formats of amateurship, except these answers do not look like definite and coherent determinations relating to theoretical models which scientists are then paid to rationalise (Teil 2004). On the contrary, they are provisional and incoherent trials, self-realising modalities, focusing on diverse and contradictory aspects of taste, moving from one to the other. The test of their validity is part of taste itself, which cannot be separated from the whole set of collective practices and long-term relationships with a repertoire of things.

Our aim, then, is not to extract from interviews and observations with amateurs the objective grounds of a pleasure, a feeling or a taste that they would ordinarily experience only as subjective, implicit representations largely blind to their own determinations. Conceiving of taste as amateurs' experimental ongoing activity, an accomplishment that continually takes into account its own results to modify itself and its procedures, we aim to promote amateurs to the rank of experts, to acknowledge their ability to be the reflexive managers of their own taste. In so doing we simply repeat the fundamental gesture of the ethnomethodologists who restore to the actors themselves the social competences employed in producing the categories of their own worlds and actions (Garfinkel 1967). At this stage one of our goals is to take advantage of the extensive know-how amateurs display when looking for what they prefer, administering their pleasure, evaluating, trying out, judging in a situation or changing their diagnoses, in order to put to the test and formulate, together with them, some of the modalities of taste. But, beyond these *ad hoc* momentary tricks of the trade, it is also in the long term that amateurs have been the architects of their own ability to appreciate things and the forgers of the frameworks of their tastes. As much at a personal as at a collective level, tastes have a history (and this is why the plural is necessary here). They are anything but pure and natural properties which have had to fabricate themselves through the invention of formats and repertoires, devices and abilities, all elements which amateurs of diverse products or domains have progressively set up by passionately debating them collectively.

This is why the neo-ethnomethodological posture for which we plead insists on taste as a reflexive and performative capacity, opposed to any possibility of seeing it as an objectified reality which scientific knowledge could account for from the outside. The reflexive nature of an activity (an issue here at its zero degree due simply to the act of putting oneself into an identified disposition) does not assume that there is necessarily reflection by actors – which implies a degree of calculation and awareness of what one does at a far higher level, and the passage from a simple variation in our modes of presence in situations to the level of deliberate action (Ricœur 1990). After its seminal presentation by Clifford and Marcus (1986), the many aspects of the reflexivity thesis, focusing on crucial problems for us, such as intimacy, the body and the use of social theories by actors themselves, have been thoroughly debated (e.g. by Beck et al. 1994). Concerned mostly with political matters and a characterisation of modernity, however, reflexivity as seen by Beck et al. applies only to the social construction of identities and agencies, inside a stable macro-sociological conception of the collective. Science and technology studies proposed a use of the word closer to ours, when addressing objects and collectives (Woolgar 1988; Ashmore 1989).

This may be too general a claim, but it happens to be very efficient in the precise domain of taste, which by now we have shown to be dramatically spread between rival disciplines, as if they were competing to give *the* definitive account of what good taste in, or *the* quality of, things is. We now raise a number of questions, present some of the results of our method and show its efficiency in getting away from aporetic binary debates in the field.

Tasting, listening to or appreciating something are essentially silent activities. Does this mean it is only tacit, condemned to its mysterious status of an internal, profoundly subjective, unspeakable reality? We do not claim to bring to a close such a longstanding debate, rather perhaps just to recall how much this silent activity constantly resorts to words by many different means, and that on this matter too it might be time to abandon radical dualisms. We simply chose an appropriate case in this respect, focusing our inquiry on great amateurs, those most likely to make extensive use of diverse types of wording for their practices. Great amateurs can be an *overt* source of information.

Another way of avoiding exteriority: interviewers' complementary experiences

One way of taking advantage of the comparison of music and wine or food was to use our complementary competences and weaknesses: one of us is a semi-professional expert wine-taster who enjoys music, the other is a music-lover and a former musicologist and a *petit amateur* of wine. We can thus use our own bodies, preferences, knowledge and prejudices as touchstones and variables implied in our experiments, instead of putting our own status as amateurs in brackets, as is usually done by social scientists, on topics where belonging to a group of great amateurs, being a connoisseur or simply 'knowing a little what all this is about' are so crucial in interviews. The interviewer's level of amateurship completely modifies the kind of discourse and observation she or he can get from great amateurs, who never enter into 'the real thing' in front of the uninitiated. And if we are among great amateurs, the danger is, conversely, of regarding the love of music or wine as an apprenticeship, a mere process of acquiring knowledge and corporal ability, the quality of the object being taken as an evidence. Our mutual lack of expertise allows us to be more symmertrical and forbids either of us to mobilise any interpretation by taking for granted that some perceptions are the good, or correct, ones and others are 'biased'. That is to say, models of taste presume that there is some direct or objective perception of any item under scrutiny and that divergence from that given, orthodox or taken-for-granted manner of appropriation constitutes a biased view. Yet we see no basis for such a presumption since all principles of perception are at the same level and have equal validity.

Music is described mostly as a *performance*, on the one hand, and is referred to as an art work, on the other, while wine is above all a *product* – even if it is interesting to note that, when trying to promote the quality of their taste, wine amateurs tend to talk about it in terms both of aesthetics and, to a lesser extent, of a physical and mental conditioning, so that tasting resembles a music concert. Our comparative method then just prolongs the amateurs tendency to use the same words to describe wine or music. Using the specific features of each product to see how they apply to the other makes it possible to describe empirically diverse formats of amateurship independently (at least relatively so) of the objects of this attention, that is to say, formats are not directly deduced from supposed intrinsic properties of either wine–food or music. It does not mean that there is no difference between listening to music and drinking wine, but an account has to be given for those differences within the taste relationship, not as the result of external predetermining factors.

Let us begin with a short example, in order to show the combination and incompatibilities of diverse forms of amateurship. We consider here the case of Raoul who is both an amateur wine enthusiast and a music-lover. He does favour specific wines and music over others. In the case of wine, he discovers and tries first those which are the best in order to guide his perception and to be sure to avoid mistakes in his perception of the quality of the wine he buys. Therefore he is very attentive to what experts say; he listens to connoisseur friends' opinions, buys many books and guides in order to increase his knowledge, and tries to adjust his perception to the described quality of wines.

He considers music, however, to be completely different from wine, in that music is something abstract that generates emotions, and, for him, the quality of the music he listens to is related to the quality of the emotions he personally perceives – emotions which are strongly related to his past experiences and the capacity of that music to evoke past experiences. Thus, where music is concerned, he never relies on others' advice; he considers it inapplicable to his case. He listens to music on the radio, waiting for a casual encounter with something he likes; he hears the music his friends play to him, but he never directly follows their opinions. He just takes his opportunities to get to know new music, and whenever he likes a piece, its creator or the musician performing it, he purchases accordingly.

Let us regard him first as a wine-lover. If taste is considered a property of a taster, then Raoul will appear to be biased according to the relevant criteria because he does not let himself express his own taste. The bias may then be explained by psychological factors: a lack of self-reliance and in its place the influence of experts on the *proper* judgement of the actor. If, instead, taste is considered as a collective process, one might interpret the case in terms of sociological categories, the belonging of the actor to a kind of structuring/structured circle of social differentiation. If one considers taste as a property of the thing tasted, then one will take this case as a probe of the necessity of an apprenticeship in learning its objective characteristics, and such an apprenticeship is best provided by scientific procedures. Then, as with each time the question is set in terms of biased perception, one needs to give explanations of those 'biases', and to explain them by, for instance, psychological factors. In any case, from diverse and sometimes contradictory points of view, one always emphasises that taste is the result of a configuration of the amateur–object relationship.

And what about music? Raoul's behaviour might be considered as fitting very well a cognitive theory of tastes, seen as a series of experiments on one's own feelings. All other theoretical explanations – aesthetic, sociological, etc. – will, on the contrary, insist on his biased behaviour, but for different reasons. The same person whose tasting of wine was biased because he was following the evaluations of others now obeys only his own feelings. He can nevertheless be said to have a biased taste, but this time because he is not aware of musical relevance. He does not engage in aesthetic judgement; he is not aware of the unconsciously determined nature of his pretended spontaneous preferences, and so on. What, then, is the case? Do we have to adapt each explanation to each empirical case? A better solution is to turn things upside down: those rationalised and incompatible principles, forcing all the practical configurations that real amateurs set up to be deciphered as diverse biases, are simply the basic elements on which amateurs themselves continually put to the test, elaborate, discuss, oppose and link together in the diverse moments and within the constraints of their taste. But, except in rare cases, they do not try to purify them and make one of them *the* only principle of taste; rather, they just try and then move on, in a much more variable and flexible way than they themselves acknowledge, describing these well-known stages which all great amateurs seem to have passed through ('Oh, you're in your "only old sticks phase"', or 'Oh, yes, French opera is just light music? Well, let's just wait to hear what you'll say in three years' time!'), and of whose character, as dogmatic and assertive as it is limited and provisional, they are keenly aware.

Taste as a reflexive and performative activity: a fourfold scheme

Things to be liked, a collective of tasters, devices and techniques, the taster's 'body and soul'

Whatever the taste device – a meal with friends, listening to a recording in the lounge, a wine-tasting in a shop, a concert, a wine contest, even a scientific experiment – the judgements on taste and quality uttered for the occasion proliferate. Most of the people present do not agree; indeed, an individual, even if isolated, may change her or his mind.

Most of the existing research works are dedicated to *explaining* the variety of such judgements. Without trying to characterise it in any essential way, we have tried to define a kind of 'scaffold', a four-legged stool, which for us simply has the provisional status of an empty frame in which attachments can be elaborated. As a sort of minimalist hypothesis (but this too can be debated), we have assumed that each leg, alone or combined, mobilises the following four main definitions:

- taste as a property of the thing tasted;
- taste as a collective process;
- taste as a result of a device;
- taste as an attribute proper (*caractère propre*) of a taster.

We could immediately add, for instance, taste as a historical process (this can be included in taste as a collective process), or taste as a behaviour (an extension of the taster's competences). But the main point concerns not the relevance or exhaustiveness of this grid but rather the status of its basic elements. Our intention is to return them to the actors themselves, and to describe disciplines as rival ways of rationalising and purifying each of them, having snatched that common knowledge from the amateurs' reflexive competences and transformed it into an objective science.

Nothing present if not made present

Let us go back to the four legs of our simple stool (they are nothing more than those displayed by most multifactor analyses of taste). None of these elements is to be taken as *given*, or natural and pre-existing. This is true of the products of *all* tasted objects. The plural form is more appropriate for, as music demonstrates, tasting is not only about *the* work or *the* 'objects' because it passes through a number of intermediate objects. These could include the grooves of a record, the sound of an instrument, the atmosphere of the room, a voice, the body of a performer, scores, gestures – all objects whose relative importance in the performance is passionately debated by music-lovers from opposed aesthetic positions. On the contrary, these elements (products, collectives, devices and things tested) are continually tested, uncertain, tentative, appearing *in situ* and in the process of performance, as they are both the means and the products of the amateurs' activity.

The same applies to amateurs' collectives. Sociology proceeds a little too quickly, as if it were the exclusive gate-keeper of this register. It takes this modality of amateurism out of the reach of amateurs, elaborates it as an autonomous, systematic, external causality, and finally turns it back against the amateurs, as the hidden principle of their activity, revealed to them in spite of their resistances and denials by a heroic sociologist. This figure of the amateur is far from any real situation. On the contrary, amateurs know well that there is no amateur as long as one is alone in front of some good things to taste. Amateurism begins with the confrontation with others' tastes: those of some other amateurs functioning as models forcing one to deprecate what one loved, and to love what one despised, and those of some other people functioning as foils helping one to get rid of inappropriate tastes. Far from being mere *snobbishness*, this collective production of a common elaborated taste is a very powerful way of experiencing the stability, durability and various types of *respondance* – that is, the ability to respond – that objects of love may have and, conversely, of producing the collective ability to perceive these differences and give them more and more worth: the antonym of love is not hatred, but indifference.

Until now, we have been in the territory of the usual debates about the objects of art, or taste, and sociology. But, the other elements open up this space, in which love may display itself, even more. The material devices of the activity are crucial because they are the concrete mediations supporting most of the real debates about taste (Hennion 1993; Teil 2001). One glass for clarets, another for Burgundy wines. As regards the baroque revival in France in the late 1970s and early 1980s (Hennion 1997), what was reported afterwards in terms of dual aesthetic and commercial oppositions between two clear camps was above all a systematic calling into question of each medium, device and object of the musical performance: pitch, voice, instruments, size of orchestra, tunings, scores, and so on. The same applies to rock music and its successive fads and fashions: nothing reveals the differences between styles more clearly than the kind of equipment musicians use or the places in which they perform.

Material and spatial devices, collective arrangements, organised spaces and times, objects and instruments of various modes, and a wide range of techniques to deal with them: such a vision of taste as a performance undertaken through a procession of mediations perfectly fits the situated, equipped and collective definition of taste for food or love for music that we are trying to clarify. It is the opposite of the false image that the 'object versus sociology' controversy gives of it, that of a face-to-face challenge between Object and Subject; nothing of the kind when it comes to real debates among music- (or wine-)lovers.

The last leg of our stool is probably the one which poses most problems for sociology: the involvement of our body and soul in taste and artistic experiences and, more generally, the acknowledgement by any form of sociology of our sensations, feelings and emotions. Far from recognising this aspect of taste, the 'embodiment' track, over-frequented, takes the opposite direction, showing how our bodies are constructed through social devices and norms (see e.g. Featherstone et al. 1991). But the question here is not primarily about how a so-called natural body is in fact determined, tamed, performed and deformed by our social environment. Even more importantly, it is positively about the co-production of a loving body and a loved object through a collective and equipped activity. No tongue, no taste for wine, no nose without the whole wine-tasting process; no musical ear without music to hear. The body – or, more accurately, our 'body and soul' equipment – is (like the objects, collectives and devices of taste) a result emerging from the activity of tasting (Teil 1998), and not a given reality, not an autonomous and pre-existing physical body just needing a musical or gourmet training. Nor is it a psychological ability to enjoy organised sounds or elaborated products, of which the cognitive sciences are quick to give us a satisfying understanding. Our bodies and souls, like musical works and techniques, like the taste of wines or like amateurs' identities, are nothing but the means *and* the products of an uncertain, tentative, ongoing performance. Taste is precisely about managing this creative uncertainty: it is not about liking something from what we already know, but about changing our ability to like from the contact with a new thing, most often pre-presented by other amateurs who serve as mediators of one's own taste.

The provisional aim of our four-legged stool–scaffold, which we use more as a provisional minimalist *aide-mémoire* than as a meta-discourse, is to allow comparisons. Sports would direct our attention more towards the long-term training which can produce a new performing body, but no sport is possible either without objects – no pole vault without a bar – and this also means no sport without records, contests, coaching, other performers, and a lot of techniques, both incorporated and objectified. The fact remains that, out of this common fourfold scheme (objects, collectives, devices, bodies), the case of sport shows more clearly the fact that there is no such thing as a given natural body. Only long training gives the performer the feeling of a *natural* act: he or she is taking possession of an incorporated collective ability. Think of this with wine-lovers or musicians in mind – and not only performers, but listeners too – and the weakness of the dual object–society model which overlooks bodies and material devices clearly appears. No music without the collective long-term production of hearing, of a specific listening, ranging from the more general frame of attention (paying attention to music *as* music) to the more local and specific habit of listening to tunes and works made available when and where we want by the record industry – a feature of music that the recording industry has developed but which existed from the early eighteenth century with the expansion of piano-making as an activity (Ehrlich 1976) and the publication of sheetmusic (Peacock and Weir 1975).

A pragmatic definition of the great amateur
An amateur always participates in the production of the product he or she likes, as does the reader. In literary theory, or even earlier, the reader as described by Proust in the Foreword to *Sésame et les Lys*, the French version of Ruskin's *Sesame and the Lilies,* is an actor of literature, made up of a set of positions 'not outside of the book, but inside it'. Taste appears in the end as both a fascinating, but also a very awkward and ambiguous, notion, hard to manipulate. Our argument is that it gains in interest if one refuses the common sense use of the word, as the mere activity of a taster face-to-face with a given object. Taste mobilises in a reflexive way a much larger conception of activity, bringing together the many facets of our relation to things: a corporal, affective and mental ability, but also a collective one; an ability induced by the products given to the attention of the taster, but also depending closely on material and technical devices of the performance of taste; and a variable, contingent and historical ability.

Being a great amateur, then, no longer means that one knows how to feel the quality of a wine or a music, and how to manage the context of the tasting situation or to use the right devices in order to get the best perception. It is not limited to a recording of the sequence of tastes or loved things, nor to the primacy of the search for pleasure. Rather, the amateur appears to be someone who selects, juxtaposes and co-ordinates ways of elaborating her or his taste. As a result, satisfaction and pleasure are no longer to be considered as direct consequences – necessarily felt by the subject – of the perfect fit between the properties of a product and the characteristics of a subject, even a social subject. Satisfaction, pleasure and emotion are objects of a reflexive questioning by the subject.

All the above points of view, which we contest, try to reduce the variety of judgements on quality to single point of reference defined by a theoretical posture, a specific device or a situation aimed at showing the factors involved. But, most of the time, these theoretical postures appear to be irrelevant to the actors. The obsession with a rational, complete and coherent search for a localised cause in a determined part of the taste device is not to be found in the actors' practices. And all these points of view postulate taste as a result that imposes itself on the actors, in spite of themselves. Yet, these points of view describe the most common issues of debate through which amateurs reflexively elaborate their taste.

Instead of taking place on the outside, among rival disciplines, each fighting to give more importance to one aspect of their love (wines and works 'themselves', body and mind, the social game of participation and rejection, material, economic and technical devices, etc.), these debates should be returned to the real experts: the amateurs. They are the ones who perform the experiments and are forced to call themselves into question through the collective trial that any performance represents. In search of effects which are never guaranteed, they are the ones who draw on aesthetics, sociology, psychology, technology and economics, always needing to put their feelings into words collectively, in order to master, multiply and share those feelings.

Conclusion: the felicity of taste

Pragmaticians speak of the conditions of felicity of a sentence (e.g. Austin 1962): are not all the good reasons there for this type of analysis, making communication depend not only upon the properties of the enunciated or of the speakers' competences but also upon the situation of enunciation, especially relevant for taste? From an analysis centred on the perceptible effects of a product on a subject, one slides towards an analysis centred on the conditions allowing an effect to occur.

In the first case, when taking the effect as the 'enunciated', as the result to be explained, the entire methodological effort aims at inventing the right devices and experiments for distinguishing the outcome of purely musical or objective effects of a product on an isolated guinea-pig from biases stemming from the context, influences, or socio-cultural determinations (indirect effects helping or preventing good taste). In the second case, when taking the effect as the 'enunciation', as a co-producer of what happens, all these elements are there too: music and wines, diverse contexts, genres, formats of taste and various determinants. But their *a priori* distribution into distinct orders of reality (external causes, favourable conditions or obstacles, purely oenological or musical effects) and the modalities of their action are not known in advance; they are the 'constructive constraints' (see Gomart and Hennion 1999) on which taste relies and from which some effects occur or do not, without any amateur or analyst able to decide on or to master them.

Like those of Becker's 1963 marijuana smokers, effects occur only when expected, named, identified and collectively learnt, and when this long-term attention has allowed the production of products responding to this demand.

Taste is a performing activity: it succeeds only when it relies on its own results and effects, in a circular way, as long as it isolates, discusses and names them. One hears music only if one hears it *as* music. Then the question is not to isolate music or food, and to understand their *own* specific efficiency (or, conversely, in the case of sociologists, to deny it and make it a social rite or a game of identity and difference), but to give an account of the way wine or music has effects, arising out of a whole set of practices, bodies, collectives, all taken and taken again by the reflexive work of taste itself. Taste is an action, not a fact; it is an experience, not an object.

The shift is important. It has a crucial consequence, in particular, on methodology. As long as we acknowledge that the effects of a product, be it wine or music, have no reason to depend only on the product itself, nor only on the consumer's abilities, a crucial characteristic of taste becomes its reflexivity. And the analyst can only accompany amateurs, observing, seeing things arise, noticing changes, noting all the work of adjustment. She or he cannot simply objectify them without falling into one of the many strategies of the amateurs, strategies that they have already tested and which, most likely, they have already shown to be outdated.

Note

1 We have limited the number of citations in order to lighten the discussion. For more details see Teil 1998.

References

Aron, J. (1989 [1973]), *Le Mangeur du XIX Siècle*, Paris, Petite Bibliothèque Payot.

Ashmore, M. (1989), *The Reflexive Thesis: Wrighting [sic] Sociology of Scientific Knowledge*, Chicago, IL, Chicago University Press.

Austin, J. L. (1962), *How to Do Things with Words*, Oxford, Oxford University Press.

Beardsworth, A. and Keil, T. (1997), *Sociology on the Menu: An Invitation to the Study of Food and Society*, New York, Routledge.

Beck, U., Giddens, A. and Lash, S. (1994), *Reflexive Modernization*, Cambridge, Polity.

Becker, H. (1963), *Outsiders: Studies in the Sociology of Deviance*, New York, Free Press.

Bell, D. and Valentine, G. (1997), *Consuming Geographies: We Are Where We Eat*, New York, Routledge.

Bessy, C. and Chateauraynaud, F. (1993), 'Les ressorts de l'expertise: epreuves d'authenticité et engagement des corps', *Raisons Pratiques*, 4, pp. 141–64.

Bessy, C. and Chateauraynaud, F. (1995), *Experts et Faussaires*, Paris, Métailié.

Bourdieu, P. (1979), *La Distinction – Critique Sociale du Jugement*, Paris, Editions de Minuit.

Camporesi, P. (1989), *L'Officine des Sens – une Anthropologie Baroque*, Paris, Hachette.

Camporesi, P. (1992), *Le Goût du Chocolat*, Paris, Grasset & Fasquelle.

Capatti, A. (1989), *Le Goût du Nouveau – Origines de la Modernité Alimentaire*, Paris, Albin Michel.

Clifford, J. and Marcus, G. E. (eds) (1986), *Writing Culture: The Poetics and Politics of Ethnography*, Berkeley, University of California Press.

Couniham, C. and van Esterik, P. (eds) (1997), *Food and Culture: A Reader*, New York, Routledge.

Ehrlich, C. (1976), *The Piano: A History*, London, Dent & Sons.

Farb, P. and Armelagos, G. (1985), *Anthropologie des Coutumes Alimentaires*, Paris, Editions Denoël.

Featherstone, M. (1991), *Consumer Culture and Postmodernism*, London, Sage.

Featherstone, M., Epworth, M. and Turner, B. (1991), *The Body: Social Process and Cultural Theory*, London, Sage.

Fischler, C. (1990), *L'Homnivore*, Paris, Editions Odile Jacob.

Flandrin, J. and Montanari, M. (eds) (1996), *Histoire de L'Alimentation*, Paris, Fayard.

Garfinkel, H. (1967), *Studies in Ethnomethodology*, Englewood Cliffs, Prentice-Hall.

Giachetti, I. (ed.) (1992), *Plaisir et Préférences Alimentaires*, Paris, Polytechnica.

Giachetti, I. (ed.) (1996), *Identités des Mangeurs – Images des Aliments* (Paris, Polytechnica CNERNA CNRS.

Giddens, A. (1991), *Modernity and Self-Identity*, Cambridge, Polity.

Gomart, E. and Hennion, A. (1999), 'A sociology of attachment: music amateurs, drug users', in Law, J. and Hassard, J. (eds), *Actor Network Theory and After*, Oxford, Blackwell.

Goody, J. (1984), *Cuisines, Cuisine et Classes*, Paris, Centre Georges Pompidou–CCI.

Harris, M. and Ross, E. B. (eds) (1987), *Food and Evolution*, Philadelphia, PA, Temple University Press.

Hennion, A. (1993), *La Passion Musicale: Une Sociologie de la Médiation*, Paris, Métailié.

Hennion, A. (1997), 'Baroque and rock music: music, mediators and musical taste', *Poetics*, 24(6), pp. 415–35.

Hennion, A. and Méadel, C. (1989), 'The artisans of desire: the mediation of advertising between the product and the consumer', *Sociological Theory*, 7(2), pp. 191–209.

Letablier, M.-T. (1997), 'L'art et la matière: savoirs et ressources locales dans les productions spécifiques', unpublished report, Paris, Centre d'Etudes de l'Emploi.

Lévi-Strauss, C. (1964), *Le Cru et le Cuit*, Paris, Plon.

McIntosh, W. A. (1996), *Sociologies of Food and Nutrition*, New York and London, Plenum Press.

Mennell, S. (1985), *All Manners of Food: Eating and Taste in England and France from the Middle Ages to the Present*, Oxford, Blackwell.

Mennell, S., Murcott, A. and Vanotterloo, A. H. (1992), *The Sociology of Food: Eating, Diet and Culture*, London, Sage.

Merleau-Ponty, M. (1964), *Le Visible et l'Invisible*, Paris, Gallimard.

Mintz, S. W. (1996), *Tasting Food, Tasting Culture: Excursions into Eating, Culture and the Past*, Boston, MA, Beacon Press.

Peacock, A. and Weir, R. (1975), *The Composer in the Market Place*, London, Faber Music.

Pitte, J.-R. (1991), *Gastronomie Française: Histoire et Géographie d'une Passion*, Paris, Fayard.

Poulain, J. (2002), *Sociologies de L'Alimentation : Les Mangeurs et L'Espace Social Alimentaire*, Paris, Presses Universitaires de France.

Ricœur, P. (1990), *Soi-Même Comme un Autre*, Paris, Seuil.

Rose, N. and Miller, P. (1990), 'Governing economic life', *Economy & Society*, 19(1), pp. 1–31.

Rose, N. and Miller, P. (1992), 'Political power beyond the State', *British Journal of Sociology*, 43(2), pp. 173–205.

Teil, G. (1998), 'Devenir expert aromaticien: y a-t-il une place pour le goût dans les goûts alimentaires?', *Revue de Sociologie du Travail*, 4, pp. 503–22.

Teil, G. (2001), 'La production du jugement esthétique sur les vins par la critique vinicole', *Sociologie du Travail*, 43(1), pp. 67–89.

Teil, G. (2004), De la Coupe aux Lèvres. *Pratiques de la Perception et mise en marché des vin de qualité*, Toulouse, Octarès.

Terrio, S. J.(1997), 'Des maîtres chocolatiers aujourd'hui: Bayonne et la Côte Basque', *Pratiques, Rites, Ethnologie Française*, 27(2), pp. 205–13.

Vigarello, G. (1993), *Le Sain et le Malsain: Santé et Mieux-Etre Depuis le Moyen Age*, Paris, Seuil.

Warde, A. (1997), *Consumption, Food and Taste: Culinary Antinomies and Commodity Culture*, London, Sage.

Woolgar, S. (1988), *Knowledge and Reflexivity*, London, Sage.

2

Standards of taste and varieties of goodness: the (un)predictability of modern consumption

Jukka Gronow

Introduction

Very broadly speaking, there are three alternative understandings of the relationship between an object and its individual user. First, the value of an object is inherent to that object's use in its capacity for satisfying its user's needs or functions. Second, value is based on the individual's subjective evaluation of the object in question, regarding its utility, capacity to give pleasure, etc. The third, culturalist, alternative is to understand the value of an object in terms of the cultural meaning assigned to it and shared by the members of a community. It is thus determined by its place in a common cultural system of classification and codification. What is common to the three alternatives is that there is in them, in fact, no place for any genuine disagreement about matters of taste. They all seem to exemplify the old maxim according to which *de gustibus disputandum non est*. Whether it depends on subjective preferences or on some inherent objective characteristics, the relative worth – or quality – of objects is not open to argumentation or any social mediation. The third alternative, in its turn, leads to cultural relativism. Within any one culture the relative value and worth of objects is taken for granted but they are not open to revaluation or critical argumentation by the members of any other cultures. In order to better understand the relation between objects and their users one has to work out the relation between the individual and the social. With the help of a conceptual framework that makes it possible at the same time to understand how one can be both a unique individual and a part of a social whole, how to have an individual taste and to share it with others, it is possible to speak of (semi-)objective aesthetic standards which, however, are not stable but, in principle, open to negotiation and therefore in a state of constant change.

Following the Simmelian idea of a modern society consisting of a multitude of social circles, the social world perspective offers an opportunity to analyse the emergence and functioning of diverse and independent socially shared aesthetic standards and etiquettes. It also explains how even those who do not necessarily share the same taste can, at least to some degree, sensibly appreciate and even criticise each other's performances and choices.

Our modern society is not a mass society; neither is it a totally individualised society, nor a society consisting of several, totally separate, cultural enclaves. There are some aesthetic standards of excellence and goodness that can be mobilised in analysing and evaluating the formation of the demand for consumer goods and services. They do not tell us what the next novelties will be, but they do tell us that to be successful any novelties will be embedded in complex social practices and rules.

In our modern food culture there are at least some such relatively well-known and clear-cut aesthetic standards and etiquettes of taste to which some particular consumer goods or product groups belong and from which they derive their special worth and value. An almost classic example is the classification of wines according to a very complex taste system, corresponding in part to their origin and cultivation. Without doubt, to many people wines are more-or-less irrelevant as objects of consumption or appreciation, and there are people who might have a totally different relation to wine appreciation, their interest extending no further than, say, a wine's alcoholic content or presumed health effects. But, just as in the case of art, the classic example of social worlds (see Becker 1982), this does not exhaust the cultural and social importance of the social world(s) of wine lovers for the marketing and consumption of wines. As will be shown, the importance of such restricted social worlds to the wider world of mass consumption depends on the degree to which such social worlds are open to 'casual visitors' and welcome tourists.

In cow-milk drinking countries over the last thirty years, one remarkable development in consumption has been the extremely rapid diversification of milk products and the subsequent segmentation of the market. From a very standardised bulk product –consisting basically of only three products: milk, sour milk and cream – hundreds of new milk products have emerged, all neatly packaged and branded. The product variety offered for sale on the cooled shelves of any ordinary local supermarket might well exceed the number of different wines on sale in the local off-licences. Different systems for the classification of milk products, in part overlapping with each other, have evolved, which in the main refer to such *objective* criteria as the chemical and nutrient consistency of the milk. In addition to several 'normal milks', which differ from each other only in terms of their varying fat content, 'luxury' products are available such as low-fat A-milk, calcium-added milk (for those fearing or suffering from osteoporosis) or special milk (for those who are allergic to cows' milk). These examples would suggest that milk has become a medicine and drinking milk part of a medical treatment. Even to those who are more interested in enjoying life's small pleasures, several alternatives are on sale, such as sweetened milk-drinks, in handy small plastic bottles or cartons, with flavours to be enjoyed as refreshing soft drinks after jogging or skiing, etc. To complete the picture, a similar array of choices can be found, too, among sour milk and cream products.

It is, however, impossible to prove that this complicated and nuanced system of product classifications would have arisen side-by-side with some standards of taste developed in a social world(s) of lovers of milk-drinks. In many ways, the development of this modern variety of milk-drinks could better be explained by the needs of the dairy industry and its initiative in diversifying its products under the pressures of changing market conditions and diminishing or stabilising demand. It would also seem to fit very well into a picture of a somewhat homogeneous market, which at regular intervals welcomes minor novelties and where price diffentials are not remarkable either. But even in the case of milk-drinks there obviously are some (pseudo) objective criteria of classification that first determine the position of each commodity both as belonging to this particular market and as having a place among potential substitutes. What makes an understanding of such markets difficult is that the relation between the supply side and the demand side is not symmetrical: the meanings and practices which the producers suggest do not necessarily find any adherence among the consumers who might *invent* totally new and unanticipated uses for these products.

The *Erlebnis*rational consumer

Gerhard Schulze's study *Die Erlebnisgesellschaft* (1991), of a society emphasising subjectivity and inner experiences, includes many valuable insights and observations concerning the changing nature of modern consumption and the orientation of modern consumers. Basically an empirical research into the various consumer schemes and the milieu of Nuremberg, West Germany, in the 1980s, it achieved the almost prophetic stature of a *Zeitgiadnose*, a diagnosis of our times, coined in the slogan *Erlebnisgesellschaft*. In Schulze's opinion a drastic change has occurred in the orientation and intentions of the consumer. From a traditional, basically instrumental, orientation to finding effective means of satisfying needs, consumers have moved towards the achievement of subjective mental states. Their inner experiences are the final and only criteria of success.[1] As Schulze formulated it, the subject becomes its own object. Such an activity is rational, but its rationality is of a rather peculiar kind. So far as the purposive activity of means' selection is concerned, this rationality does not differ from instrumental rationality, the effective choice of means by which to achieve some definite ends.

What is peculiar about it is rather the character of the *ends* themselves. The goals of actions are ephemeral subjective states, which change constantly, of which the consumer is often uncertainly aware. Consequently, the selection of means for their achievement also becomes problematical. It is difficult to know when those goals have actually been reached or to judge whether they have been optimally achieved. Needs can be satisfied in principle but one can never know whether the mental state reached – often only for a fleeting moment – was really worth the effort. Perhaps one could have done better and experienced something more exciting or pleasurable by some other means, elsewhere. Furthermore, the same means that helped to gain satisfactory results at one time could equally well fail at some future time: there can be no guarantee of success (Schulze 1991: 116–17).

By the phrase *Erlebnissociety* Schulze intended to strongly emphasise subjective experiences as the peculiar goal of the activity of consumers in a modern consumer society. As Pasi Falk (1994), for instance, has pointed out, it is to be doubted that consumption in any society, ever, has been characterised by the satisfaction of only objective needs.[2] Therefore it would be better to treat Schulze's two types of rationality as pure – ideal – types of action. Obviously most acts of consumption unite, to a lesser or greater degree, both aspects. As Csikzentmihalyi (1981) argued, even though there are expressive activities where instrumental concerns play no role (making love, listening to music, climbing a mountain, etc.), it is difficult to conceive of purely instrumental activities where a person would be unaware of how much or how little gratification is derived from the experience at the moment.[3] In many cases, however, it makes good sense to speak of consumption as predominantly oriented towards inner experiences (*Erlebnisse*) as compared to more directly needs-oriented or instrumental consumption. Schulze's own examples range from dining at a gourmet restaurant – which, to some people, might be just an ordinary business lunch but which to most would be a special treat to be remembered – to a tractor – which might be driven in races or be an object of adoration to the afficionado but which is mostly 'consumed' as a work instrument, plain and simple. However, not even tractors are *just* tractors any more, their makers claiming, for instance, to offer their drivers a sense of exquisite luxury and comfort. Similarly there are not only gourmet restaurants that cater to the social elite and workplace canteens with crude spoons and plates for the workers, but many intermediary food outlets which also claim to be luxurious, at least to a moderate degree.

Pure examples of 'inner-directed' consumption are to be found in the cultural artefacts, services and products of the culture industry, from movies and TV programmes to recordings of music and concerts, from sports events to literature, from charter flights to southern destinations to Sony PlayStations – none of which so much as pretend to serve any useful purpose: they are there 'just for fun'.

The five principles of consumer demand

Despite or, rather, because of the strong emphasis on the individual's subjective experiences which are typical of the new rationality of consumption, the social patterns emerging from that rationality are far from *individualistic* in any common sense of the word. On the contrary, the society of inner experiences is characterised by a very strong degree of social conformity and homogeneity of behaviour. *Erlebnissociety* is typically a society of (relatively homogenous) mass consumption, admittedly with many individual, social and periodic minor variations, but with very little by way of more daring expressions of people's genuine subjectivity or any excessive individuality of life styles. This paradoxical conclusion follows from the basic uncertainty and indeterminacy typical of the situation facing a modern consumer. Five interesting principles follow in Schulze's analysis (1991: 433–4). They are all means of coping with the ephemeral nature of consumer goals and the basic subjective uncertainty concerning their achievement.

The principle of correspondence
Singular actions are tied together by some criterion, such as the distinctive style of an individual consumer: things are somehow thought or felt to 'go together' or to fit together. Even that strategy, however, is problematical in relation to ephemeral goals: for instance, the desire to experience something 'exciting' but without being able to articulate what that might be ('I want to visit a new, exciting and stylish restaurant, but, at the same time, I probably wouldn't feel at home there after all.')

The principle of abstraction
This is a strategy based on optimising the outcome of consumption habits or of long-term consumption rather than of single acts. It means using some *abstract* criterion of selection over a wide variety of concrete objects. Typical examples are the preference to consume things sequentially, like TV or radio series, journals or books, or with common threads, such as movies with the same main actors or concerts with the same singers, or restaurants with some typical ethnic cuisine ('I like Chinese food' or 'I only go to real Irish pubs').

The principle of accumulation
Based on the idea of accumulating singular similar experiences, this principle leads to a tendency to repetition. What was successful once is probably worth trying again. On the other hand experiences tend to lose value when repeated. The paradox, which concerns also the principle of abstraction, is that the best experiences often come unexpected, as if by chance, walking along the street ('I always go to my local pub, but something exciting might be happening in the pub just around the corner').

The principle of variation
In compensation for the inherent tendency to repetition, variation is welcomed. It is, however, important to note that this is a question strictly of variation – preferably within a genre – not of real novelty. One changes one's pub, but not the neighbourhood; or one looks for a pub with a greater variety of ales, not for the diversity of its wines. The modern *Erlebnis*rational consumer is not adventurous.

The principle of autosuggestion
This is the main reason for social conformity, and for the close observance of the habits of one's own social milieu. Since one can never be sure of the 'real' worth and value of one's experiences ('I might have missed something more

exciting; was this all there was to it after all!') one constantly looks up for one's peers for the confirmation of their authenticity and value. ('I visited this new pub across the road because my friends now go there and they told me it's nice.' More generally, the surest sign of a good venue is that it's full of people – even better if one has to queue in order to get a table, while next door is a similar place with lots of empty tables.)

As Schulze pointed out, modern consumers are inclined to social conformism not because they feel embarrassed of being different or are afraid of behaving themselves improperly: it is not social propriety that guides them. They follow the example set by others out of personal *uncertainty*, because they are afraid of missing out on something more exciting and important that presumably all others are enjoying. There is no other criterion of the value of an object than one's own belief in it. It is as good as one believes it to be. It is also important to note that such consumption and its validation are beyond the question of manipulation or any false promises since there cannot after all be any objective criteria to prove that there are some other, more real, values attached to the object of consumption.

The main conclusion, then, is that the often presumed individualisation of consumption, for example its liberation both from social restrictions or ties and from the constraints of physical necessity, does not lead to increasing heterogeneity but to increasing homogeneity of consumption, and, more concretely in the case analysed by Schulze, to the formation of a few massive and internally relatively homogenous schemes and milieux of consumption. Novely and change are welcomed, but only in small, well-proportioned doses. Such variation is not allowed to break with the more general principles of connectedness and uniformity.[4]

The varieties of goodness

The main problem affecting Schulze's position – and in this respect it shares the destiny of many other diagnoses of the goods or ills of modern consumer society – is that in his scheme there is no place for any socially shared principles, or criteria, of goodness other than repetition and the imitation of the 'generalised' other: either you like what all the others seem to like or you are left all on your own to choose according to your own personal whims and wishes. In his scheme the social milieu in which an individual is living is there mainly to confirm by the observable example of others that the individual experience was truly real, that he or she 'was not just making it all up'. The principle of the mass is the only etiquette or guideline of taste, or, if you allow for social segmentation, the example of one's social group. There cannot be any scales of goodness – unless the strength of one's own experiences and their possible resonance with those of others is taken as such. (For an interesting account of broad taste classes, see Gans 1974.) Consequently there cannot be any sensible discussion about the worth of one's taste: one cannot possibly present arguments to convince others of its worth; at most one might seduce others into trying it. This leads to a state of uncertainty. There is a strong need of aesthetic definition in an *Erlebnissociety*. As Schulze emphasised, following a discussion among German academics about the aestheticisation of everyday life (Gronow 1997), these experiences are aesthetic by their nature, or at least they resemble and can be described as such: they are 'exciting', 'enjoyable', 'interesting', etc.

To take an example used by Schulze, cars are commonly advertised as having capacities that, obviously, are practically useless to any ordinary driver. Since there is a speed limit of some 70 miles per hour in every European country (except, of course, in Germany, the land of Mercedes Benz), one could not, without breaking the law, enjoy to its full capacity a new car capable of a speed of 200 miles per hour which accelerates from zero to 100 in 6 seconds, not to speak of the other technical attributes advertised in new cars. Many drivers would probably still regard these cars as objectively better than many slower and technically less advanced cars. As we know, utensils of home technology, and computers and mobile phones are regularly marketed in similar terms to emphasise their technical superiority – thus, its accumulator lasts a week longer; it is ten times faster than any other; it can be programmed to complete various distinct tasks; the sound output is greater and its quality higher, etc. – and announce capacities mostly never utilised by, and of little practical value to, the great majority of their buyers. A bottle of fine champagne, a Bordeaux wine or a particular caviar might, in the world of food, be equivalent to a Mercedes, though most people would perhaps care very little, and would say that any decent sparkling or red wine or fish roe does equally well. Many might even argue that what in fact they eat or drink is not only cheaper but also tastes much better than other alternatives.

In Schulze's understanding such technically superior qualities as exist are advertised to make a general impression on the buyer and to enliven her or his imagination (whatever subconscious motivations ever presumed). They are symbols of something else (to take a trivial example, fast car = masculine power), which presumably arouses and appeals to the inner mental states of consumers: they promise some exciting experiences and participation in the good life (Falk 1991; Gronow 1997: 442). As such it would not matter at all if the car could not perform as promised, since the owner could not possibly ever test it in practice. For the owner it would be quite satisfactory, so long as he or she is convinced that the car is capable of such performance – and that some other cars are not.

What makes this kind of reasoning somewhat suspect is that, despite the inner-orientation of the consumers, many products are nevertheless presented to them as having presumably technically – and in some sense objectively – superior qualities and capacities. This is true in particular of many items of consumer technology, both domestic and other, but also of more amorphous items, such as foods and drinks. They not only offer a general promise of good life with youthfulness, love and sunny beaches (like Coca Cola) but often refer (and people refer to them too) to their nutritional value and healthfulness, not to speak of other, less concrete, characteristics, such as better taste or propriety according to some social etiquette, convention or tradition. For people who wish to taste *real* champagne, a 'ready-made' etiquette advises them on what would be the *proper* occasion, manner and place to enjoy it. In other words, they could, like tourists, 'visit' a social world of 'champagne drinkers' and borrow its standards of taste for the occasion. One might, of course, claim that such characterisations as make possible the evaluation of the goodness or fitness of a product are basically inherited remnants from an older culture of use oriented more to instrumental consumption (or of a traditional, ritualistic consumption). People not only want to say that something is pleasant or lovely: they are also rationalising and giving reasons for their preferences and likings, explaining and convincing others of the superiority of their own choices.

What I argue here – in line with my earlier work on the sociology of taste (Gronow 1997) – is that it is reasonable to claim both that modern consumers make their choices on their own, often free from both physical and social constraints, following their personal wishes and whims, and that there are nevertheless some (semi-)objective aesthetic schemes, codes or guidelines of taste which help us to evaluate and choose specific objects of consumption. These guidelines are changing and not fixed; yet they are shared – and often taken for granted – by various groups of people. In following them one can make use of various value scales to evaluate the internal and relative goodness of the objects and services offered. Therefore they can also convincingly be utilised in marketing and advertising. From this it follows that one can improve, even perfect, one's own performance and evaluate the performance of others. This is a possibility which is not restricted to certain virtuoso shoppers (cf. the role Weber reserved to some rare religious virtuosi) but one that is left open to practically any ordinary consumer. Just as one can perform better on the sports field or as an artist, so one can perform better as a consumer or shopper – say, of mobile phones or Italian sausages and cheese. Although such performance might appear to many as irrelevant and uninteresting, all that is needed is that there are *some* significant others who acknowledge its value and are ready to appreciate it.

What I argue here is that such criteria of goodness and improvement of both taste and 'technical' performance do make sense, though not as plain and simple objective criteria of technical superiority as such, nor simply as symbols which refer to some deeper, inner, subjective meanings. There are objective – in the sense of socially shared and binding – aesthetic codes that determine the inner value and relative worth of things to people. They are socially constructed and negotiable, and as such (semi-)objective, aesthetics which are taken for granted by the participants in any – smaller or bigger – social world. They are utilised as reference points even by members of the 'wider' society not necessarily directly involved in their creation and legitimation processes.

This should be evident in the case of such consumer goods as wines, beers or spirits, in relation to which there are readily available systems of classification of taste and quality. But even in the case of the newly created variety of milk products, both the producers, advertisers and marketers, on the one hand, and the consumers, on the other, can have recourse to such aesthetic standards and seek advice to find new uses for old products or old and new uses for new products. This would not, however, take place in quite the same way as in the case of wines – where the commercial classification and the classifications of the social world(s) of wine lovers coincide and dynamically reinforce and support each other – but in a less pronounced manner. The obvious difference is that there is no such clear-cut social world under whose auspices all or most of the products of this branch of food industry would fall. They are not as essential to the core activities of any social world as, for instance, wines.

The social world perspective

The social world perspective, formulated well over thirty years ago by symbolic interactionists, offers the best conceptual tools with which to develop such an idea of an objective aesthetics which is all the time open to change and which, in principle, encourages the creation of standards and is potentially receptive to new consumer goods (Noro 1995). Social worlds, according to their classic definition, emerge and are organised around some core activities that 'are believed to be legitimate, fun, appropriate, aesthetically right, morally right, leading to truth' (Strauss 1983: 128). Such social worlds can be more or less amorphous or they can be organised, varying from thematic chatting groups and lovers of particular art forms to more organised hobby clubs (like a sport-fishing club). Probably the ideal types are to be found among the many well-established free-time clubs, keeping in mind, however, that their constituency is not restricted to an inner core of ordinary members or activists but includes people who are more loosely attached to them and who often outnumber many times the real activists. The main idea is, however, that there is some kind of an involved inner core of members in addition to any amorphous circles of more loosely attached participants with lesser degrees of involvement. According to Strauss, it is when people start taking their collective activities seriously that the need for organisation develops. Members of the group will

> design their own sites, regularise their meetings, produce literature for their internal and/or external consumption, inventing/testing/improving/producing/ distributing the technology brought into being by the core social world activities; building networks of relationships with necessary external agents (suppliers, distributors, purchasers, promoters, service people, even travel agents); and sometimes, of course, formalizing internal relationships by founding of associations, complete with constitutions, official positions, rules and regulations.
> (1983: 128)

As the list of activities and agencies in and around any social world suggests, many aspects of commercial consumption naturally become attached to it; most social worlds can equally well give rise to various forms of commercial activity and application. The rapid development of sports gear and wear offers an illuminating example.

What distinguishes social worlds from other kinds of social organisations is their voluntary nature. And what distinguishes one social world from another is the legitimising process specific to each: in the final instance each has a set of aesthetic rules and procedures, an etiquette or a code, enabling the setting of standards and evaluation. The purpose of aesthetics is two-fold: the identification of objects with aesthetic value ('*Is* this art?') and of authentic issues, i.e. issues which belong, or are part of, this particular social world; and the establishment of the quality or worth, the aesthetic value, of any single issue that has been acknowledged as authentic ('Is this *good* art?') (Becker 1982; Gilmore 1990: 150). As Strauss (1982: 180) formulated it,

> this question of authenticity is a different issue than whether a given product or performance measures high, medium, or low on some scale: that is, the question of how useful, beautiful, safe, or moral it is . . . The former issue pertains to the boundaries of the social world or sub-social world; the latter involves not a question of boundaries but of the differential embodiment of in-world values.

It is part of the unofficial nature of most social worlds as well as of aesthetic judgements in general that there are no – and in principle cannot be any – explicit rules or regulations concerning such issues. They are learned in a process of socialisation into the world, new members often following the example set by other, more experienced, members (learning by doing). Hence the importance to social worlds – as well as to education in general – of exemplary figures and models.

Types of involvement in social worlds

Most, if not practically all, people belong, in one way or another, to several such social worlds, or circles. The extent of their involvement, however, varies greatly. The typology propounded by David R. Unruh (1979 and 1980), which is based on degrees of involvement, differentiates four types, ranging from the near total life – encompassing the involvement of insiders – to the total non-involvement, or disinterestedness, shown by outsiders or 'strangers', who must nevertheless be somehow 'taken into account' by others more involved in the social world.[5] These types are (counting from most involved to least involved) the insiders, the regulars, the tourists and the strangers. Insiders and regulars are the elements most constitutive of a social world. Insiders, whose entire social existence and worldview can centre around a single all-important social world, 'seek control, direct, and create social worlds for others'. Their role is one of 'creation and intimacy'. They also take care of the recruitment of new members and arouse the interests of potential new participants. Regulars act as if the social world is their home; they are familiar with its 'etiquette', to which they tend to make few adjustments. Their attitude is characterised by 'integration, familiarity and attachment' (Unruh 1979: 121ff.). The legitimacy of the etiquette of any social world is achieved by the unquestioning loyalty of the regulars, who mostly take for granted the rules, the relevance of the issues and the scales of worth of that social world, and to a lesser extent, by the interest shown by the tourists.

Tourists, as the name indicates, are occasional visitors to a social world. They do not show any long-term involvement, being motivated by mere curiosity. They must be reasonably aware of the social world to be interested in visiting it, but they are committed to that world only insofar as it remains 'entertaining, profitable, or diversionary' (Unruh 1980: 281). Some social worlds are more dependant on the interest shown by tourists than are others which are more exclusive.

Strangers, in contrast to the other three types, have no involvement at all in the social world. They are not interested in, indeed are not necessarily aware of, its existence or activities. What Unruh evidently has in mind in saying that any social world must take strangers into account is that they are the others, the outsiders, the strangers against whom the other, more involved, participants can contrast their own experiences and worldviews. The term 'stranger' is borrowed from Simmel's *Soziologie*, first published in 1908 (see Simmel 1992: 764). For Simmel, a stranger is an outsider who brings with her or him other and more objective standards and criteria into a social world and so can inspect it impartially. In this way, the presence of a stranger can help to relativise the standards.

Any social world thus has an established and legitimised set of aesthetic evaluations of its own concerning both the authenticity of the issues (the kinds of activities, objects and techniques which belong to that social world) and the evaluation of their relative worth or goodness within that social world. Some social worlds are conservative and are doubtless more concerned to preserve their activities and issues in as stable and unchanging a form as possible, whereas ongoing development and refinement might be a major interest in others. The rules and practices of a social world are always *in principle* negotiable, and can therefore be in a state of constant change. A social world perspective presents only a phenomenology of social worlds, and gives no reasons and explanations as such for the variation and multiplication of social worlds. However, so far as social worlds are either interested in expanding their field of influence and recruiting new regular members (or attracting tourists) or are concerned to maintain the interest of the current insiders and regulars, one would presume that they have some inbuilt mechanism of renewal. Such renovation would more naturally lead to a continual refining and an increasing complexifying of 'the rules of the game' than it would to any drastic changes concerning these basic issues or the value of the 'game' itself.

The segmentation process of social worlds

There is, however, another mechanism, the segmentation process of social worlds, or the emergence of new social sub-worlds from established ones.

The segmentation in the social world of *haute cuisine* through the repeated emergence of *nouvelle cuisines* is a good example of such segmentation (see, for instance, Mennell 1985).

According to Anselm Strauss (1983), one can describe such a segmentation process in seven stages:

1 forming a new social sub-world;
2 defining and building its legitimate core activity;
3 differentiating and defining the new borders;
4 writing and rewriting its own history;
5 competing for resources with the old one;
6 elevating and manoeuvring in arenas;
7 further segmentation.

In their exemplary study of recreation specialisation Ditton et al. (1992: 36–7) analysed the ways in which new sub-worlds can distance themselves from their 'parent' worlds. In their own case – sport-fishing – segmentation took place

- around spatial distinction or topographic characteristics (different stretches of the stream are important);
- around different objects (fish species);
- around technology and skill (fishing equipment and its use);
- around an ideology (delineating real and authentic experience);
- along the lines of the intersection of social worlds (emerging new hybrids);
- through recruitment. (According to the authors new members tend to maximise chances for new lines of activity, uses of technology, ideological positions and further segmentation; but, in principle, different means and channels of recruitment could, as such, give rise to further segmentation, too.)

One would expect that segmentation in one of these aspects would lead also to differentiation in other aspects and, finally, to the emergence of a separate new social world.

This process of social world segmentation is only a descriptive account; it gives no tools with which to identify the kinds of social worlds which are given to segmentation, say when they will segment and why. One could, however, claim that the greater the number of the insiders and regulars in a social world the more encouraged is the emergence of new sub-worlds, which gradually turn into separate worlds. In such social worlds there may be insufficient room for new insiders wishing to take an active part in the creation and maintenance of the rules and rituals and who therefore are tempted to establish a new social world of their own. In the beginning it will differ only slightly from the old one ('We play only indoors' or 'We eat only simple and stylish food', that is the real thing), existing alongside it, but gradually will develop into an independent form of an activity with a particular etiquette of its own. One could probably claim that in our societies such segmentation processes have been greatly accelerated, at least within free-time activities: for instance, in the world of sport new sub-worlds seem to emerge all the time and at an accelerating tempo, often also demanding official recognition as legitimate games (there is, for instance, a growing list of sports waiting to be approved and taken into the official programme of the Olympic Games).

The inner development of the 'rules of the game' (in a social world) and the emergence of new 'games' (in a social sub-world) are the two parallel mechanisms that explain the renovation and change of social worlds and their aesthetic standards.[6] Whereas the first leads mainly to refinement and increasing complexity inside an existing social world, the second concerns the very core activity and the authenticity of its issues (something totally new becomes interesting, exciting and worth promoting.)

The principles of supply

It has already been pointed out that the rationality of producers and suppliers is different from that of consumers; yet they must somehow admit of being matched and coordinated. We also know that to most – if not practically all – social worlds some commercial activities are closely attached. Sometimes a social world finds such commercial activities as it needs already in the market where they have been used and consumed in other contexts and for other purposes. They must, however, be redefined in the social world that now utilises them for its own purposes.[7] Often, by contrast, a new social world will give rise to new commercial activities (the opening of specialist shops, production units or meeting points; the founding of journals; or the promotion of travel arrangements, etc.); and, occasionally, new social worlds emerge around technical innovations and their commercial applications (recently, for instance, various social worlds have emerged around new computer and information technology). A third alternative is that such social worlds have initiated and actively promoted the process of innovation and product development (e.g. the development of the Linux operating system, created with the contributions of thousands of enthusiasts all around the world who are members of a loosely organised social world of computer programmers).

One of the merits of Schulze's study is that, in addition to analysing the principles guiding the orientation of demand in a *Erlebnissociety*, it described principles governing the supply side. According to him, there are four such principles of, or strategies for, rationalising the supply of products and services (Schulze 1991: 442–3).

- Schematisation is a strategy that helps to incorporate supplies into schemes which are relatively stable over longer periods of time and groups of customers (e.g. musical genres).

- Profiling exists in order to create an aura, or image, of uniqueness around one's products in order to differentiate them from others.
- Transformation creates and offers novelties for sale (again, safe variations of the old rather than real novelties).
- Suggestion corresponds to the principle of autosuggestion on the demand side (since growth of production is inbuilt in the whole economic system there is no need for a principle corresponding to the fifth principle of accumulation on the side of the consumers).

Both sides, the demanders and the suppliers, are thus interested mainly in everyday schemes: producers attach some familiar key stimuli to their products; and consumers have a need for simplification to help their orientation. Change is welcomed, and producers are ready to satisfy it, but there is no big motivation to produce any unexpected and radically different products and services: it is wiser and better, in general, for both sides to play safe.

The social world perspective adds to such analyses an important dimension: it can better explain both consumers' willingness to approve and adopt real novelties of all kinds (they make sense as soon as they become essential issues, objects, services, techniques in any new or old social worlds) and the use of semi-objective social aesthetics regulating the value and worth of various items. This offers the producers no straightforward strategy for determining their future supplies or the marketing of novelties. But it certainly means that the alternatives available are not just those of sticking to old practices, earlier proven successful, or of blindly probing one's way by throwing bait to consumers. There are genuine criteria of authenticity, worth and goodness which make sense to consumers and that can also be utilised, at least to some extent and in various ways, through marketing and design.

Hennion and Méadel (1989: 192) emphasise the crucial role of advertising agencies and marketing institutions in defining what a product really is. They formulated a mediating position in which advertising works as operating in

> a world where there is neither technical necessity nor determining needs, without for all that being able to refer comfortably either to the equivalence of all objects or to the arbitrary nature of all desire. Experts of advertising understood their work as mainly to mediate – or fulfil a gap – between these two extremes, to give the product new dimensions. The product is not treated as a ready-made artefact with predetermined objective functions. It changes in their hands going through different steps in various marketing and advertising departments or offices. This is, in their own words, a model 'where it is no longer possible to draw a distinction between the technical characteristics of the product and its signifying character, because everything, from marketing to conditioning by way of product tests, of measurements of the competition and of the internal mobilization of the enterprise, functions on the double register of the object: it is a thing, but a thing for a person. A technical product and a product, which communicates. A product that fulfils a need if it knows how to create the needer. (p. 199)

What the social world perspective adds to this very illuminating account of the role of advertising is to show that in accomplishing all this the advertising agencies operate in a world inhabited by distinct aesthetic schemes in which various objects and services can be placed or have already a well-established position. The schemes and places inhabited by the object are not stable but in a permanent state of change and transformation, new schemes emerging while old ones wither away. This is identical to the way in which individuals inhabit modern society. As Georg Simmel (1955) suggested, individuals normally belong to several social circles, investing various degrees of involvement in each, and their very individuality is determined by the specific combination of such social worlds. Thus, one could claim that, normally, any one artefact or service can simultaneously belong to several social worlds and play a more-or-less similar or different role and have a different meaning in each of those worlds.

The social world perspective does not, of course, offer any simple solution to the problems of marketing, still less guarantee commercial success. Whether any one new object or service offered for sale and marketed to the members of a social world (presuming that it would be possible to identify them with sufficient precision) really finds some resonance and stimulates demand depends, finally, on the insiders and regulars' recognition of the object as their own – as having an intrinsic value in this particular social world. The relations between the producers and these involved members of social worlds are asymmetrical and not reciprocal: a producer's rationality is not the same as that of a consumer. Producers themselves are not usually – and in many cases could not possibly be – members of these social worlds. What the producers can do is to try to be well informed about such social worlds and their particular aesthetics, which might be or become relevant for consumers of their products. In any case, there is an objective reference point, a socially valid frame, between the subjective image of the product and its objective characteristics – which actually first helps to determine them – to which both consumers and producers, in their respective ways, can refer. (These frames are also, however, transformed constantly due to their own activities and interests.) This is equally true in the worlds of fashion and home electronics, of cuisine and cars, wines and beers, PCs and mobile phones, etc.

The point was made earlier that at times new commercially successful enterprises emerge directly from the activities of (non-commercial) social worlds. Insiders who started as enthusiastic volunteers, with a particular hobby as their passion, may gradually turn it into a profession, open shops, workshops or service centres. They might thereafter become pure businessmen, though some will preserve or even strengthen their former status as core members in their social worlds. In a similar way, one could claim that producers often are their own best customers (think, for instance, of the various art worlds whose producers, mediators, critics and managers frequent exhibitions, buy each others' works). In this way, there could be, at least in some fields, a closer relationship, even cooperation, between certain producers and key consumers. For example, Pierre Bourdieu (1984: 367) suggested that members of the new middle class, in particular those active in new professions, often were their own best customers.

The food scene: how to identify social worlds

One of the main problems in the empirical study of social worlds is of knowing how to identify them. It is evident that one can identify in food culture (defined here as cooking and eating), as in almost any important sphere of human life, numerous more-or-less well-organised big social worlds. No systematic empirical research has been conducted about them and therefore the following remarks are preliminary and hypothetical.[8]

It would understandably be impossible to identify all the members of a social world – not to speak of tourists and strangers – lacking any formal organisation and membership status. Their identification becomes obviously more difficult the less involved the members are. Howard Becker (1982; see also Unruh 1980: 291) suggests that the best way to recognise a social world is to identify its core product – loosely defined as objects, experiences or events (for instance, wine-tasting) – and trace it back to all those who contribute to its production and circulation (in addition to the obvious wine producers and sellers, connoisseurs, experts, critics, etc.). Equally important as key products for the identification of social worlds are their communication centres since the limits of effective communication are also the limits of any one social world. Such centres vary from authorised publishers and publications, to information sites and key informants (e.g. wine journals and media programmes). Also, social worlds often present themselves to outsiders in specific places and spaces, such as specialist outlets (a gourmet shop or a wine exhibition) where members gather.

The social worlds perspective can explain one of the surprising features of modern food culture. It has been argued that eating and culinary delights are not, as a matter of course, the central issues in the lives of most people. The meals of most Scandinavians, for instance, are by no means notably imaginative or varied (Kjaernes 2001). And yet popular culture tells a different story: many TV programmes on food compete with the most popular soap operas in terms of viewing figures; the most popular food journals have large circulations; newspapers feature popular food columns; every year hundreds of new cookery books, many of them big editions, are published for Christmas; and sampling the local cuisine is a 'must' for holidaymakers wherever they are. Judging from this one would imagine that culinary culture, both at home and in restaurants, would occupy a prominent place in the lives of most people and that people generally would be extremely concerned with issues of eating.

The secret is that social worlds of food, probably because they are relatively familiar and offer ease of access to practically everyone, seem to seduce many tourists willing to visit them at least occasionally to have a taste of – or only a look at[9] –what they have to offer. Thus, many people offer themselves and their families occasional 'treats', Sunday lunches or dinners with friends, at which something 'special' is served; and to do so, they have merely to 'visit' some relevant social worlds. For tourists, the 'relevance of a social world is often times pre-packaged, directed and coached' (Unruh 1979: 124), and often for sale too. Regulars and insiders have an important task to enact their social worlds for the benefit of interested tourists and offer their treats in nice ready-made packages.

Judging by the popularity of food columns in newspapers and food and health journals, many tourists visit these social worlds with regularity. The origins of all public discourses on food cannot, by any means, be traced back to any social world in the strict sense. Much of the programmatic, ideological, entertaining or persuasive talk about food in the media most certainly does not have any direct relation or relevance to any existing social world. They are mostly just recycled items from the very rich historical cultural knowledge of food accumulated through the ages and offered for public entertainment by journalists; and, like other retro-fashions they are often wrapped up in new packaging. Therefore, in order to identify interesting social worlds of food one should, following Becker's advice, look out for various recommended standards of taste and etiquette, but also, and primarily, for products and 'services' (in the wider sense of the word), techniques, instruments and tools, as well as for communication centres of various kinds and key figures.

With these reservations in mind, one could as a preliminary divide the social worlds of food into two big groups. One group is concerned mainly with culinary taste, cooking skills and table etiquette. Further division by such criteria as the presumed cultural or geographical origin of foodstuffs, preferred methods of preparation or kitchen technology, preferred venues for and company with whom to share the experience, the importance of cooking versus eating, or some natural classification of dishes (fish, vegetarian, beef, etc., or according to their provenance). If one adds the dimension of drink one easily finds several more (beer-lovers versus wine-lovers, fans of single-malt whisky versus Russian vodka, abstainers, mineral-water enthusiasts, traditional sour-milk drinkers, etc.). It would be relatively easy to find in almost any European country clubs, journals, publications, restaurants and other meeting places that cherish one or more of these or similar 'core' issues. Evidently there are also tens of thousands of insiders and regulars who treat them with gravity.

One of the most influential and interesting recent examples of this kind of social world is the Slow Food (SF) Movement, which originated in Italy but has become a worldwide phenomenon (see Murdoch and Miele, chapter 7 of this volume). It started as a reaction to the opening of McDonald's restaurants in Rome and around Italy in the early 1980s, its main task the promotion of local and regional cuisines. It has developed a formal organisation and very elaborate standards of culinary taste that are used to judge whether any given food or dish is 'authentic', i.e. real slow food, and what its relative worth is. SF is interesting because it has had commercial implications from the very beginning. During its short life it has already experienced segmentation and change as ecological concerns and agricultural policy have become increasingly important issues on its agenda. SF offers an interesting example of a social world that has evolved into a social movement. What separates a social movement from a 'pure' world is that it has a political agenda and a platform from which to defend the importance of its concern, with varying degrees of activity and aggression, to others, or 'strangers'.

The other important, and rapidly increasing, visible group of social worlds is centred around the issues of health and fitness. The most popular and organised ones inevitably are concerned mainly with weight-watching. The worldwide enterprise Weight Watchers is probably one of the best organised and biggest, but new dietary programmes, with their own techniques and methods, promises and ideologies, and with (inconsistently) serious and involved practitioners, emerge all the time. Weight Watchers has an added dimension, which makes it, like Alcoholics Anonymous, akin to a religious sect: one can become 'hooked' on it. Losing weight following the programmed steps becomes a lifelong struggle for adherents, just as a virtuous life is the goal of a believer wishing to please a god. On the other hand, any 'tourist' can make a visit to this world by, for example, buying a ready-made Weight Watcher's meal from the supermarket.

In general, however, such social worlds could be called 'dietary worlds' as opposed to 'taste worlds'. They recommend tightly organised and restricted diets (from strict vegetarians to vitamin freaks, from those who eat only 'living food' to those who cook everything in an oven, from those who follow the rules of official nutrition science to those who practise some self-made or 'folk' dietary beliefs – diet variations are endless). Many insiders find that such social worlds fill their time and give life meaning, whereas regulars might follow the diets recommended but not make that their main duty. At the same time numerous tourists continue to visit one or more of them periodically, not necessarily staying loyal to a single world for any extended period of time, not taking them necessarily all that seriously, either, but, anyhow, following and adopting their aesthetics in some relevant aspects. In ultimate cases, a social world can become almost private. In such cases a dedicated insider faces the danger of receiving the stigma of deviancy or mental illness. Such would be the case, for instance, for a private collector who keeps her or his collection totally secret or has value standards that are not intelligible to anyone else.

Good and bad food

How does all this help us to determine the goodness of any food product, a dish, a dinner or a drink? The question is problematical and its answer can be determined only within the limits of a certain social world. Many products, just like individuals, can participate in numerous social worlds at the same time, and therefore their measuring stocks can be diverse and often even negate one another. Anyone interested in marketing a product can therefore choose from two distinct strategies. One is to try to convince as many social circles as possible that the product is of special value to them, even though to each of them it would be so in a different way: it can be tasty, nutritionally balanced, an essential part of a traditional national cuisine, local, vitamised, easy to cook, festive, etc. The more 'hooks' the product has the better – up to that certain point when they start competing with and eliminating each other and cease to be at all convincing. To many regulars and insiders products with multiple dimensions might also feel inauthentic.

The other marketing strategy is to concentrate effort to convey the merits of the product to just a single social world, one to which, however, it is understood to be extraordinarily important – possibly the product without which that social world could not exist at all. This leads to specialisation and emphasises the uniqueness of the product. It is easy to name numerous, already classic, examples from the social world of haute cuisine, such as truffles, oysters, *foie gras*; champagne or wines from Bourdeaux; or, in their own right, traditional British ales; and, to take some Finnish examples, caviar from white fish, river crabs, or some particular wild mushrooms or berries. One could equally well name several such products that are important and very specific to certain dietary social worlds (milk products to people who do not tolerate milk, margarine without any fat at all, products with calcium added to people fearing osteoporosis, ecological products cultivated without any possible 'unnatural' technical means, etc.). Most social worlds are open to tourists from other worlds who can often make use of such special offers and by experimenting with them or redefining them incorporate them into their own aesthetics and thus enrich their own culinary experiences. This process of crossbreeding, and the ensuing potential for the emergence of new social sub-worlds, seem to be accelerating in our times.

There is a group of social worlds related to food and eating that enjoys a peculiar position and a certain hegemonic privilege in defining certain generally applicable aesthetic standards. These comprise state officials and experts who enjoy the legitimising status of science and whose task it is to take care of national health and guard us from the risks or harmful effects of food and drink. Insofar as such experts and their organisations have alone acted as guardians of food safety their authority has been undisputed (cf., however, the cases of food scares and scandals like mad cow disease). When, with developments in biotechnology and preventive medicine, they are increasingly expected to identify not only what is dangerous and harmful but also what is good and healthful, their role becomes more problematical. To the extent that they can issue legal restrictions and punish those who break them (for instance, in such clear-cut cases when 'false' vodka kills people, or when there is a danger of food poisoning) they play a special role, not quite like those of other social worlds active in food culture (such worlds are more organised and have clear rules restricting their membership, too).[10]

On the other hand, so far as they act as experts who give advice and information, and make recommendations about healthful eating habits, their social institutions do not, in fact, differ much from those of other social worlds. They have their loyal followers as well as tourists, their occasional, rather mildly interested, visitors. What marks them out as different is that they speak with the – undoubtedly great – authority of science and the State. At least as far as product development in the food industry is concerned, these 'semi-official', and at times pseudo-official, social worlds which enjoy the authority of health sciences are at present the central points of reference. Even though the numerous new milks, sour milks and creams sometimes taste unusual and some people might claim to enjoy the taste of one more than that of another, in the main the dividing lines between the products are based on their presumed health effects. At one level one can choose between different degrees of fat content in milk; at a more sophisticated and, as a rule, expensive level, one can choose from all kinds of health-promoting or illness-preventing additives and ingredients of milk. But, ultimately, we do not really know whether these classifications – readily offered by the producers, with the support of the social worlds of science and printed on the packaging or declared in advertisements – are, in fact, regarded by their users as relevant to the attainment of the desired inner experiences. Some of them might be considered totally irrelevant, and people's real reasons for buying them might lie altogether elsewhere. Some again might be made to fit into a very different context of aesthetic evaluation.

Thus, the social world perspective offers a discursive way of understanding quality and claims to quality. It allows for the fact that people in distinct social circles make different judgements about products and foodstuffs. Such judgements are not reflections of personal idiosyncracies, but tend to conform to the standards (though these are subject to regular alteration) upheld within particular social worlds. Quality, or rather the identification of relevant qualities, is therefore part of an ongoing process of negotiation, of claim and counter-claim, both within a social circle and across boundaries to other circles. There is, on this view, no generic consumer whose behaviour can by modelled outside of particular, and often specialising, social contests.

Notes

1 This is, of course, reminiscent of the idea of a more general cultural change from instrumental to expressive orientation, or from work to leisure and pleasure, presented in theories of post-industrial society (see, for instance, Bell 1974).

2 Even though it has a particular emphasis of its own, Schulze's diagnosis resembles, in some respects, the characterisations of many recent analysts concerning the essential novelty of a modern society of consumption. In his early work Jean Baudrillard (1981), for instance, contrasted the economy of signs with the production of use values. Colin Campbell (1986) identified the daydreamer who is always striving for something new and previously unexperienced as the model of the modern consumer. It has also obvious resemblances to Pasi Falk's eternal

seeker for the substitutes among the world of commodities as a substitute for the maternal symbiosis lost in early childhood. Falk's modern consumer (1994) can, in fact, never be satisfied. Bauman's diagnosis (2000) of the 'lonely', always wishful, consumer, faced with the hopeless task of finding real satisfaction, reached almost existentialist dimensions. The modern consumer is, in Bauman's understanding, forced to live in a condition of perpetual uncertainty and angst. Such an existentialist interpretation of the human condition of the modern consumer as something that never can genuinely be shared with others is deeply rooted in the general suspicion concerning leisure, pleasure and expressive activities as something purely subjective and therefore less essential than instrumental activities like productive work (see Csikszentmihalyi 1981).

3 Cf. Mukerji's comment (1978: 349) that 'the tendency to conceive of plastic combs in people's pockets and paintings in museums as completely unrelated kinds of objects obscures an important connection between the two: both are designed to have cultural meanings and social ones'.

4 This conclusion supports Gronow and Warde's argument (2001) in another context: that one should pay more attention to repetitive behaviour, routines and 'ordinary' consumption. In fact, in most cases of everyday consumption (for instance, eating) hardly any exciting subjective experiences are sought after (this is related to the problem of 'high involvement' versus 'low involvement' in consumption).

At first glance there would seem to be a contradiction between the tendency to conformity and fashion. One can, however, solve the contradiction between the demand for novelty and surprise as expressed in fashion and the schematisation and the consequent monotony of consumption identified in Schulze's principles. Despite the principal novelty, contingency, unexpectedness of fashion, it represents a pacified and not a 'revolutionising' mode of change. Typically, fashion fulfils the criteria of variation within a genre. As Herbert Blumer (1969) argued, fashion is a relatively harmless means of learning to tolerate and cope with perpetual social change.

5 As C. W. Park and Mittal Banwari (1985) have argued in discussing the notions of low and high involvement widely used in consumer research, to be involved presumes some emotional intensity and awareness. Some items of consumption might, however, be very important to a consumer simply as part of his daily routines, in which case it would not be natural to say that he or she is highly involved with them. By distinguishing between insiders and regulars one can avoid the problem, at least in part. Insiders are really involved in their social world, while regulars take it more routinely for granted. The social world and its objects, issues and activities are important in the lives of both of them, and could not easily be replaced by others.

6 In Bourdieu's (1984) analysis of the processes of distinction both of these mechanisms are present. Competition with a social class tends to lead to refinement, whereas the emergence of 'new classes' as challengers tends to redefine the rules of the game. In the latter case the value of the former aspirations is totally denied and new standards of worth established.

7 One of the best examples is the redefinition which necessarily accompanies the transformation of ordinary objects in daily use into valued collectibles. To take another good example used by Mukerji (1978: 354): 'some features of pot fragments in museums may interest potters, and other may interest anthropologists'.

8 See, however, Gary Fine's exemplary (1996) study of the social world of food producers and restaurant cooks, and the aesthetic standards of their craft as well as their relationship to the economic interests of their trade.
9 Reading or collecting cookery books can also be a serious hobby.
10 The character and the role of the legally authorised rules of food safety which exist in every country could be compared with the building codes of plumbing, used as an example by Muckerji (1978: 356): 'today plumbing and other craft traditions are protected and innovations in plumbing techniques limited by building codes which are meant to distinguish between good and bad work, but also to allow for a large amount of good work to be both created and legitimated. Codes are strict enough to discourage massive amounts of amateur work, making the work of professional plumbers more valuable, but they are not detailed enough to distinguish outstanding from adequate work. In this system almost everyone can have good plumbing (or plumbing that is recognizable within the traditional value systems), but probably little rare and independently valuable plumbing is identifiable.' Present-day Russia is an instance of a country with many such codes that often are not followed and where hardly anyone actually believes in their functioning. For instance, according to some recent reports 40 per cent of all instant coffee on sale in Russia is faked and one-third of the inhabitants of St Petersburg report having suffered from food poisoning during the last year.

References

Bauman, Z. (2000), *Liquid Modernity*, Cambridge, Polity.
Becker, H. (1982), *Art Worlds*, Berkeley, University of California Press.
Baudrillard, J. (1981), *For a Critique of the Political Economy of the Sign*, St Louis, LA, Telos Press.
Blumer, H. (1969), 'Fashion: from class differentiation to collective selection', *Sociological Quarterly*, 10(1), pp. 275–91.
Bourdieu, P. (1984), *Distinction: A Social Critique of the Judgment of Taste*, London, Routledge and Cambridge, MA, Harvard University Press.
Campbell, C. (1986), *The Romantic Ethic and the Spirit of Modern Consumerism*, Oxford and New York, Blackwell.
Csikzentmihalyi, M. (1981), 'Leisure and socialization', *Social Forces*, 60(2), pp. 331–40.
Ditton, R. B., Loomis, D. K. and Seungdam, C. (1992), 'Recreation specialization: reconceptualisation from a social world perspective', *Journal of Leisure Research*, 24(1), pp. 33–51.
Falk, P. (1991), 'Miten "hyvää" myydään', in Salin, V. (ed.), *Maailman merkkejä*, Helsinki, MV.
Falk, P. (1994), *The Consuming Body*, London, Sage.
Fine, G. (1996), *Kitchens*, Berkeley, University of California Press.
Gans, H. (1974), *Popular Culture and High Culture*, New York, Basic Books.
Gilmore, S. (1990), 'Art worlds: developing the interactionist approach to social organization', in Becker, H. S. and McCall, M. (eds), *Symbolic Interaction and Cultural Studies*, Chicago, IL, University of Chicago Press.
Gronow, J. (1997), *The Sociology of Taste*, London and New York, Routledge.
Gronow, J. and Warde, A. (eds) (2001), *Ordinary Consumption*, London and New York, Routledge.

Hennion, A. and Méadel, C. (1989), 'The artisans of desire: the mediation of advertising between product and consumer', *Sociological Theory*, 7(2), pp. 191–209.

Kjaernes, U. (ed.) (2001), *Eating Patterns: A Day in the Lives of Nordic Peoples*, Report No. 7, Lysaker, National Institute for Consumer Research.

Maffesoli, M. (1994), *The Time of the Tribes: The Decline of Individualism in Mass Society*, London, Sage.

Mennell, S. (1985), *All Manners of Food: Eating and Taste in England and France from the Middle Ages to the Present*, New York, Blackwell.

Mukerji, C. (1978), 'Artwork: collection and contemporary culture', *American Journal of Sociology*, 84(2), pp. 348–65.

Noro, A. (1995), 'Kulutussosiologian mallit and figuurit', *Sosiologia*, 1, pp. 1–11.

Park, W. C. and Banwari, M. (1985), 'A theory of involvement in consumer behavior: problems and issues', *Research in Consumer Behavior*, 1, pp. 201–31.

Schulze, G. (1991), *Die Erlebnisgesellschaft: Kultursoziologie der Gegenwart*, Frankfurt and New York, Campus.

Simmel, G. (1955), 'The web of group affiliations', in Wolff, K. (ed.), *The Sociology of Georg Simmel*, New York, Macmillan.

Simmel, G. (1992 [1908]), *Soziologi: Untersuchungen über die Formen der Vergesellschaftung*, Frankfurt am Main, Suhrkamp.

Strauss, A. (1978), 'A social world perspective', *Studies in Symbolic Interaction*, 1, pp. 119–28.

Strauss, A. (1982), 'Social worlds and legitimation process', *Studies in Symbolic Interaction*, 4, pp. 171–90.

Strauss, A. (1983), 'Social worlds and their segmentation processes', *Studies in Symbolic Interaction*, 5, pp. 123–39.

Unruh, D. R. (1979), 'Characteristics and types of participation in social worlds', *Symbolic Interaction*, 2, pp. 115–29.

Unruh, D. R. (1980), 'The nature of social worlds', *Pacific Sociological Review*, 23, pp. 271–96.

3
Quality in economics: a cognitive perspective[1]

Gilles Allaire

Introduction

The importance of food quality issues in the contemporary global context is well established. Since the early 1990s we have seen developments in nutrition, life sciences and biotech programmes; the setting up of food quality standards in Europe as well as in other OECD countries; the heightened focus of the media on food issues and a series of food safety crises. On the market side these trends have included a reconsideration of business strategy on the part of firms and their implementation of quality standards, which, as a result, are profoundly renewing and extending food differentiation. Moreover, two complementary tendencies are emerging from the 1990s, which can be viewed as *dis*organising food markets and as a manifestation of postmodern reflexivity:

- an increase in public concern regarding health and environment, including animal welfare and
- the questioning of the legitimacy of the 'institutions' which provide knowledge about food: mothers as the experts, public agencies and even 'science', which together functioned in a way that guaranteed the productivist model of industrialisation and the safety of food during the so-called modern period.

The approach developed in this chapter is for food quality to be viewed in terms of emergent cognitive paradigms sustained within food product networks that encompass a wide range of social actors, from farm to fork, with a wide variety of intermediaries, professional and governmental. There has been a new and historical problematising of the quality of food, partly in relation to food crises, partly in relation to the globalisation of food networks. But to arrive at this theoretical approach, a critique of orthodox economic accounts of quality is advanced, and in particular their failure to explore deeply enough issues of consumption. Quality issues, in various guises, have been central to economic approaches and their understanding of markets and competition. Mainstream approaches offer a normative view to consumption to cope with the differentiation of goods. The general underlying critique is that they find it difficult to accommodate the increasing complexity of quality, conflicting understandings and contradictory paradigms of quality, that have become a historical feature of contemporary food markets. They tend to reduce these processes of ever-increasing heterogeneity to restrictive accounts where 'information gaps' can be mitigated. Although the heterogeneity of goods is controlled by standardisation, both in local settings, through routines, and in global markets, through the institution of quality standards, the quality issue is not about to end.

Quality refers to the social performance of a product or a service. The view of qualities as cognitive paradigms is developed in counter-position to the normative orthodoxy, by examining its deficiency in order to present alternative solutions. Thus the structure of this chapter is divided into two broad sections, following a brief description of the historical moment of the 'quality turn' in food. In the first, economic theories of quality, and of the central dilemmas addressed by these, especially in relation to food quality are explored. In succession, we critique normative views of measurement and standardisation of quality assumed necessary for (food) markets to function; views of how consumer and producer technologies and labour are substitutable in co-production of food; the role of certification, labelling and credence and brand reputation, supported by many market intermediaries as a response to 'market failure'. In the second, I develop a different approach, arguing that now a broader perspective is necessary to meet the challenge of heterogeneity and change, in order to understand how shared cognitive integrations, embracing producers, intermediaries and consumers, is essential to the overall constitution of food quality. I call these *cognitive paradigms*, and identify a central tension between two fundamental tendencies: the tendency towards experimental decomposition and combination; and the tendency towards holistic quality based on identity. I thus see the social process of qualification as a dynamic one, in which quality conflicts and quality hybridisation are central features of global food markets, provisioning and consumption.

The 'quality turn'

The differentiation of food by quality concerns the whole system of food production and provision. The diversification of food services (prepared food, lunch services, various information services, etc.) and of food items in the marketplace rests on an increasingly complex circulation and mixing of ingredients. The universe of quality features 'immaterials' (or signs). Lash and Urry (1994) distinguish two kinds of signs according to whether they have a primarily *cognitive–informational* content, which they refer to as 'post-industrial goods', or an *aesthetic* content, which they refer to as 'postmodern goods'. I argue that the diffusion of aesthetic goods lies in the realm of politics and that aestheticisation is not limited to a particular domain of consumption practices but rather corresponds to the individualisation of agencies. In the context of globalisation, aesthetics and more generally 'immaterials' (Allaire and Wolf 2001) allow for the mobility of goods and for polymorphism. Markets tend to be global, and thus food is becoming more public and diverse, both in terms of norms and opinion. In the last decade, the differentiation of quality as a driver of innovation has been due to several factors, which include the aestheticising and individualising of food consumption patterns, on one hand, and citizen and public concerns about the environment and health, on the other.

Professional, industrial and public strategies to develop the production of labels indicate a much more polymorphic world than does the representation of quality in conventional approaches to agro-food studies. Components of this 'quality turn' comprise the immaterialising of food and the institutional-ising of quality (qualities), as suggested by Goodman (2002: 272): 'organic production, other alternative agrofood networks, quality assurance schemes and territorial strategies to valorise local food product'. However according to Goodman, consumption has been under-theorised in the research devoted to the political economy of agrofood, and this has led him to call for an integrative approach to production and consumption. To integrate the con-sumption point of view in innovation studies regarding food chains is still a challenge for both sociologists and economists.

One may observe that food markets and industry have historically consti-tuted a barrier between farmers and final consumers (the eaters). The story is well known: industrial norms, homogenised mass food, farmers became sup-pliers of raw materials, consumers concentrated in towns, displacing forms of supply, and so on. But this story is incomplete if we do not take into account important transformations in consumption patterns with the development of services. In the early days of industrialisation, food products were still ingre-dients for family cuisine. The development of food processing services and the trend towards eating out (Warde and Martens 2000) correspond to structural changes, which have introduced the basis for the multiplication and the mar-ket differentiation of food goods, and hence new issues regarding quality for the globalisation of food networks. In the last decade, rural sociologists and geographers, while generally not abandoning the macro perspective of the political economy of the agro-food system, have shifted to an analysis in terms of 'actor networks' (Arce and Marsden 1993; Marsden and Arce 1995; What-more and Thorne 1997; Murdoch and Miele 1999; Murdoch et al. 2000). According to Lockie and Kitto (2000: 15; see also Goodman 1999), this lit-erature has neglected the analysis of the hybrid nature of the networks 'prior to their destabilisation by bio-activists or alternative food networks' and failed to 'problematise the relationships between "consumers" and "producers" in the networks through which they are constituted'.[2] Nevertheless, all these works have introduced quality as a network-based property, rather than an individual preference. The following sections will show that this perspective is still challenging for economists.

One way to define the 'quality turn' is as a change in the demand regime: other factors than prices are taken into account by consumers situated in a global market developing a differentiation of services. The notion of 'turning-point' implies structural evolution. Institutional supports are necessary if we invoke factors other than price to circulate knowledge about product qualities. These institutional supports are referred to as the 'economy of quality', following Karpik (1989).[3] In terms of societal change, 'economy of quality' can be associated with 'knowledge economy' or 'risk society', although each notion has its own story. What is at stake in the 'turn' in agro-food studies is the attribution of analytical salience to food knowledge and opinion. In order to embrace the whole issue, 'economy of quality' applies both to specific quality products, in the restricted sense of identity-based products, and to 'functional food', which integrates food with dedicated health services (Kalaitzandonakes 2000). Both genetically modified organisms (GMOs) and organic foods imply institutional innovation, which during the entire decade of the 1990s was one of the major concerns of American and European food authorities and policies. A new regime of innovation has developed through the extension of *alternative* foods, even if these types of niche market have grown, and even if those alternatives have been recognised by public policies and play a role in popular representations of food which extend far beyond their markets. Quality differentiation, however, concerns also the large industrial and distribution food systems. Private brands have been investing in 'green' and 'security' attributes, especially after the recent food scare crises (Allaire 2002). These different developments introduce and rest on a change in the 'institutional forms of competition': to engage private behaviours and strategies and to penetrate into the world of consumers, quality differentiation processes imply changes in market institutions.

In previous papers (e.g. Allaire 1995), I have related institutional change, or change in the 'mode of regulation', of the sector of agriculture to crises in 'conventions of quality' developed in the markets under the Common Agricultural Policy (CAP). In that approach, a 'quality crisis' arises from a gap between current market generic quality norms and users' expectations which call into question prevailing conventions of quality. On the one hand, a local quality crisis appears when a local system of production does not adapt to the market; that can occur in various settings, both in the industrial poultry sector in Britain (as today) and in an area of production labelled for its origin. It can be attributed to problems of collective competence. On the other hand, at a macro level, a quality crisis can be seen as an institutional crisis, i.e. as challenging the whole system of market institutions that participate in and regulate the design of quality. Thus, the CAP (prior to the reform of 1999) normalised a generic market quality by fixing intervention prices and defining a minimum level of quality below which products had to be removed from the market. These minimum norms, by polarising the market, limited market differentiation (to varying extents in different product markets). Under this type of regulation, paradoxically, the more saturated the market, the less able it was to satisfy new demands for quality. That gave rise to an argument for more market-oriented agricultural policies, with quality regulation becoming an important part of these policies. But my analysis of the socio-economic developments leading to an institutional quality crisis and to the agricultural policy changes initiated in the 1990s is now proving insufficient to address new quality conventions emerging with the globalisation of food. This chapter's interest is with exploring how economists' theories take into account the process of the creation of quality in the period of the current quality crisis.

Limits of normative approaches to food quality

Standards and quality

The fact of the heterogeneity of goods is obvious – particularly in agriculture and food, due to the idiosyncrasy of the conditions of production and consumption. Standards allow for comparability of goods in the marketplace and for technical compatibility, both in production and consumption. There are measurement standards (grades) and definition standards (norms) which specify a type of good. To be a tradable good, a product or a service comes with a body of information referred to by economists as standards. As Kindleberger (1983) says, standards extend to private, collective and public goods according to whether they relate to contractual specifications, professional community repertoires or public norms. Less formal information is generally referred to by the notion of 'convention'. Conventions of quality have historical consistency and, as regularities, they provide frameworks for coordination.[4] Quality is not natural; rather it is a mode of ordering the natural and the social.

To become generally established, a quality convention involves both types of standard. How information is construed is central to the design of quality: it is institutional knowledge, analogous to a 'constitutive rule' in Searle's sense.[5] The emergence of quality standards and designations signifies that both producers and users potentially have some control over a relevant characteristic and are able to understand it in common terms, so quality is constituted within a social and institutional space. In a context that is becoming more global, in order for quality to be effective it must be understood as a 'complete' set of rules.[6] Product 'characteristics' are physical features, intrinsic (composition) or extrinsic (place and context of production or consumption). Quality involves knowledge (or rules) for determining a characteristic that *counts as* distinguishing a good within a family of goods or establishes a particular relationship between different goods. Quality characteristics and standards may relate many aspects, such as the process of production, or the product or the service it delivers to the consumer in a given context. They designate public domains of norms and conventions. The so-called 'quality turn' extends the reach of standardisation to 'alternative foods' as they are integrated within the referencing system. However, this introduces new cognitive ambiguities and complexities into the notion of quality. Scientific controversies and the recent food crises reveal the instability of knowledge of quality and of the institutions regulating it.

From a standard economics point of view, the gains from comparability, both private and social, are the driving force for standardisation (Katz and Shapiro 1985), supported by positive network externalities. The setting up of standards and the referencing of activities and products form the baseline process for the globalisation of technical systems and market extension. They are also a normative basis for economic theory. In the basic framework of the theory of market competition, goods are homogeneous, meaning that they are perfectly known as distinct from other goods. Qualifying information is considered as an objective and constitutive part of goods, and, as shown by Stigler (1961), the costs of searching for and communicating that information are part of the equilibrium price. 'Quality' relates to the creation and evolution of the nomenclature of goods. Mainstream theories limit themselves to the identification and correction of failures in the maintenance of a given nomenclature resulting from asymmetries in the distribution of information, and in failure of its public character. In this account, the institutional and cognitive process relating to the creation of product characteristics is exogenous in relation to the 'natural', or objective, properties of goods. I see this account as restrictive when considering how goods multiply when new information concerning their properties is revealed, thus introducing controversial issues of pertinence and coherence of established informational norms. Competition is supposed to result in efficient allocation, and in a predictable world, relies on perfectly decomposable pieces of information. The identities of goods must be generally established for the development of competitive adjustments, as can be seen from the devastating effects that follow the emergence of critical suspicions about the identity of goods (e.g. 'mad cow', dioxin and other food scares). In the following sub-sections I examine two aspects of the classic economic approach to quality, the first referring to the technology of consumption and the second to quality labels (or signs) and information intermediaries. The conclusion of that discussion leads to a more global analysis of the process of the creation of quality.

Normative consumption technology approaches

Variations in quality characteristics are brought about by the variability of technologies, resources, places of production and the variability of producers' skills. Differences within supplied products and services also result from the market process itself. As initially noticed by Sraffa, the producer desiring to increase her sales can attempt to break down consumer indifference regarding the producer's identity (to which, theoretically, the market is blind) and try to move up the product's individual supply curve. That strategy generates variety and the market rapidly becomes a network of differentiated and more-or-less isolated individual markets. Classically, according to Chamberlin (1933), these markets of differentiated products are monopoly-like, meaning that producers have some control over their pricing strategy, but a control limited by lateral substitution within qualities. Thus producer rationale functions to exploit variations in the characteristics of similar products, and to develop the art of marketing. But Chamberlin, who considered product variations qualitative 'in their essence', viewed the consequence of this process of differentiation as the quasi-impossibility of aggregating individual supply curves into a unique supply curve. The theory of reputation has been developed to incorporate the residual qualitative differences in a market perspective. If the differences are relevant for the consumer, they impart 'true quality' to the product.[7]

Economists have introduced the notion of consumption technology (or the consumer function of production) to make a distinction between goods in the market and the consumer use of goods in a process designed to obtain expected effects or affects that are the final goals of consumption. The consumption function proposed by Lancaster (1966) links goods and their objective characteristics with the services they display for the consumption process, which are the true arguments for the consumer utility function. Relevant characteristics are integrated capabilities to perform given services. In contrast to Chamberlin's view of quality, Lancaster's 'characteristics' are objectively quantifiable as well as objectively identifiable, similar to physical features. The characteristics which count in the first instance (e.g. the consumer prefers and pays for a car's size and then chooses the colour) are assumed measurable. No measurable characteristic corresponds to subjective attributes, which are not considered as market structures.

Goods for the consumer are multifunctional and can deliver a bundle of characteristics. In this way, food may combine nutrients and very possibly undesirable ingredients. A service may be assured alternatively by several types of good or service possessing relevant capabilities. A dinner at home may involve variable domestic work or be substituted for by a meal at a restaurant. Some activities may shift from production to consumption, or the reverse. According to Becker (1965), services that intervene in final consumption are produced using purchased goods and personal time, combined in the production function of the household. This theory provides insights into two factors of developing consumption activities: the content in the services of supplied goods (consumption opportunities) and the value of time for individuals (time resources). Stigler and Becker (1977) have added consumer skills and specific capital to this function. The consumer in the consumption process is thus represented as playing a more active role by including the accumulation of consumption capital (routinised consumption patterns) and the building of competences (learning processes). Allowing for trade-offs of goods for time and time for consumption capital, Beckerian models explain observed consumer behaviours which do not adapt directly to price variation, but are *rational* considering the consumption function parameters. The market integrates this social variation of consumption patterns, which is constrained by the distribution of incomes and time budget. However, the foundations of neo-classical approaches to consumption technology are challenged if we aim to consider reflexive dynamics (changes in preference and innovation by demand).

To safeguard the normative theory of competition, the Lancasterian matrix needs to be comprehensive or integrative, allowing for homogeneous understanding of the goods/characteristics, nomenclature and for homogeneous perception by the consumers of each product's distribution of qualities.[8] A characteristic has to be presented in the same way and according to common references to result in identifiable information; in other words to make sense in a context of multiple sources of propositions. To satisfy this condition, innovation is limited to the permutation of characteristics and the displacing of capabilities between the spheres of production and consumption. Technical change remains compatible with the model as long as the structure of preferences for characteristics stays stable. And the model rests on an assumption of perfect substitutability of the capabilities diversely integrated in various products and services. In Lancaster's terms (1979: 20–1), 'goods are simply a transfer mechanism whereby characteristics are bundled up into packages at the manufacturing point . . . [and] opened up to yield their characteristics again at the point of consumption'. Good design counts for technical and economic reasons, but one can say that the technology is perfectly substitutable between spheres: the producer adapts on her side, through analysis of the market characteristics, but is indifferent to the user and the consumer/user adapts on her side, being indifferent to the particular product or producer. Although Lancaster or Stigler and Becker (with the idea of consumption capital accumulation) and followers found many reasons for rational consumers to escape such a rigid model, the model has continued to be considered as the consumption rationality norm. No economist will pretend that such a model can really be comprehensive if we admit some product-particular identity ('true quality') that is behind reputation models, but the mainstream continues to adhere to the normative theory of consumption. In such a view, deviant behaviours (based on subjectivity) are classed as 'inefficient'. Classic explanations invoke a lack of consumers' managerial skills or consumption capital or experience, with all factors reduced to a lack of information. Assuming that relevant information is provided to consumers, the rational consumption model is the normative horizon.

The technology of consumption approach is capable of explaining transformations in systems of food production, distribution and consumption which can be analysed as technical substitutions, assuming that on both sides – goods and consumption patterns – innovation is decomposable into its corresponding capacities, implying generally complementary goods or skills on the part of the consumer. For example, assuming a stable preference for the reduction of the domestic working time of individuals, the theory suggests the development of a line of innovation that allows for that substitution. The prediction fits well with the 'Fordist' period. But such a development was sustained by other socio-economic changes which allowed for the separation of activities in time and, notably, some private control of individuals over the use of their 'own time'.[9] Furthermore that development implied the technological identification of the capacity of products and services to make economies in real preparation time. The objective technology approach had a certain relevance in a period when, under public initiative, basic nutritional and food hygiene knowledge was being diffused, when accounting had become a generalised practice in households, and when consumption awareness and skills were being strengthened by information provided by advertising, social workers, magazines, consumer organisations and other institutions. Information that was undoubtedly partly contradictory, was embedded in a homogeneous discourse on the theme of a 'sane and happy' modern way of life (Barthes 1972).

This approach however, would appear unsuitable for the contemporary and more controversial world. Today, the complexity of the consumption process is more cognitive than technical. Many developments make this account of perfect substitutability and switching difficult to sustain. Firstly, products integrate more services and the diversity of goods multiplies rapidly. While the process of domestic consumption (including meals) often requires less working time, the process of investment in consumption capital is more subtle. The evolution of food behaviours in this regard appears as a structural change in consumption technologies. Secondly, food services are largely outsourced in various forms, while purchased food products and services are heavily encapsulated with symbolic burdens and public and ethical responsibilities. Thirdly, activities devoted to food and 'foodism' (the culture of food) are blends that make it difficult to split working from leisure time. And, fourthly, outsourced capacities include information services and all public or collective bodies contributing to the formation of consumption capital. Immaterial food services include, for example, membership in a wine club or a 'community-supported agriculture' programme, as well as consulting a paediatrician about what to feed a baby. All these changes in 'consumption technologies' imply changes in belief in quality attributes.

Certification and credence intermediaries

In mainstream economics, it is considered a normative result that asymmetry of information about quality leads to sub-optimal choices by consumers and to market domination by the lowest quality as shown by Akerlof (1970). Following Akerlof's line of argument, because of opportunism producers do not reveal the quality of their offers; price information cannot do the job; and, consequently, a market does not exist for quality. As a result, producers acting to escape pure competition become motivated to escape a market where quality is not valued by differentiating themselves and making quality significant. Certified labels and reputation investments are complementary mechanisms assumed to restore market coordination. Through reputation mechanisms, by which consumers' expectations are assumed to form the firm's reputation, the market is supposed to be able to introduce a coherent signalling system. A firm invests in its own reputation if it can rely on a process of consumer learning about its products' 'true quality'. Premium price represents returns on that reputation investment and incites the producer to continue her quality approach. The existence of premium prices – which seems to give rise to a reduction in welfare compared to a situation of perfect information – should not be regarded as a market failure, but rather as a cost due to imperfect information, which is as real as production costs (Shapiro 1983). The essential hypothesis of the model is thus the existence of an effective process of consumer learning, offering private incentives to invest in quality. The critical issue is thus the mechanisms of consumer learning.

Reputation has important collective aspects which condition consumer learning and drive strategies to maintain collective reputation in a changing environment. A technological change which decreases the production costs of a generic product or extends its basic capacities can weaken 'high quality' positions if producers of the 'higher' segment do not benefit from the same change, making it more costly and risky to 'invest in reputation' by keeping to traditional quality norms. On the other hand, technical change that, ex-post, is regarded as affecting the quality characteristics of a product may reveal superior characteristics of the original product and indirectly provide an opportunity for producers to maintain their previous method of valuing those characteristics, as in the case of 'artisan' or 'traditional' or 'hand-made' products, which have in this way become investment arenas. Another factor in the disturbance of the quality order is the change in the identities of the leading actors in the design of quality.[10] Many food stories that combine such different disturbances of quality positions could be told. Reputation and quality orderings are challenged to design quality by structural changes and by competition between collective actors.

As pointed out by Nelson (1970), goods can be distinguished on the basis of how they convey information to the consumer: 'search goods' which exhibit their characteristics to the consumer in search (e.g. consumer chooses yellow or red apple prior to the purchase) are opposed to 'experience goods' the properties of which are revealed by the act of consumption, after the purchase (e.g. when eating, the consumer assesses the sweetness of the apple). These distinctions do not lead to fixed types of good: *search* and *experience* are complementary processes from a technology of consumption viewpoint, allowing the consumer to learn (e.g. the consumer can associate the yellow apple with sweetness according to her own taste). Search needs experience and experience changes search orientation. In many cases, individual experience is insufficient to assess the product or service characteristics. Consumers benefit from knowledge acquired by others, experts and connoisseurs, and are confronted with private or public signalling initiatives, including the mandatory label. Finally, if the product information were complete and comprehensively formalised, search goods would correspond to standardised goods, allowing for large expansion in transparent markets. Indeed intermediaries compete to label product properties and the informative effectiveness of labels is conditioned but threatened by the plurality of signs.

A third category of knowledge attributes attached to goods is generally distinguished in the recent food economics literature as 'credence attributes', denoting such features which are important to the consumer, but which the consumer is unable to discover by the consumption experience. They refer to contextual product properties related to certain public goods and values, such as environmental or social justice, or to cultural values that may be community-specific. The 'quality turn' may be related to an opinion, developing in the specialist literature, according to which food markets feature these immaterial (or external) attributes. While 'experience goods' refers to individual kinds of experiences that can be substituted by information, 'credence goods' refers to a social (or distributed) experience. Credence involves reliance on intermediaries to assess those characteristics. Food safety and nutritional properties are examples of such attributes that combine reported personal experience and credence in various sources of knowledge. Credence attributes include immaterial virtues of specific characteristics, such as denomination of origin, whether GMO-free, or the extent to which the production process is environmentally friendly or treats animals humanely. They extend to cultural and political concerns that have developed out of public controversies related not only to food quality, but to more global issues such as the multi-functionality of agriculture and trade and development debates. Corresponding characteristics of the production and distribution processes cannot be traced in the final product and will not be revealed by experience of the product. Third-party action is needed to make the quality judgement, in the way that experts in the art market and connoisseurs in deluxe food markets judge quality.

A distinction has to be made between knowable characteristics, on the one hand, about which individuals may lack information due to the cost of investigation, and, on the other hand, global quality constitution, which is not assessed according to universal norms. While the certification of the characteristics not assessable by the client is assumed to mitigate the lack of information, the issue of credence appears if we consider that these certifiable, and thus measurable, characteristics do not exhaust the entire significance of the quality. Credence is manifested when experience (which verifies searched characteristics) is shared.

While the cost of experience is lessened by reference-sharing and public information, socialisation of experience engages 'experts', and credence issues arise due to the evident fact that expert knowledge is always incomplete and thus liable to challenge. It was with this meaning that the term 'credence' was initially introduced in economics by Darby and Karni (1973) to analyse markets in which sellers are also experts who determine consumers' needs, such as 'medical, automotive, and other repair services'. In general, professionals are in the situation of experts, and professional services involve trust. What, for example, specifically determines the quality of products 'made on farm' and directly sold by a farmer to a consumer is the credence in the expert-specific skills of the farmer who manages the whole chain down to the consumer. More generally, food services involve professionals and can be characterised by the notion of 'credence goods', from the master chef's cuisine to the school-lunch programme designed by a nutritional expert.

In 'credence goods' we are confronted with several conceptions of quality, although the current mainstream literature generally addresses isolated food credence attributes and assimilates them to levels of quality, retaining a Lancasterian technology perspective (credence attributes are in this account considered to be objective characteristics combined with the others in constant terms). It is assumed that regulation is effective, transmitting a perfect definition of the quality similarly to all consumers, even if the given quality may be valued only by some. More importantly, while the definition of the space of quality is considered to be an exogenous problem, that space is assumed to be coherent and information unambiguous. Nevertheless the notion of credence introduces a particular type of knowledge by linking identifiable characteristics (signs) with a not fully assessable quality and confronts the normative view with fuzzy goods established by loose linkages between signs and quality.

Credence, or trust, refers to the fact that consumers, unable to judge the intrinsic characteristics of the product or service, make their choice on the basis of an act of faith in the producer or service provider, the characteristics of which appear as significant cues for the consumer decision. Such cues include personal elements, if the exchange is made in a community context, or objective references, such as the place of production, membership in a profession, or certification of the production process or producer capabilities. In large markets, credence relies on actors who impart a particular identity to the product, i.e. immaterial attributes. These may be the name of the distributor, the trademark of the producer, the name of a certification body or some public guarantor, but they may also be various intermediaries speaking for the product (word-of-mouth networks, specialist magazines, etc.). Such intermediaries, if they are effective, add value to products by qualifying them in the sense that they provide elements of judgement. The issue of credence is one of the credibility of the source, which of course introduces the possibility of credibility gaps. Uncertain costs spring from the incompleteness of the quality specifications, while credence intermediaries are assumed to supply producers, consumers and various stakeholders with relevant knowledge. Thus, markets for credence goods are made possible by supplying consumers with a substitute for the information and trust they lack (Tirole 1988). While third-party, or public, regulations are generally viewed as perfectly mitigating such information failure, they themselves can fail. Since certification procedures, and in general quality signs, are imperfect substitutes for quality knowledge, they are necessarily completed by other sources of opinion in order to have credence effects. A sign, as a physical informational object, comes without direct significance. Its sense is inscribed in contextual quality conventions, and comes from the quality representations of those who give significance to it. All signs potentially display multiple significations. A sign is able to clear up the quality market if the consumer is able to pass judgement on and get meaning from it, generally by combination of information. This raises the more general issue of the potential increase in instability of credence attributes with increasing complexity and globalisation of quality.

Anania and Nisticò (2002) present a model which aims to explain the persistence of credence failures by comparing three institutional scenarios: no regulation; imperfect regulation; and perfect regulation. They conclude that producers, both individually and collectively, can have an interest in sustaining imperfect regulation, and for that reason quality labels must be considered an imperfect substitute for credence. However, the example the authors describe, that of products under the EU regulation for marques of geographical indication (where a food product originates, or PGI) and marques for denomination of origin (specific types of product, or PDO), is insufficiently analysed. They link imperfect regulation to the fact that the quality attributes of certain new PGIs remain heterogeneous due to compromises within different groups of producers, leading to the definition of loose quality rules. While it is in fashion in economics to admit 'imperfection' in the sense of a certain amount of fraud or cheating as an economic lubricant, other explanations of the ambivalence of the rules and of the product can be offered if we take into account the plurality of signs it conveys. If the imprecision of the production rules associated with the label is the problem, and several studies show that this can indeed be the case, we are confronted with a situation à la Akerlof, where a specific quality market does not exist, and this is generally confirmed by the fact that the PGI sign does not receive a premium. In the case of a longstanding reputation related to origin, a PDO (say, Bordeaux wines), however, we are again confronted with a heterogeneous product and market. The name 'Bordeaux' is engaged in a design quality system (and network) which was evolving over time, along with the evolving of market structures and actors strategies. According to Barjolle and Sylvander (2002), a sign loses credibility if the product heterogeneity increases, but this depends on market structure and the play of signs. Oversimplifying the Bordeaux story, it can be said that such a loss has happened to the name as a result of the growth of a large market for *generic* Bordeaux wines. For consumers, Bordeaux has become differentiated into 'low' and 'high' levels of quality, according to whether or not the wine label refers to a particular *terroir*, and the most reputed terroirs no longer make any reference to the name Bordeaux. In this case, the regulation is 'imperfect', not in fact because rational producers have commercial interests in maintaining some fuzzy definition of the quality of the wine, but because they are competing to define the *true* quality, and we are confronted with the differentiation of signs in a same region.

Complementary recent works assessing consumer response to protected geographical identification labelling show variable combinations within quality dimensions. Loureiro and McCluskey (2000) calculated consumers' willingness to pay for the PGI label 'Galician Veal' (known by 48 per cent of shoppers in Spain) and found it to generate a high premium only for certain meat cuts, according to a vertical classification, specifically the high quality meat cuts, while it does not at the extremes (the 'low' and the 'very high', or deluxe, parts). This suggests that the PGI label is effective only in combination with other indicators. The authors conclude that to use the PGI label for products that are not of 'high' quality (here according to the type of cut) is not an efficient marketing strategy and possibly could damage the collective reputation. Hassan and Monier-Dilhan (2002), comparing the value for the consumer of a PDO label (Camembert, a recently recognised PDO intervening in a longstanding market) with marques of processor (national brands) and marques of distributor (private brands), show that the label of origin is valorised more in combination with distributor marques than with processor marques. Finally, credence goods are not one-dimensional and signs do not combine linearly.

Another example of credence complexity and fallibility comes from 'alternative foods'. The intricate and tricky links between expertise and credence issues in the process of innovation can be seen in 'organic' agriculture and food. Organic producers consider that they are experts in what is good both for the 'health and the earth' (as expressed in their own literature). However organic producers are not the original experts, just as physicians are not the original experts behind the procedures they follow, even if they are autonomous in their diagnoses. The idea of organic production emerged as a holistic set of 'principles'. Steiner and Howard, the founders of the two main traditions, have had a number of followers, recognised as 'masters' – a form of expert – by both producers and consumers in what can be called 'organic' community networks. Within these networks credence systems have developed, including dedicated direct provision networks and confidential trademark supports (e.g. 'Demeter', since 1928).

In this context of 'domestic' and 'inspired' types of quality convention (to use the classification of Boltanski and Thévenot 1991), incipient organic farming professional networks eventually led to the normalisation and emergence of 'industrial' and 'market oriented' organic quality conventions (Sylvander 1997). As a result of several evolutionary factors in both the social and the market role of 'organic quality', the globalisation of that quality is today supported by a public system of certification and of signalling. Products exhibiting the official logo have to be certified by agreed independent certification bodies, which today is 'good practice' for public quality policies.

The extension of organic networks has introduced the need for public guarantees. The worldwide normalisation of the quality 'organic' by homogeneous public standards in the 1990s instituted that attribute in the global food market, but not without controversy. This has resulted in a structural change in the institutional definition of what can be called 'organic' quality. While the economics literature has discussed the comparison between public or private systems of certification in formal terms (free of space–time reference), we are here confronted with an historical change in the institutional form of quality. This change has not led to a complete quality convention substitution. In other words, the standard and the logo have not fulfilled their promises. Thus one can observe an uneasy combination of the two institutional forms: community-based and professional networks supplement public standards to shore up fallible credence (Sylvander 2003).

While the word 'organic' is still something of a mystery in terms of credence, the term 'organic standard' is nothing more than an objective attribute allowing for the introduction of organic products into more varied patterns of consumption. I stress here two impacts of that development. First, while 'organic' quality is defined by standards, as a global attribute it has been introduced as legitimate knowledge in the public sphere of law and research. Public interest being high, information and issues around organic products have become popularised, with legal and scientific 'facts' mixed in with health and foodist imagery in numerous magazine and media stories (Allaire and Wolf 2001). Second, somehow 'organic' quality is in competition in the public's conception with what is referred to as 'healthful' and hygienic food, a quality inscribed in law as a consumer right. While organic standards may not claim to be more healthful, they do put a negative value on the use of chemicals, irradiation and GMOs. Hence they play a role in the deconstruction of a previously unquestioned public credence and they displace public debate.

The credence complexity issue extends to public policies controlling food attributes. For example, a certification procedure for 'good environmental practices' may be of uncertain significance in terms of impact on the environment, however strictly the farmer follows the codes of practice on the ground. No isolated sign, specification or norm is capable of constituting a classification. Quality designates a class of positions against other classifications. This is a type of relation that cannot enter in the 'objective' consumption technology view. The introduction of the notion of credence into the normative approach highlights the radical incompleteness of knowledge of the properties of goods. But the standard economic approaches that reduce knowledge to information, and hence to problems of distribution of the information, are inadequate in understanding the development of a polymorphic quality universe where information is dynamic. Unlike information, food knowledge corresponds to beliefs regarding distant effects of production or consumption. Beliefs constitute a major dimension of food quality. In shifting from an information paradigm to a knowledge paradigm, according to the terms of Nonaka (1996: 3), we introduce 'a dynamic human process of justifying personal belief toward the "truth"'.

Quality and cognitive paradigms

Although neo-classical consumption theories do not ignore the cognitive limitations of individual consumers, endowed with routinised consumption patterns, nothing has been said in that theoretical perspective about the process of the emergence of the common knowledge that makes the characteristics of goods objective (Requier-Desjardins 1999). The availability of objective knowledge seems immediate (no forms of knowledge accumulation are presented in information theory), while forms of quality knowledge are contradictory.[11] Hence, while room for collectives and intermediaries is denied within the homogenising normative framework, we nonetheless see them creeping into economic argumentation as benchmarks, in order to direct consumers to various credence networks. Collective cognitive resources are considered in the maintenance of technical coordination in a chain, as well as in the formation of reputations and in convergent consumer perceptions of qualities.

In this section, I focus on the cognitive nature of those collective resources, referring to them as cognitive paradigms and conventions of quality. Concretely, if we observe the developments of quality crises and their adjustments, such as the European beef crisis, we see, according to Hirschman, collectives taking 'exit' (e.g. vegetarian advocates) or 'voice' solutions (e.g. beef labelling). Indeed quality problems are precisely those which concern the diffusion of quality standards so that they become 'public'. According to Thévenot (1998), we cannot speak of innovation without the successful establishment of a new *doxa* that materialises the way in which a quality is identified, stabilised both in norms and in technical procedures, and thus made reproducible, i.e. guaranteed. This process occurs not in a vacuum but in a world where such stabilised qualities still exist and where some of them oppose the current process. While public investments and services, such as public research, facilitate adjustments by intervening within the local and collective structures of learning, conversely, creative groups invest in and work to take part in public knowledge.

The multiplication of credence goods related to food in a globalising consumer world reflects the multiplication of uncertainty domains in large and complex markets. But, for a long time, heterodox economists have considered that uncertainty in transactions is a distinctive feature of the market economy, not its antithesis. A common objective of the constructivist visions of the economy emphasised knowledge divergences and uneven distribution. The development of the normative economic framework has overridden approaches which address knowledge dynamics, principally the Austrian tradition and evolutionary economic theories. These latter two theories have in common a rejection of the equilibrium perspective and the determinist view of the evolution of economies and societies. They argue that change comes from the variety of the outputs of agents' interactions. The notion of 'market' (or economic competition) corresponds to an 'economic process' where innovations are selected. An economy is a dynamic system, where structures and institutions result from the interactions of individual plans and constraint agents.

While evolutionary economists have developed an organisational point of view of production with the notion of routines (Nelson and Winter 1982) and more extensively the notion of competence, the Austrian economists (notably Hayek) have developed a general theory of the creation of economic knowledge corresponding to entrepreneurial agency. Today these approaches are gaining the interest of economists in a context where innovation occurs in an uncertain world. An active field of research is developing that is engaged in linking heterodox views of institutionalism, Austrian and evolutionary economics, constituting a 'cognitive turning point in economics' (according to Orléan 2002). I now offer a critique inside this general perspective, making the point that, while these theories address knowledge, they have not until recently focused on the consumption process and the creation of quality, an essential part of the general process of the creation of competence. The focus then moves to the integrative capacities of agencies and, finally, to cognitive paradigms in innovation.

The market process challenged by reflexive consumption

The rigid equilibrium approach is rejected by evolutionary economists for whom the creation of variety is at the core of the functioning and progress of the economy, and by the Austrian economists, for whom the aggregation of economic variables make no sense. Consumer choices and habits cannot be summed up in a preference function; nor can producer outputs be represented by a global production function. Capital is essentially heterogeneous because it conceals alternative capabilities, which are not given features but depend on individual yet interactive anticipations. The economy is a complex of interconnected institutions that provide a context of meaning for the actions of individuals. Information available to agents is not systematically cumulative and coherent, and knowledge is changing and distributed within agencies. I discuss the heterogeneity of goods and the consumption process from that perspective, addressing the problem of the frontier between production and consumption and how quality crosses that frontier.

In the Austrian economic tradition, the 'market process', which ultimately designs individual frameworks of production, is a process of discovering opportunities. What is at stake is the discovery of some consensual knowledge able to make production organisation and product design workable . In this sense, the market process includes the process of the creation of quality we are studying. Coming from that perspective, the selection of entrepreneurs' plans interferes with the definition of the functions goods can provide. This observation suggests two sets of questions. First, selected plans are not only monetary investment programmes to procure productive assets but include product design according to the perception of consumer needs and the mode of production organisation. The entrepreneur chooses a means–ends combination and is capable of adapting it from experience. This capacity to choose a framework is generally seen as the defining competence of entrepreneurs, meaning in some ways a reflexive capacity. Second, the pressure of price is not sufficient to transform such complex designs. Entrepreneurial action is one not of maximisation (that is subsequent) but of selection of a productive

framework (or organisational design). The knowledge dynamics which under-
lie the discovery of designs must be analysed in a manner complementary to
the market dynamics.

As several authors have observed, heterodox economics failed to integrate
both firm and consumption within a cognitive view of the market process as
a subjective process of discovery (see, for instance, Metcalfe 2001; Nooteboom in press). The 'resource-based' or 'capabilities view' of the firm has
offered a behavioural approach to the producer.[12] Producers do not find productive knowledge as 'blueprints'; rather productive knowledge is a matter
of capabilities (Richardson 1972). Langlois and Cosgel introduce this
approach into the consumption process, arguing that the analysis developed
in the context of production can translate well both into the domain of consumption and into 'the problem of boundaries between consumers and producers' (Langlois and Cosgel 1996: 5; 1998). In response, it may be said that
the consumer faces the same multi-level decision problem as the producer,
first with the choice of an action framework and then with the choice of the
means (parameters) to achieve the action. The consumption process, as it is
a process of action design, has a hierarchical structure similar to that of productive design (Clark 1985). A particular choice made at one level conditions
subsequent decision problems and the alternatives available, in regard to the
resources available after previous choices, including the allocation of time in
the consumption perspective. To engage in the discovery process, consumers
as well as producers have to identify new resources, recognise them as relevant and match them with their plans and their own competencies. As in the
production process, capabilities in consumption consist of various routines
that help in solving problems. Because producers and consumers bring their
individual intentions and interpretations of opportunities to exchange relations, they project individual meanings of products. Thus, the challenge for
the innovator is to monitor, anticipate and (attempt to) channel the range of
meanings different consumers attribute to the products. The consumer is
confronted with an equivalent challenge. To include both production and
consumption organisation in the global market process implies coping with
the issue that agents do not automatically share common knowledge of the
structure of production and consumption, or of the choices available in each
case (Langlois and Cosgel 1998). The economic problem therefore is one of
coordination : 'discovering – or, rather, helping to create – an interperson-
ally shared structure of transaction'. To put the issue in terms of transaction
is not innocent, because it extends the scope of requiring 'common knowledge' to clear the market. As will be seen, if we extend the capabilities
approach from the organisation of production to consumption, the product
itself cannot be absent from the picture. I then move on to identify a set of
tensions between the producer, the product and the consumer.

In traditional Austrian economics, the figure of the entrepreneur represents the single agency ultimately reading the market, even if the sources of
knowledge are various. Can we attribute to the consumer the status of an

entrepreneur, assuming that the consumer possesses the power to allocate her own time? We are presented here with two different issues: the organisational form of consumption; and the frontier between production and consumption. Contrary to the capitalist form of production, the process of consumption as such does not include work contracts. The organisational form of consumption is not enterprise-like. Consumption competences are distributed in families, communities, cultures and civil networks in a polymorphic world. In extending the organisational approach of the enterprise to consumption, one must consider the substantial problems arising from the confrontation between quality design (products) and a consumption world not structured as a market. As suggested in previous sections, the issue of time allocation for individuals and households was and still is an important societal issue that significantly conditions innovation in food as well as other domains of domestic consumption. It cannot be seen as a market process, although it does interact with the market.

The second problem with the entrepreneurial view of the consumer, is the problem of the 'boundaries between producers and consumers'. As presented by Langlois and Cosgel (1996: 14), the problem is considered one-sidedly: 'what determines [the boundary is] the extent to which producers will provide the knowledge and routines the consumer needs for successful consumption and the extent to which the consumer *soi-même* will provide them'. This statement reflects a diffusion of knowledge from producers to consumers. While the authors present consumers as active, they are not proactive.

To complete the market process, what appear as gaps in consumer knowledge need to be filled by intermediaries. Langlois and Cosgel emphasise that the problem of explaining boundaries between the market and the final consumer, when considering personal and domestic domains of consumption (food, clothing, housing, transportation, health, education, culture, entertainment and so forth), is different from the explanation of the boundaries of the firm (as, for example, in Langlois and Robertson 1995), because the scope of the substitution between production and consumption is limited and consumers are 'necessarily limited in their production capabilities' (Langlois and Cosgel 1996: 18). Consequently, innovation in consumption routines is viewed as coming essentially from an external source, dependent on the offerings of producers and on the 'technological characteristics of the products'. Innovation by consumers is limited to the recombination of existing possibilities.

Making up the interface, intermediaries, be they merchants, banks or experts, offer a specific service. In this sense they are independent entrepreneurs, as are the other actors in the market process. However, it is assumed that both consumer and producer can invest in the function of intermediation (e.g. buy a travel book or connect with the travel organisation services of an airline company). To describe the capacity of the intermediary entrepreneurs, the authors use the metaphor of the problem of communication between different languages. Intermediaries are translators. But where these intermediaries get their knowledge from is not specified. What distinctive kind of intermediating knowledge is developed and accumulated, and by whom? What is the special expertise of translation between producer and consumer knowledge, and how is that role of translation institutionalised? These issues are not addressed, and the view of quality they propose here finally is not essentially different from the normative approach I presented in the first section.

In contrast to the building of producers' competences, which have serious constraints of coherence, the impact on the market of the diffusion of consumers' knowledge is generally seen as more erratic, such as the role of fashion in clothing or of food scares and fancies. The entrepreneurial vision of the market process can provide a realistic understanding of the evolution of consumption patterns by giving capabilities to the market intermediaries who operate the correspondence between goods and quality, 'that entail "sense making" rather than rational explanation' (Nooteboom in press). But, both in the normative and in the capabilities approaches to consumption (both adopting a methodological individualist perspective), ultimately products and quality do have not concrete existence as such, because they are totally reconstruable: any product/quality can be freely decomposed and recombined.

Towards products as quality networks

Consumers are intermediaries for other consumers: 'recipes' circulate in every domain, formalising user experiences into consumption repertoires on which local patterns of consumption draw. In this respect, it is similar to the way production routines evolve by the circulation of repertoires from the production front. The previous economists' view of consumption is precisely a view from the market actors. A view from consumption itself, i.e. the study of the social (cultural) patterns of consumption, normally the disciplinary preserve of sociologists or anthropologists, sees the problem of the boundary between the market and the consumers from a different standpoint. From the consumption point of view, if an initial problem is to access the basic knowledge necessary to use purchased things, the enduring problem is how to maintain or enhance the capabilities of those purchased objects and obtain effective and safe service from them during their lifetime, given that things have 'social life' (Appadurai 1986). For example, supposing a consumer already holds a driver's licence, she will quickly learn to drive a car from the point of sale. But the major problem of car consumption today is how to organise financing, car maintenance services, and to enjoy the capabilities offered by the car in safe conditions. From the point of view of the evolution of consumption patterns, contrasting stories of the interface of households and domestic groups and the market could be told (Hareven 1990). Innovation springs not only from market opportunities and changes in the organisation of work in firms and services but from domestic and civil organisations, and from the evolution of communities and individual agencies. If seemingly few technical capabilities are extracted by industry from domestic routines, that does not signify that innovation in consumption, i.e. the evolution of consumption patterns, does not transmit knowledge to the production sphere. In such an alternative view of the frontier, intermediaries appear more as integrators than as simple translators.

If we adopt a holistic view, consumers, intermediaries and producers create quality definitions to which a 'product' has to conform from its origin to its final disappearance in the consumption process. The notions of the origin and disappearance of a product (or service) are relative, as are its boundaries. Fundamental debates around credence qualities concern both these types of frontier of the product. Does a food product disappear, and with it the responsibility of its manufacturer, once it has been eaten? Or are unforeseen impacts on the future health of the consumer part of the product and its quality (what economists call stock externalities)? Is it possible to locate definitively an origin for particular characteristics (prions in BSE, for example)? Neither technical decomposition of the product nor property rights approaches give a complete response to these accountability issues as they emerge. Things (and thus goods) have life because they retain properties the scope of which is determined by the social context, as, for example, with the performance and the duration of a car or food. Certainly some institutional arrangements can help the market deal with that problem and to mitigate it through quality agreements or conventional understandings (and economists can reflect on how to design such mechanisms). But such questions are persistent and jeopardise quality conventions; they even grow in the context of globalisation. Ultimately, a product cannot be considered as having a finite set of properties as it reveals evolving qualities along its undetermined life-cycle and gives rise to unexpected uses or capabilities. This observation invites us to consider products, and thus product quality, as networks across the market and consumption. A product is an intermediary node in a network, whose meanings are continually problematised with the globalisation of markets.

In a network perspective, quality cues and intermediaries are condensers that provide some contextual and often contested, yet global, knowledge of a product. Qualities in globally criss-crossing networks cannot be combined and recombined at will, contrary to Lancasterian characteristics. The essence of quality resists technical and logical decomposition. A bundle of specified characteristics, as the product presents itself in a contractual transaction, does not make sense in itself, but acquires quality only by mobilising mental images, provided by networks in which the product is embarked, in the transactors' brains. In that perspective, a credence attribute refers to a quality that cannot be broken down into components to be mapped, one-to-one, on to itemised consumer experiences.

I propose to distinguish between material characteristics corresponding to the sheer features of the product and immaterial non-experience- based attributes. The Lancasterian approach to the market frontier (see pp. 66–9) works as long as immaterial qualities are linked with materials. It is generally possible to show some linkages, such as those between the sensation of speed and the power of the car engine, but this is of little interest in the real consumption process. Imagine all the intermediaries that intervene in the relationship between time, distance and the performance of a car, and beyond that, the fact that all of the intermediaries overlap in a complex world, including traffic conditions and regulation. In such a network speed-limit regulations are 'immaterials'. By that I mean more than that the speed-limit signs are interpretable by normal drivers: these injunctions qualifying traffic infrastructures result from a globalised and distributed experience. Food is a comparable world, yet much more polymorphic. Immaterials in a product network function as global quality references. Immaterial attributes of food products include tradition, origin, hygiene, health, etc., as well as the product names in general. It is by naming and designing such immaterials that quality has found itself as constitutive rule.

Actor-network theory aims to dissolve modernist categories, such as nature and society, structure and agency, or micro- and macro-analytical distinctions, arguing that these antinomies emerge only in the processes of network formation. Network-building involves heterogeneous materials and immaterials in intermediary entities. The network's ability to exchange capabilities within these entities constitute them as intermediaries. In that perspective, a new sociology of food gives salience to 'the status of nature' (Goodman 1999), including anthropological perspectives (Poulain 2002), and reintegrates nature through the construction of food quality in recursive agro-food networks of production and consumption (Stassart 2003). Quality attribution comes from politics, as an interaction of global networks. Referring to Urry (2000), Murdoch and Miele note that 'the traditional forms of stability associated with discrete societies have given way to a world of flows in which goods, images, peoples, technologies and other artefacts criss-cross long established boundaries and borders'.[13] Thus complex processes connect demand and consumption (Harvey et al. 2001). In my view, the implications of particular interest for economists derivable from that approach are related to the unsatisfactory economic notions of 'externalities' and 'quality' (see Callon 1998). Both refer to problems brought on to the public agenda in certain circumstances and appear as social constructs rather than as purely natural or technological properties of the production process. An actor-network approach argues that capabilities acquire material, organisational and cognitive supports that are integrative for a network, but only as an emergent property. This stress on the emergence of integration draws us towards evolutionary economics perspectives, and it is fruitful to explore a convergence of approaches in relation to the emergence of conventions of quality, including their institutional and cognitive supports, for their integrative capacities.

Integrative capacity, as defined here, is a cognitive nexus that allows for some continuity of behaviour by adaptation to changes in context. Considering quality as integrative (global) knowledge, the deployment of integrative capacities results in a process of establishing quality, or 'qualification'. To 'qualify' goods (to condense quality networks), integrative knowledge incorporates an adaptivity or flexibility to factor variations. According to the evolutionary approach (Nelson and Winter 2002: 29), 'the basic behavioural continuity issue can be addressed in terms of skills, routines, learning and cognition'. The notion of routine provides the basic integrative knowledge that assures the feasibility (or the coherence) and the efficiency of the tasks that individuals and organisations have to perform, in a given framework but in variable contexts. The problem of behavioural continuity is, however, multi-scaled:

> [I]n particular, continuity derives from sustained commitments to organisational strategies and heuristics that presumably involve higher-level cognitive processes in the individuals involved . . . In a still broader context, cognitive frameworks and paradigms are known as a source of long-lasting influence and continuity for both scientific disciplines and industrial technologies. (Nelson and Winter 2002: 32)

To add a consumption perspective, I would include identity commitments and the cognitive frameworks constituted through quality networks.

Evolutionary models distinguish between a 'superior' level of regularity, referring to a whole productive organisation (firms or other types) or to the institutional settings of an economy, and an 'inferior' level where the routines emerge through individual and collective learning from experience. Evolutionary theorists stress that linkages between emergent regularities at 'superior' levels and integrative processes at 'inferior' levels are the outcome of a complex co-evolution in time (Dosi and Winter 2003). While structures with integrative power can be considered as quasi-invariants for a period of time, they remain provisional and retain ambivalence. Credence goods can be seen as an example of this quasi-invariance in relation to certain product networks.

Three types of support of integrative capacity can be distinguished in the literature: the classic figure of the entrepreneur (discussed earlier); (quality) convention as collective learning (see Favereau 1998); and routine in the evolutionist approach. In the above definition, routines are integrators at the first level. The figure of the entrepreneur corresponds to an integrative economic capacity, and, if the true capacity of the entrepreneur is in the design of organisations (choice of a 'framework' in the above terminology), this can be seen as meta-routine. A meta-routine has the character of a *regularity* and not of a *rule* due to the ambiguous co-evolution between the levels of integration. In the same perspective, it has been seen, a network product is a complex integrator. Quality conventions that structure a product network as knowledge integrators can also be seen as meta-routines, designing the particular combinations of knowledge acquired in a product's lifetime capabilities. The same methodological comments apply. The combination constituted by a quality represents some regularity of the understanding of the characteristics of the product within different contexts, including production and consumption.

But quality by itself is not an intangible set of rules, even if in certain hierarchical or formalised cooperative contexts a convention of quality can be inscribed in a set of rules. Furthermore, as I have argued, the frontiers of product networks are pushed away by globalisation processes.

Although quality represents 'common' knowledge, this commonality cannot be seen as the sharing of the same imaginative representations. While the circulation of quality knowledge allows for the recognition of capabilities integrated in the product in different contexts, to a certain extent these are idiosyncratic contexts of integration (or disintegration) of the product capabilities which can be seen as co-evolving rather as determined one after the other in a linear diffusion of knowledge. In that perspective, what I have called a product network articulates several contexts of integration and several quality conventions, which are knowledge integrators on characteristics more-or-less in competition with each other in local, variably-bounded, contexts of fabrication or of usage. Emergent food product networks overlap each other in the food quality economy. It is at this meta-level, that we can speak of cognitive frameworks and paradigms.

Integrative cognitive paradigms in food innovation
To reconcile emergence and integration, continuities and discontinuities, we need to consider innovation in terms of the dynamics of 'knowledge systems' (Foray 1998). While some approaches discussed above seem to allow for an infinite differentiation of products, I emphasise the critical role of integrative capacities which sustain quality systems and product networks at different levels, from the individual producer or consumer competence-building to policy design. Following Allaire and Wolf (2001), two alternative cognitive paradigms are introduced which function as meta-routines in the process of quality creation. I call them the logic of decomposition and the logic of identity.[14] Learning or knowledge creation, in Hayek's perspective, results from changes in a constituted 'cognitive map' by elementary processes of 'reclassification' and 'recombination' of knowledge. While these two processes are joined in the design of new knowledge, they separately offer, as 'rational myths' (according to Hatchuel 1995), innovation paradigms that shape expectations and the representations of problems. In the first logic/myth, the variety of goods is made possible by the decomposition into single traits of functional attributes and their subsequent recombination into product capacities. The complementary process of reclassification is ignored. This logic fits with Lancaster's model and functions only on the hidden assumption that current quality conventions allow classification precisely due to their integrative capacities. The second integrative paradigm is rooted in a claim to establish distinctive identities. It refers to classification as a process of incorporation into holistic frames of knowledge that precludes decomposition. These two logics/myths nourish innovation paradigms and they competitively and complementarily structure knowledge systems, or, in other words, the quality creation process. While the first is representative of the technological

logic of the production viewpoint, the second corresponds more to the client logic of marketing.

As a pattern of complementary innovation, I see decomposition/recombination applying to agronomic inputs and food end-products by entailing a conception of an agriculture and food premised on a splitting down of information and material into discrete 'bits' in a serial linear process. The decomposition paradigm gives valuable representations to the evolution of information structures in the agriculture and food global system of innovation premised on the collection of highly detailed data through continuous automated monitoring at all stages of production and marketing. According to this paradigm the creation of new products, markets and consumption arenas is predicted by permutations within rapidly expanding databases (Allaire and Wolf 2001). Communication technologies in the production and marketing domains, such as bar-coding, electronic data interchange and precision farming, contribute to an overall database integration. These technologies offer a potential means by which to enhance efficiency and the capacity to differentiate over time through a kind of automated learning (modularity).

The second paradigm, the logic/myth of identity, is exemplified by products, referred to as credence goods, bearing transcendent identities (Allaire and Wolf 2001). Allaire and Wolf include in that paradigm all forms of product individualisation, such as trademarks or other names and cultural attributes, making up the class of immaterial external product attributes. In different contexts – direct marketing, certification procedures and labels, competitions and rating guides, medical consultations, etc. – consumers are provided with global evaluations on food products and services. In this chapter, the emphasis is on the development of this myth as an heuristic device for understanding the notion of quality.

The decomposability paradigm corresponds to the cognitive logic of the experimental method that breaks down a function into independent factors. What is called 'function' in logical or formal terms corresponds to what I earlier defined as integrative capacity. Consider the classic agronomic function of production for a given parcel of land. The problem is one of identifying, in a given situation, the factors which contribute to the yield and those which limit it. Only a realistic but decomposable framework can offer a solution, albeit one limited to that framework. Factors on which we can carry out experiments are extant material and immaterials. Classic contributing agronomic factors such as minerals, the soil structure, available water and sunlight all exist in accumulated scientific agronomic knowledge as measurable characteristics. This scientific knowledge can exist both in private corporations and in the public domain. The decomposable existence of 'factors' makes it possible for the emergence of an integrative capacity that allows actors to design, for example, a fertilisation procedure. In turn, this procedure becomes a given which can be considered in further experimentation as an extant factor. Digital monitoring, as in precision farming, offers a prodigiously enhanced set of experience records as the entire farm and entire sets of farms became related in seamless sets of recorded data (presented here in an optimistic light; see Wolf and Wood 1997). Super databases seem to attribute infinite power to that logic in order to attract significant investment. The power of that logic/myth in ordering the industrial world is not to be denied (and it is dependent on the distribution of property rights and on prevailing conventions regarding the circulation of knowledge, but those are other issues). But the efficiency of that process is limited by the unstable linkages between co-evolving levels or contexts of integration, discussed earlier. We cannot add attributes corresponding to immaterial qualities, such as the qualification 'organic', or even certain qualifications produced by labelling, as factors independent of agronomic technical functions as such. To include such issues, the problem would need to be broken down into different levels of integration (reclassification).

The identity paradigm offers heuristics to qualify a capacity as a whole (and not in the form of a decomposable function). As Appadurai (1986: 5) puts it: 'even though from a theoretical point of view human actors encode things with significance, from a methodological point of view it is the things-in-motion that illuminate their human and social context'. To return attention to the things themselves, some 'methodological fetishism' is needed for the social analysis of the world of commodities. I emphasise that the analyst, in so doing, works in the same way as do ordinary consumers, to whom quality representations are fetishistic heuristics rooted in fetishistic metrics and mottoes. We are confronted here with qualification resources that have an identity power or which bring 'transcendent' qualification (Allaire and Wolf 2001). Within the identity paradigm, for example, origin cannot be reduced to the physical characteristics of the product. Transcendent resources not only have a strategic power, but as rational myths they offer a cognitive structure to integrate quality. Philosophical principles are embedded in organic food, aesthetics in natural food, solidarity in fair-trade food, and so on. These immaterials are incorporated by products throught images that ultimately make these identity resources recognisable in the form of product networks engaged in the economy of signs.

A paradox inherent to identity-based innovation is that diffusion of identity resources does not require symmetry among actors' commitments and competences. Identity networks retain coherence in the face of the transfiguration of quality imagery, when such changes are consonant with actors' commitments and competences. Diffusion of identity in large markets is premissed on individuals manipulating and interpreting images. Product networks expand as identity diffuses through acculturation, and emergent networks may coalesce through politics. Alternative food images include, for example, representations of community-specific resources, while the current local rural development strategies developed under the EU Agenda 2000 regulation generally include representations of food alternatives (direct sales, farmers' markets, organic products, etc.). Organic standards prescribe non-GMOs, which is a quality not justified by publicly recognised objective effects of GMOs, but by a global representation of genetic engineering. People who feel nervous about GMOs tend to turn to organic products (an alternative quality framework) or at least to include perspectives from the organic discourse in their quality framework. The same (unstable) link appears when one reads: 'You dreamed it, Sony does it.' But, in the previous example, alternatives (the organic dream) refer to (integrative) community values, while the message of Sony refers to the values of individuals. Mechanisms of image translation create, reshape and transmit knowledge, thereby extending markets for differentiated products. Integration mechanisms that extend identity networks by replacement and transfiguration of imagery are poorly recognised by purists within the myth of identity, while the key objective for cooperation among proponents is to extend such networks. Here concern is with the ways in which the logic of identity is confronted by accountability demands from those who desire entry, and thus want the identity to become public. As Allaire and Wolf (2001) emphasise, identity networks that expand via commerce and various social movements invite accountability challenges, as industrial trademarks have done. Each time, network extension obliges products to conform to various qualities. The standards of evidence associated with such challenges of legitimacy will often be incompatible with the information structures of immaterial resources on which the distinctive identity rests. But, within that framework, it is possible to develop an analysis of the institutional hybridisation of quality networks.

Conclusion

In this chapter, through a survey of consumption and quality theories in mainstream and heterodox economics I have contrasted a normative approach to quality based on information theory in which quality appears as meta-information to a subjective and reflexive approach to knowledge which presents quality as an ambivalent integrative capacity, or meta-routine (or convention). The normative approach extends to the analysis of private, collective and public initiatives to mitigate any asymmetry of information related to products on the market. However, the knowledge that enables signs to circulate with products is left out of the picture. The production and consumption worlds are assumed to be coherent as a theoretical consequence of the equilibrium perspective, and perhaps as a cultural credence to 'science'.

In questioning this approach to quality as market failure and a substitute for information, insight is gained into theoretical problems arising from persistent and renewed diversity in globalised markets. The characterisation of goods by the information they are able to display ultimately depends on market institutions and consumers' collective behaviours. The radical incompleteness and ambiguity of the market nomenclature and of qualification mechanisms have thus to be thought of from an institutional and evolutionary perspective.

To adopt the 'quality turn' stressed in the specialised literature, we need to do more than develop a theory of consumption, even a theory including learning and capabilities in the manner of institutionalist theories of production. The domain to be embraced extends from farm to fork, and importantly the reverse, which is the current challenge for innovation studies related to quality. In orthodox economic approaches, the solution to the information gap concerning quality and capabilities is sought in improving ways that producers can monitor consumers' changing needs and preferences in global markets. I have argued, however, that the information gap is not organisational but *societal*, and that knowledge cannot be reduced to information messages.

Concrete products result from complex networks. To analyse the stabilisation of quality conventions, I have distinguished two cognitive logics, that are also myths in the sense that they refer to only one of the two aspects of the knowledge creation. The first, the logic/myth of decomposability, faced with an expanding number of product attributes, attempts to deepen standardisation and synthesis by producing ever more public standards aimed at clarifying and securing final consumption markets. While this vision sustains procedures of public accountability, it is challenged in a context where different qualities proliferate. Differentiation in a knowledge-based economy involves differentiation both of products and of people. Innovation, which formerly was oriented by specialist professional networks, now develops in complex and open innovative networks. A critical role is played by coordinating structures in processes of learning and by integrative capacities in quality innovation. While, in the global market, contractual and certification procedures have emerged as a central arena in which control over quality is regulated, the debate on accountability reflects a pattern of more immaterial and service-oriented consumption. The second logic/myth relates to immaterial resources which develops an ever-expanding universe of different quality identities, based on holistic cognitive frameworks. At the same time, food scares have put the construction and articulation of agro-food networks under interrogation by bringing to light the hidden relations between food and nature.

A wide diversity of examples of hybridisation in quality creation is to be found in the studies presented in the present volume. Local markets exhibit at the same time both fashion cues and certified labels. Organic and other alternative foods can be found in supermarkets, threatening the preservation of identity by antithetical logistical procedures and contrary standards. Both in their development and in their solutions, crises in large distribution systems, such as the BSE crisis, show the same result: the multiplication of knowledge of quality and the complexification of the world as product networks expand. In western eyes, two myths that shape that world are in a constant dialectic. The myth of Prometheus, the mission of science at the endless frontier of the decomposition of knowledge in defiance of the unknowable domains of the gods, is constantly vying with the myth of the origin of knowledge which is at the inner core of identity.

Notes

1 The author thanks Steven Wolf and Jean Gadrey for the initial inspiration for this work, Mark Harvey and Kate Mailfert for very helpful editing contributions, but remains entirely responsible for any insufficiencies in the text.

2 The agro-food 'actor-network' literature has been in English, except for the recent work of Stassart (2003), who developed outstandingly the conceptual repertoire of the actor-network theory in the treatment of the food provision system through the study of two Belgian beef *filières*. Comparable research published in France refers to the 'convention' theory. The critique offered by Lockie and Kitto (2000) concerning the focus on 'alternatives' as the operators for food deconstruction can be extended to those comparable in the French literature of the 1990s. But, this critique is harsh because the authors consider a restricted corpus. Besides the rural sociology literature both convention or actor-network approaches have developed in domains of research connected with food issues such as the sociology of risk, and have shed light on complex hybrid networks. Agro-food networks are revisited in the second section.

3 Karpik (1989) distinguishes social tools that create and diffuse quality judgements and social tools that build trust regarding quality definitions. These two dimensions of the notion of quality are generally emphasised by economic sociology, innovation sociology and heterodox economics.

4 The notion of 'convention of quality' (Eymard-Duvernet 1989) introduced a plurality of modes of qualification, corresponding to different modes of the assessment of quality. Conventions of quality do not support isolated worlds, but rather a plurality of conventions of quality coincides today with the polymorphic world emerging from the 'quality turn'.

5 A constitutive rule, one that can be noted 'X counts as Y in C' (in a context C), 'determines a set of institutional facts and institutional objects where the Y term [quality characteristic, e.g. "vitamins added" or "no GMOs"] names something more than the sheer physical features of the object named by the X term [the product components, e.g. "nutritional fact" or "less than X per cent of GMO ingredients"]. Furthermore, the "counts as" locution names a feature of the imposition of a status to which a function is attached by way of collective intentionality, where the status and its accompanying function [in other words, the capacity named by Y] go beyond the sheer brute physical functions that can be assigned to physical objects' (Searle 1995: 44).

6 The norm ISO 8402 defines quality as 'the totality of features and characteristics of a product or service that bear on its ability to satisfy stated or implied needs'.

7 Through information theory, reputation mechanisms can be seen by economists both as making possible the ordering of qualitative differences in respect of a product type and as a trait functioning as an economic signal. But, on their side, organisation scholars generally see corporate reputation as rooted in the meaning-developing experiences of employees (Fombrun and van Riel 1997), thus introducing complex intermediaries to the process of reputation-building. This second approach fits better with the developments outlined in the second section.

8 While consumer behaviour and the marketing literature favour perceived quality or quality attributes, the food sciences literature addresses measurable properties, counting them as product characteristics. Although these literatures deliver heterogeneous knowledge, they are formally integrated by economists in Lancaster's

framework, in which the market outcome for quality is determined by the supply of characteristics, the demand for attributes and the information of the consumer regarding the distribution of attributes.

9 The seminal paper by Becker is devoted to the issue of the allocation of time. It provides a framework for the development of household economics, including the classic producer–consumer model of the peasant household. The substitution trend I am evoking developed, in part, in the household. But more generally, and in particular when services are at stake, the time–goods substitution concerns personal consumption: eating out, phoning, professional training, entertainment, and so on, are more personal than are household services. Their development implies a certain degree of individualisation of the usage of time and purchasing decisions. It is through that individualisation that health issues related to consumption became a large public concern.

10 The main role in the design of commercial food quality has shifted from the merchants (who formerly used the source or origin of the products as a benchmark in quality assessment at a time when agricultural resources were localised) to industrial companies and then to retailers. To some extent active industrial restructuring and concentration have weakened the role of industrial trademarks, while more global concerns about consumption that involve the entire chain (e.g. green labels) seem to be more easily handled by retailer networks.

11 The normative framework integrates qualitative attributes only if they are reduced to an homogeneous system of functions of objective characteristics (see the first section).

12 See Montgomery (1995).

13 Quoted by Murdoch and Miele (2003: n.p.); the authors introduce a note of caution to Urry's argument: 'while, on the one hand, networks might appear to be increasingly mobile, that is, increasingly disconnected from given spaces they also, on the other hand, act to condense space (and time)'. They explain how networks condense space or territories by using the conventionalist approach. We find a parallel with the idea of network condensation of quality which we have referred, on our part, to 'transcendent' attributes (Allaire and Wolf 2001).

14 In this sub-section I draw on Allaire and Wolf's paper (2001), the purpose of which was to analyse contemporary differentiated ways in which food evolves through various networks of knowledge diffusion and creation. We opposed the two paradigms as alternative ways of differentiating food networks, providing 'functional' versus 'identity' food, but emphasised that the globalisation of agro-food networks was combining governance institutions related to those two paradigms. My intention here is to relate these cognitive frameworks to the discussion of the economic approach of quality.

References

Akerlof, A. G. (1970), 'The market for lemons: quality uncertainty and the market mechanism', *Quarterly Journal of Economics*, 84, pp. 488–500.
Allaire, G. (1995), 'Croissance et crise en agriculture', in Boyer, R. and Saillard, Y. (eds), *Théorie de la Régulation: L'Etat des Savoirs*, France, La Découverte.
Allaire, G. (2002), 'L'economie de la qualité, en ses territoires, ses secteurs et ses mythes', *Géographie, Economie et Société*, 4(2), pp. 155–80.

Allaire, G. and Wolf, S. (2001), 'Cognitive representations and institutional hybridity in agrofood innovation', Toulouse, INRA-ESR, forthcoming in *Sciences, Technology and Human Values*, 2004.

Anania, G. and Nisticò, R. (2002), 'Public regulation as a substitute for trust in quality food markets: what if the trust substitute cannot be fully trusted?', Working Paper, Italy, University of Calabria.

Appadurai, A. (ed.) (1986), *The Social Life of Things: Commodities in Cultural Perspective*, Cambridge, Cambridge University Press.

Arce, A. and Marsden, T. (1993), 'The social construction of international food: a new research agenda', *Economic Geography*, 69(3), pp. 293–311.

Barjolle, D. and Sylvander, B. (2002), 'Quelques facteurs de succès des "produits d'origine" dans les filières agroalimentaires européennes', *Economies et Société* (September–October), Cahiers de l'ISMEA, Série Systèmes Agroalimentaires, 25, pp. 1441–64.

Barthes, R. (1972 [1957]), *Mythologies*, trans. Lavers, A., Paris, Editions du Seuil, and New York, Hill & Wang.

Becker, G. (1965), 'A theory of the allocation of time', *Economic Journal*, 299(74), pp. 493–517.

Boltanski, L. and Thévenot, L. (1991), *De la Justification: Les Economies de la Grandeur*, Paris, Gallimard.

Callon, M. (ed) (1998), *The Laws of the Markets*, Oxford, Blackwell..

Chamberlin, E. (1933), *The Theory of Monopolistic Competition*, Cambridge, MA, Harvard University Press.

Clark, K. (1985), 'The interaction of design hierarchies and market concepts in technical innovation', *Research Policy*, 14(5), pp. 235–51.

Darby, M. and Karni, E. (1973), 'Free competition and the optimal amount of fraud', *Journal of Law and Economics*, 16 (April), pp. 67–88.

Dosi, G. and Winter, S. G. (2003), 'Interprétation évolutionniste du changement économique: une étude comparative', *Revue Economique*, 54(2), pp. 385–406.

Eymard-Duvernay, F. (1989), 'Conventions de qualité et pluralité des formes de coordination', *Revue Economique*, 40(2), pp. 329–59.

Favereau, O. (1998), 'Notes sur la théorie de l'information à laquelle pourrait conduire l'économie des conventions', in Petit, P. (ed.), *L'Economie de l'Information: Les Enseignements des Théories Economiques*, Paris, La Découverte.

Fombrun, C. and Riel, C. van (1997), 'The reputational landscape', *Corporate Reputation Review*, 1(1–2), pp. 1–16.

Foray, D. (1998), 'The economics of knowledge openness: emergence, persistence and change of conventions in the knowledge systems', in Lazaric, N. and Lorenz, E. (eds), *Trust and Economic Learning*, Cheltenham, Edward Elgar.

Goodman, D. (1999), 'Agro-food studies in the "age of ecology": nature, corporeality, bio-politics', *Sociologia Ruralis*, 39(1), pp. 17–38.

Goodman, D. (2002), 'Rethinking food production–consumption: integrative perspective', *Sociologia Ruralis*, 42(4), pp. 271–7.

Hareven, T. K. (1990), 'A complex relationship: family strategies and the processes of economic and social change', in Friedland, R. and Robertson, A. F. (eds), *Beyond the Marketplace: Rethinking Economy and Society*, New York, A. de Gruyter.

Harvey, M., McMeekin, A., Randles, S., Southerton, D., Tether, B. and Warde, A. (2001), 'Between demand and consumption: a framework for research', Discussion

Paper No. 40, Manchester, ESRC Centre for Research on Innovation and Competition, University of Manchester.

Hassan, D. and Monier-Dilhan, S. (2002), 'Signes de qualité et qualité des signes: une application au marché du Camembert', *Cahiers d'Economie et Sociologie Rurales*, 65, pp. 24–36.

Hatchuel, A. (1995), 'Les marchés à prescripteurs', in Verin, H. and Jacob, A. (eds), *L'Inscription Sociale du Marché*, Paris, L'Harmattan.

Hirschman, A. O. (1970), *Exit, Voice and Loyalty: Responses to Decline in Firms, Organizations and States*, Cambridge, MA, Harvard University Press.

Kalaitzandonakes, N. (2000), 'Functional foods: technical, institutional and market innovation', *AgBioForum*, 3(1), pp. 259–60, available: www.agbioforum.org.

Karpik, L. (1989), 'L'économie de la qualité', *Revue Française de Sociologie*, 30(2), pp. 187–210.

Katz, M. and Shapiro, C: (1985), 'Network externalities, competition and compatibility', *American Economic Review*, 75(3), pp. 424–40.

Kindleberger, C. (1983), 'Standards as public, collective and private goods', *Kyklos*, 36(3), pp. 377–96.

Lancaster, K. J. (1966), 'A new approach to consumer theory', *Journal of Political Economy*, 74(2), pp. 132–57.

Lancaster, K. J. (1979), *Variety, Equity and Efficiency*, New York, Columbia University Press.

Langlois, R. N. and Cosgel, M. M. (1996), 'The organization of consumption', Working Paper 7, Storrs, University of Connecticut.

Langlois, R. N. and Cosgel, M. M. (1998), 'The organization of consumption', in Bianchi, M. (ed.), *The Active Consumer*, London, Routledge.

Langlois, R. N. and Robertson, N. (1995), *Firms, Markets and Economic Change*, London, Routledge.

Lash, S. and Urry, J. (1994), *Economies of Signs and Space*, London, Sage.

Lockie, S. and Kitto, S. (2000), 'Beyond the farm gate: production–consumption networks and agri-food research', *Sociologia Ruralis*, 40(1), pp. 3–19.

Loureiro, M. L. and McCluskey, J. J. (2000), 'Assessing consumer response to protected geographical identification labelling', *Agribusiness*, 16(3), pp. 309–20.

McMeekin, A., Tomlinson, M., Green, K. and Walsh, V. (2002), *Innovation by Demand*, Manchester, Manchester University Press.

Marsden, T. and Arce, A. (1995), 'Constructing quality: emerging food networks in the rural transition', *Environment & Planning A*, 27(9), pp. 1261–79.

Metcalfe, J. S. (2001), 'Consumption, preferences, and the evolutionary agenda', *Journal of Evolutionary Economics*, 11(1) (special issue), pp. 37–58.

Montgomery, C. (1995), *Resource-Based and Evolutionary Theories of the Firm*, Dordrecht, Kluwer Academic.

Murdoch, J., Marsden, T. and Banks, J. (2000), 'Quality, nature and embeddedness: some theoretical considerations in the context of the food sector', *Economic Geography*, 76(2), pp. 107–25.

Murdoch, J. and Miele, M. (2003), 'Culinary networks and cultural connections: a conventions perspective', in Hughes, A. and Reimer, E. (eds), *Geographies of Commodity Chains*, Harlow, Pearson Education.

Nonaka, I. (1996), '"Knowledge has to do with truth, goodness, and beauty": conversation between Professor Ikujiro Nonaka, Tokyo, and Claus Otto Scharmer', available: www.dialogonleadership.org.

Nelson, P. (1970), 'Information and consumer behavior', *Journal of Political Economy*, 78(2), pp. 311–29.

Nelson, R. R. and Winter, S. G. (1982), *An Evolutionary Theory of Economic Change*, Cambridge, MA, Harvard University Press.

Nelson, R. R. and Winter, S. G. (2002), 'Evolutionary theorizing in economics', *Journal of Economic Perspectives*, 16(2), pp. 23–46.

Nooteboom, B. (forthcoming), 'Discovery and competence in production and consumption', in Backhaus, J. (ed.), *Recent Developments in Austrian Economics*.

Orléan, A. (2002), 'Le tournant cognitif en économie', *Revue d'Economie Politique*, 112(5), pp. 717–38.

Poulain, J. (2002), *Sociologies de l'Alimentation*, Paris, Presses Universitaires France.

Requier-Desjardins, D. (1999), 'Producer–consumer approach: from consumer's [sic] preferences to consumption technology', Centre d'Economie et d'Ethique pour l'Environnement et le Développement (C3ED), available: www.c3ed.uvsq.fr/eeesdp_line/maqt_DRD/preftec.pdf.

Richardson, G. B. (1972), 'The organisation of industry', *Economic Journal*, 82(327), pp. 883–96.

Searle, J. R. (1995), *The Construction of Social Reality*, Harmondsworth, Penguin.

Shapiro, C. (1983), 'Premiums for high quality products as a return to reputations', *Quarterly Journal of Economics*, 98(4), pp. 659–79.

Stassart, P. (2003), *Produits Fermiers: Entre Qualification et Identité*, Brussells, Peter Land.

Stigler, G. (1961), 'The economics of information', *Journal of Political Economy*, 69(3), pp. 213–25.

Stigler, G. and Becker, G. (1977), 'De gustibus non est disputandum', *American Economic Review*, 67(2), pp. 76–90.

Stiglitz, J. (1987), 'The causes and consequences of the dependence of quality on price', *Journal of Economic Literature*, 25 (March), pp. 1–48.

Sylvander, B. (1997), 'Le rôle de la certification dans les changements de régime de coordination: l'agriculture biologique, du réseau à l'industrie', *Revue d'Économie Industrielle*, 80(2), pp. 47–66.

Sylvander, B. (2003), 'Crédibilité et flexibilité de la certification dans un contexte de globalisation et de crises alimentaires: le cas de l'agriculture biologique', Le Mans, INRA-UREQUA (Department of Rural Economy and Sociology).

Thévenot, L. (1998), 'Innovating in "qualified" markets: quality, norms and conventions', paper presented at the workshop 'Systems and trajectories for agricultural innovation', 23–25 April, University of California, Berkeley.

Tirole, J. (1988), *The Theory of Industrial Organization*, Cambridge, MA, MIT Press.

Urry, J. (2000), *Sociology beyond Society: Mobilities for the Twenty-First Century*, London, Routledge.

Warde, A. and Martens, L. (2000), *Eating Out: Social Differentiation, Consumption and Pleasure*, Cambridge, Cambridge University Press.

Whatmore, S. and Thorne, L. (1997), 'Nourishing networks: alternative geographies of food', in Goodman, D. and Watts, M. (eds), *Globalising Food: Agrarian Questions and Global Restructuring*, London, Routledge.

Wolf, S. and Wood, S. (1997), 'Precision farming: environmental legitimation, commodification of information, and industrial coordination', *Rural Sociology*, 62(2), pp. 180–206.

4

Social definitions of *halal* quality: the case of Maghrebi Muslims in France[1]

Florence Bergeaud-Blackler

In French mosques, the rules surrounding the consumption of food and drink (such as pork and alcohol), as well as table manners (using the right hand rather than the left to convey food to the mouth) and eating patterns (fasting during the month of Ramadan), are subject to frequent inquiry, along with those concerning marriage, sexuality and dress code. All such questions have one point in common: they question the limits of Muslim coexistence with non-Muslims. May a meal be shared with a non-believer? May a Muslim marry a non-Muslim? In whose presence may a Muslim woman remove her veil? The religious authorities at all levels – *fuqaha*, *oulema* and *imam* – face the difficult task of finding answers to these modern-day issues while relying for guidance on ancient religious texts. The situation is further complicated by the fact that Islam recognises certain practices inherited from the two preceding monotheisms, Judaism and Christianity, religions with which it maintains special relations. For Muslims, there exists a relative exogamy[2] with the 'people of the Book'.[3]

Food is an area in which the principle of continuity with and tolerance towards the practices of the two older religions conflicts with specific Islamic instructions. In Europe, outside of *Dar el Islam*,[4] imams' opinions are divergent and can be divided roughly into two main tendencies. Some consider that halal meat is the result of a precise technical ritual described in the Islamic texts. Others, quoting a verse of the Koran, consider that meat is lawful as long as the animal has been killed by someone considered to belong to the 'people of the Book'. These distinct tendencies result in diverse practices: some Muslims argue that the only way to abide by Islam is to purchase meat exclusively from halal butchers' shops; others deem such strictness unnecessary for those who live in a Christian country; still others believe that slaughtering one's own meat is the only sure way to guarantee its legitimacy and lawfulness.

These competing practices illustrate the diversity of interpretation arising out of Muslim religious texts. They reflect, or induce, the heterogeneous dietary practices and habits of Muslims in France. If a consensus cannot be reached on what criteria define *halal* meat in religious terms for Muslims in

Europe, it is perhaps because the production–consumption of this product – non-existent in the Maghreb[5] – is primarily a commercial business. This statement must not be taken to mean that halal food is devoid of religious significance. Rather, studies show that buyers spontaneously 'define' it as the product of a religious ritual. It appears – indeed, it is the hypothesis developed in this chapter – that a religious rationale is applied more to the finished product than to the production process as such. The definition of halal meat belongs to the consumer who recognises and attributes its specific qualities.

Before developing this hypothesis and drawing conclusions from it, it is necessary to explain the empirical observations on which it rests. In France, halal meat sold in halal shops is produced by the standard industrial production chain in the abattoir and follows the same steps, in the same order, as 'ordinary' (i.e. non-halal) meat. In the abattoirs that I visited, the difference is more one of manner than of process. In both cases, halal and non-halal, the animal is killed by the drainage of all its blood. When the carcass is intended for sale to halal butchers, the act of slaughter is performed by a Muslim, who makes no use of stunning, while the animal is held in a 'restraining pen'.[6] Unlike *kosher* slaughtering (Nizard-Benchimol 1997), where the carcass is ritually examined (*bedika*) and, if found non-conforming, withdrawn from the circuit,[7] the carcass to be sold as halal does not undergo a particular treatment. Unlike the Jewish *chekhita*, where a mark is made on the flesh by the *chokhet* to indicate to the Jewish controller–puncher at the end of the slaughtering chain that the animal has been slaughtered and examined according to ritual procedures, there is no means of tracking to guarantee that the carcass stamped halal has really been slaughtered by a Muslim. At the end of the chain, the carcasses are weighed and marked with legal and halal stamps by the same operator. After the post-mortem veterinary inspection, carcasses are dispatched to the fridges of wholesalers. From there, most of the carcasses marked halal are sold and conveyed to butchers' shops; in cases where there is a surplus, the wholesaler can decide to sell the carcasses to non-halal retailers, preferably after having removed the signed portions of flesh. Thus carcasses stamped halal can be distributed in both non-Muslim and Muslim shops: halal carcasses do not systematically end up being sold as halal meat. Consequently, the meat obtains its halal status outside of the abattoir – in the halal shops, once cut by the butcher, and through its unique presentation. There, its particular shape and presentation render it recognisable by the customer as halal meat. This does not mean that such meat *will* be recognised by the customer as truly halal, but the possibility will at least arise, whereas that same cut according to French methods in a non-Muslim butcher's shop will not be seen as halal at all.[8] In this food chain, it is the customer in the act of purchase who appears to be the first to authenticate the halal status of the meat.

What renders meat halal is not a material process in strict conformance to an imagined uniquely Islamic prescription; to understand what is halal for meat or food it is necessary to go beyond the abattoir. I suggest in this chapter that the quality 'halal' is rather the result of a social and economic consensus between the different generations and cultures of migrant Muslims as distinct from the non-Muslim majority. The production of halal meat seems to adapt to the differing viewpoints of Muslim groups, despite the lack of a clear religious definition.

In the first part of this discussion I sketch a brief history of the development of the halal market from its origins in France, taking the region of Bordeaux (in south-west France) as an example,[9] and showing, notably, that the Muslim authorities took very little part in that development. Lacking a definition of what is unique to halal meat, the halal market grew relatively rapidly. In the second part I give my reasons for suggesting that the end-consumer, through the retailer, possesses control over the definition of the halal quality of meat. In the third part I present two consequences of my hypothesis. Being consumer-driven, the halal market responds rapidly to its social and economic context, as is shown by the development of a new definition of halal built by subsequent generations of Muslims born in France to whom halal is, first of all, a guarantee that food is free from any *haram* substances.[10] This definition leads to a conception of separate circuits of production and a separate Muslim 'diet'. Another consequence of this consumer-driven market is that its growth appears compatible with the recent institutional reorganisations of the food control institutions and the food industry at the European and international levels, designed to take greater account of the choices and ethical concerns of consumers.

The development of the halal market

In 1990, a study was done for the French Ministry of Agriculture in which economists calculated that 200,000–350,000 tonnes of meat annually are required to meet the demand for halal meat by the 4 million Muslims living in France (Nefussi 1995a). My study, based in Aquitaine, estimates that over 1996–2000 the number of halal meat retailers doubled in the St Michel neighbourhood of Bordeaux alone (Bergeaud-Blackler 2001). A combination of economic, practical and religious factors in the late 1990s led to the rapid expansion of a market that had not even existed until the 1970s. As I show, six factors contributed to create and develop a halal meat market:

- the search for new market outlets;
- the increased severity of regulations governing slaughter in the context of European integration;
- the availability of a low-cost and flexible labour supply;
- the multiplicity of religious interpretations of halal ritual;
- the withdrawal of religious groups from the struggle for control over halal meat;
- the virtuous economic effects of the suspicion of 'false' halal meat.

One of the deciding factors in the growth of the halal meat market was the desire of the operators of beef and lamb chains to find new outlets for a commodity that the market's evolution had diverted from its former destinations. Improvements in productivity and new policies promoting 'quality' led to a pattern of 'protected chains', the side effect of which was to produce animals classified as non-conforming. For instance, in Gironde, the producers of lamb shifted from classical production to production labelled 'Agneaux de Pauillac'. To be classed as conforming to this label, animals must comply with certain characteristics. When this is not so, the animals cannot be sold in the protected circuit. After the inception of the European free market and the development of quality schemes under the pressure of food crises, public institutions such as prisons, hospitals, school canteens and the processed-food industry proved incapable of absorbing all these surpluses. The search for new outlets became a priority for local producers and the slaughterhouse industry.

From the 1980s, French regulations governing the slaughtering of animals (Decree 80–791), and EC pressure for its better enforcement, required all slaughtering of animals by Muslims to be undertaken by competent workers inside a properly equipped slaughterhouse. Industrial production chains of halal meat developed rapidly while respecting strict divisions of labour: Muslims contented themselves with the retail sector, while non-Muslims controlled the production and distribution. There were no obstacles to this rapid development, not even the strict hygiene inspection regime governing such perishable products. Halal butchers have not been subjected to regular inspections as the authorities consider it relatively unproblematical, from the point of view of both public health and tax revenue, that the animals are slaughtered in recognised abattoirs and sold in established outlets rather than illegally slaughtered, sold and consumed.[11]

Confronted with this rapid development, the State sought to regulate the halal market in order to prevent the potential rewards brought about by its profits falling into the hands of Islamist groups which do not conform to the ideal of 'republican integration'. In 1990, following the terrorist attacks in Paris of September 1986, the 'Rushdie affair'[12] and the first occurrence of the 'headscarf affair' in Creil,[13] the Interior Minister Charles Pasqua (in charge of religious matters) sought to encourage the creation of an institution representative of Islam in France in order to have only one interlocutor in his negotiations with the Muslim population. One of his first initiatives was to attempt to establish a national monopoly on halal certification. He arranged a meeting between the Fédération Nationale des Exploitants d'Abattoirs Prestataires de Service (FNEAP), the most powerful representative of the interests of the slaughterhouse industry, with the director of the Institut Musulman de la Mosquée de Paris, the oldest (although not the most popular) Islamic institute in France. This initiative led to a written agreement giving the halal certification exclusively, and with it potentially great economic power, to the Mosquée de Paris. But the members of the FNEAP refused to implement the agreement: its conditions were for them far less advantageous than the contracts they had already negotiated at the local level with wholesalers. However, immediately after this convention was signed, the economic actors started to speculate in the halal market. Consequently, numerous slaughterhouses invested in costly stunning pens suitable for ritual slaughter and in recruiting qualified Muslim slaughterers. Some wholesalers contacted Islamic associations requesting information on halal consumption or investigated the possibilities of opening halal butchers. If the State failed to regulate the halal market, it indirectly – and involuntarily – favoured its growth.

While the processing sector was becoming organised, the distribution sector benefited from a flexible labour supply made up of Maghrebi unemployed construction workers, metal workers and farming hands. These job-seekers entered the butchery trade with very little initial capital, often supported by family members or other personal connections. Helped by tax exemptions granted by the State and voluntary labour by family members, together with, in some cases, non-declared sales or continued social welfare benefits for families, a number survived the difficulties and established what developed into successful businesses,[14] though some experienced excessive competition and closed their shops within a year of opening them. The competition did not favour a cooperative spirit among butchers and resulted in the failure of any attempts to regulate retail meat prices. Wholesalers speculated around these disagreements and their consequences. The halal market, considered by non-Muslim wholesalers as particularly unstable and unpredictable, was treated with little consideration and sometimes with disdain. The general attitude, as it was understood by one non-Muslim wholesaler, was 'that one doesn't fight over crumbs'. In rural areas, for instance, halal business was silently left to the monopoly of a single operator by the others. This operator could then put pressure on the grocer, imposing low quality of carcasses at relatively high wholesale prices.

During the 1980s, when the need for Muslim establishments (schools, mosques and cemeteries) was being expressed more widely, the State systematically refused to make any public contribution to Muslim groups due to its policy of non-involvement (laïcité) in religious matters. The leaders of Muslim organisations envisaged a tax on halal meat to ensure the creation and maintenance of Islamic establishments. However, the supply chain for Islamic butchers had already advanced too far, and the retailers refused to enter into 'quarrels' that they felt did not concern them. They did not wish to form alliances with mosques or other institutions, disagreements with which could potentially lose them an already volatile clientele. As a result, the Islamic associations decided not to directly engage in these debates. Some did express support for the creation of independent associations of halal certification, but had no further involvement.

In Aquitaine, the mid-1990s saw a period of deflation in halal retail meat prices. In addition to the presence of strong competition, a dynamic arose of a great suspicion of 'false' halal meat. Halal shops were opening at an increasing rate, always promising to be 'more halal'; while, several years later, the market arrived at a quantitative saturation and successive food crises began to have an effect on buying practices; qualitative differentiation appeared and prices stopped falling.[15] The halal market entered into a new phase. Grocer–butchers started dealing directly with farmers in the cattle markets, trying to contact the competitors of their wholesale butchers and seeking to impose their own employees as 'sacrificateur' in the abattoirs (despite a French regulation mandating that such work was to be done only by slaughterers accredited by one of three approved mosques). They also better acquainted themselves with the cutting techniques, aiming to improve the output of the carcasses. They decorated their shops with images evocative of tradition and the 'local butcher'; and, to combat concerns over British beef (which was thought to carry BSE), displayed in their shop window, next to a large halal sign, a notice guaranteeing their beef to be 100 per cent French.

To conclude this first part, it can be noted that the butcher experienced a competitive situation preventing him from controlling retail prices, while the consumer enjoyed an advantageous position. The qualitative differences offered choice to consumers while prices were low compared to supermarket prices. Rumours of 'false' halal meat proliferated, resulting not in the decline of the market but rather, conversely, in the virtuous effect of pushing shop-owners to offer higher quality and service at a low price.

Devaluing the act of slaughtering

My study of the production and consumption of halal meat shows a certain independence between the actual conditions of halal meat production and the consumer discourse. Consumers know little about the process of the production of halal meat. When questioned, several people asserted that halal meat is paler than non-halal meat because, unlike the latter, it is drained of its blood. In fact, this difference is attributable to the age of the slaughtered animal rather than to the method of slaughter. Like butchers in the Maghreb, Muslim butchers in France tend to buy the meat of young bovines because it is considered to be more tender. This meat is particularly low in price on the French market because it is discarded by non-Muslim butchers whose consumers consider it undesirable, 'neither veal nor beef'. This ignorance about what goes on before the delivery of the meat to the butcher is not unique to the Muslim population. Rather, it reveals the physical and symbolic distance built by urban society towards all that reminds people of animal death (Agulhon 1981; Vialles 1987). The fact that some claim to be able to distinguish halal from non-halal meat just by its appearance reveals that consumers have appropriated the product without need for control over its production.

As will now become clear, the societal and cultural changes produced by immigration can, at least in part, explain this rapid acceptance. The migrant women who entered France to rejoin their spouses under the 'familial regrouping procedures' have played a major role in setting up Maghrebi shops and in determining the ingredients stocked by those shops. The particular place of meat in North African cuisine has changed under the influence of other culinary traditions. Finally, Maghrebi men were not included in the production processes as much as they were in their home country.

Prior to 1974, Maghrebi immigration was mainly of males and was considered largely temporary. Then, the French Government decided to stop all primary immigration other than family regrouping. As men could not go back to their country without risk of being unable to re-enter France, they preferred to bring their spouses and family and settle permanently in France. When they arrived in France the Maghrebi women revolutionised the networks of small local shops, which the larger supermarkets and factories had nearly overtaken. Supply and distribution systems developed rapidly and were able to provide these women with all the necessary products for their recipes. Several new Maghrebi retail shops opened in the residential areas of these families. Fresh produce such as fruits, vegetables, meats and other animal products were purchased through local wholesalers; spices, dried fruits, teas, flours, tinned foods and certain cereals were bought from specialist national suppliers to the sub-Sahara African, Turkish and Asian communities. The essentials for preparing North African dishes were then available to Maghrebi women. Despite often being unable to read the labels, the women learnt to distinguish and choose products, and were rapidly dictating their choices to the retailers. They also imposed on grocers their preferences regarding the quality and presentation of meat, which had an impact on the entire organisation of the supply of food and the spatial lay-out of shops. To meet the women's desires, the grocers had to ensure a permanent supply of freshly slaughtered meat and to adapt their meat-cutting skills to the requirements of the different cooking techniques required by Maghrebi cuisine (Hal 1996), a task particularly difficult with very fresh meat.[16] When a piece of meat was not sold within three days of being delivered to the retailer and had started to discolour, the butcher would convert it into a ground-meat product, such as *kefta* or *merguez*, in order to sell it before the next weekly delivery. The bowls of marinated olives and bags of spices and herbs were placed near the refrigerated windows, where perishable items are normally displayed, to suggest quality and freshness. In return, the ground meat benefited from the 'flavour principle' particular to Maghrebi cuisine, giving the idea to those entering the shop that the meat could even have originated in the home country.[17] The job of skilfully cutting and dressing the flesh, which contains very few bones and little fat, greatly impressed clients attracted by mounds of bright-pink flesh suggestive of power, luxury, abundance and satiation.

Whether they live in the city or in the country, all immigrant families in France, regardless of income, are able to buy meat for daily consumption. The price of meat is significantly lower in relation to average income than it is in the Maghreb, where it is essentially a luxury food item and is consumed infrequently by the majority and regularly only by a small group of urban families.[18] Where variations in meat price exist between shops – particularly since the recent period of quality differentiation – they do not reflect a seg-regation of the market, as is the case in Morocco, for example, where different types of butcher serve distinct social groups (Bergeaud-Blackler 2002). In the Maghreb, there is a clear differentiation between meat for daily cuisine (scant portions consisting mainly of bones and fat, and used more as a condiment or seasoning) and meat for special meals (sizeable portions of good fresh meat). In France, this differentiation no longer exists. Fleshy meat can be consumed fairly regularly by the majority of families, so that its con-sumption is no longer a distinctive attribute of the higher social classes. The distinction rests no longer on social but rather on cultural and religious criteria. For consumers, to eat halal is perhaps not the same as eating in Morocco, Algeria or Tunisia, but neither is it to eat like the French. Eating halal meat is to eat as Muslims do.

In France, animal slaughter has become a clandestine act, whereas tradi-tionally in the Maghreb it was an act of honour (Bonte et al. 1999). Animal slaughter is discretely practised by Muslim families living in rural areas and by a minority of urban families despite potential penalties. But this function of putting to death and selling, that was traditionally passed down to men, seems to be fading, even during the festival of *Aïd el Adha* (Feast of the Sacrifice, also called *Aïd el Kebir*). French and European regulations have deprived the Muslim father of his prerogative as *sacrificateur* by ordering the killing to be delegated to a qualified slaughterer in a proper slaughterhouse. The Islamic authorities for their part insist that the ritual act represents a manifestation of obedience to God, but at the same time they offer alterna-tives to the sacrifice such as monetary gifts for the sacrifice of a sheep in Chechnya or Iraq, the meat of which could feed a Muslim family living there. Studies carried out over the last twenty years (e.g. Brisebarre 1998) affirm the great popularity of Aïd el Adha among immigrant Muslim families. But if the ritual steps (choice of animal, preparation of the 'victim', sacrifice, sharing of the pieces, ritual meals) are adapted to new contexts by a majority of the families, the *sacrifiants* (those on whose account the sacrifice is made) are far more numerous that the sacrificateurs (those who carry out the slaugh-ter). The delegation of the sacrifice tends to become the rule rather than the exception. During the three days of the festival, the ritual cuisine of the Aïd el Kebir (the commensal, collective and female dimension) is taking over from the ritual sacrifice of Aïd el Adha (the religious, individual and male dimension). The feast becomes orientated more towards commensality (Deti-enne 1979: 21) and the sacrifice itself diminishes in importance, the symbolic dimension of the act fading to the benefit of the material nature of the ani-mal. Hence the animal is the focus of the feast – and of its controversies.[19]

Having shown that the control of the slaughtering process has escaped from the religious authorities as well as from the male Muslim, and that in doing so it did not prevent the exceptional growth of the halal meat market in France during the last two decades, it can be said that that market has followed the preference of the consumers. This can explain why the halal market seems so heterogeneous throughout Europe and can even present different facets within a single country such as France. Being 'consumer-driven', this market can respond relatively rapidly to the changing demands of consumers. The past five years have seen an increasing circulation of halal products for urban consumers: ready to eat, convenient, in small portions. This market meets the conception of halal for the generation of Muslims born and educated in France.

Towards a globalised halal market?

One of the factors accounting for the rapid establishment of halal butchers is certainly the absence of pork. While doubts are always possible concerning the method of slaughter, the buyer knows that she or he will never encounter a pork product in a halal butchers. Perhaps because for the younger generation the cuts of halal meat resemble those sold in any other type of butcher's shop, or because they often consume industrially prepared meals, they demonstrate particular concern about the presence of pork or pork products in the food they purchase. As I now show, the act of choosing halal expresses a cultural and religious belonging as well as a rejection of certain foods for reasons of both identity and health. Halal is certainly an exclusive discriminator; it is, however, anything but limiting, in that it opens up to Muslims of all generations and all countries a world halal food market. The new halal products of a 'globalised' Islam (Roy 2002) can today circulate easily across the five continents, particularly since 'halal' is today standardised by the Codex Alimentarius, an institution recognised by the WTO.

The taboo of pork pre-dates Islam and was upheld in Judaism and other religions situated in the general area of the near and middle east (Simoons 1994). Inscribed explicitly in the text of the Koran, the interdict has always been respected by the majority of Muslims.[20] When this law is broken by individuals, it is often a way of contesting religious authority (Douglas 1971; Detienne 1979). For the anthropologist Mohammed Benkheira (2000), the pork prohibition is so well internalised in Maghrebi Muslims that it must be distinguished qualitatively from the alcohol prohibition. Consumption of alcohol is overt, declared, conscious, voluntary and leads to repression. The pork taboo is so internalised that it can be compared in its intensity to the taboo of incest: 'We avoid incest not only because the laws, both written and unwritten, forbid it and therefore because we fear chastisement if we violate this law, but also because even the idea of incest revolts and disgusts us' (Benkheira 1995: 80). In other words, the distaste for pork in Muslim societies is so profound that it is hardly even necessary to forbid its consumption.

The recent episodes of food crisis have revitalised the pork taboo among many Muslims living in France. The origins of the diseases related to them are interpreted in religious terms: the 'mad cow' has been turned into an 'omnivore', like the pig; and in spontaneous discourses, the pig is also positioned at the source of foot-and-mouth disease.

The presence of any trace of pork derivatives, alcohol or any other prohibited substance has become a new subject of discussion. The Muslim discussion forums on the internet drive, develop and at the same time 'democratise' the debate about the border between what is considered edible and inedible, permitted and not permitted in Islam. These forums are an ideal window through which to observe the Islam of Muslim youth. My systematic investigation of messages in two Internet sites' discussion forums show that the technical aspects of slaughtering are considered less important than the issues of food content and questions related to commensality. The varied interpretations of religious texts are problematical for young Muslims, particularly when they concern the fundamental questions of marriage or relationships. Several interpretations continually feed these anxious debates. For example, certain Muslims believe that the Koran's assertion 'the food of the people of the Book is permitted' authorises the sharing of meals with non-Muslims provided that the Muslims do not eat pork. A different reading of the verse permits the sharing of meals with a non-Muslim only when it is certain that the entire meal contains no pork or pork products. Yet another interpretation opposes this latter principle of 'abstention in case of doubt' by another affirming that pious Muslims should not be suspicious and should refrain from inquiring about the composition of the food served. In these more-or-less subtle debates, there seems to be but a single certainty: pork is haram.

The plurality of such social definitions of halal products explains why there are several halal certifications and why all attempts to reduce them to one have thus far failed. Currently, in France, fresh meat is sold mainly according to 'domestic convention', while processed foods and poultry are sold according 'industrial convention', though this situation may well change in the future.

Until now, halal butchers have not seriously considered creating a protected label. In the region I surveyed, fresh halal meat in butchers' shops is always sold according to a 'domestic convention' (see Sylvander and Melet 1992) based on personsal trust.[21] The responsibility for the meat's freshness and halal qualities is placed by the customer squarely on the butcher. The exchange rests on an agreement formed by what Pierre Bourdieu (1994: 181) would call the 'taboo of the explicit', according to which 'to declare the truth of exchange . . . is to annihilate exchange'. 'What is expected of social agents is not that they perfectly follow the rules, but that they submit to these rules, give visible signs that, when possible, they will respect the rules.' In this type of domestic agreement, a label would be a 'practical euphemism'.[22]

Commercial halal labels exist in France. They apply to processed foods containing meat or non-fresh red meat, such as non-pork charcuteries or industrial poultry. In these cases, the halal label is the only means of assuring the consumer that the wrapped food is free of pork, alcohol or any haram substances. Halal conventions exist also in certain French abattoirs which prepare meat intended to be frozen for export. They usually take the form of bilateral conventions between the abattoir and the wholesaler of the importing country. Since the 1990s, the international business of halal products has developed so intensively that on 17 July 1997 the Codex Alimentarius adopted a guideline for the use of halal claims in order to prevent different conceptions of halal from becoming obstacles to global trade. The international halal trade of frozen beef and lamb benefits exporting countries such as Australia, New Zealand, the USA and Ireland to a lesser extent. The exporting countries supply frozen meat to such countries as Egypt, Iran, Saudi Arabia, the United Arab Emirates, for the region of the near east, and especially the flourishing markets of Indonesia and Malaysia. The principal exporters of poultry, a much smaller market, are Brazil and France.[23]

Whereas for numerous primary immigrant Muslims in France halal is related to slaughtering and the necessity of 'draining the blood', the international rules insist rather that halal products be purified from any haram, or unauthorised, substance and kept from contact with non-halal products. For the primary migrant halal rests on a domestic convention to which personal relations are central, whereas the Codex Alimentarius gives consistency to the label halal. The skill of the butcher, the basic requirement for achieving halal quality according to the oldest of the surveyed interviewees, has no primary importance in this new system of halal food. The international trade responding to the demand of growing urban Muslim populations gave a different meaning to the quality 'halal'. Further investigation is necessary to ascertain whether this new conception of halal is a pure 'invention' of international trade or whether the countries more advanced in this trade have imposed their own definition. The Malaysian market, for instance, is one of the more aggressive markets for halal products. Malaysian companies do not intend to sell the EU countries just halal meat or foodstuffs but also halal confectionery, halal food supplements, toiletries and cosmetics.[24]

One can imagine that in France in the near future the role of the sacrificateur (certain imams prefer the term *executant* – see Oubrou 2001), who is in some poultry slaughterhouses simply replaced by a machine, will be less and less technical and concerned more with controls to confirm that the slaughtering chain is not polluted by some haram substance in the abattoir and that the labels do not mislead the final consumer. With the general spread of labelling, the consumer will be in the position of ultimate controller, which should lead the retailers to ingenious marketing methods in order to attract a clientele who will no doubt become increasingly sceptical and even mistrustful. To date, no fixed definition of the quality halal has been successfully imposed, which has probably helped the market to grow, and with an energy that twenty years ago, when it was predicted that halal food would disappear with the second generation of migrants, was certainly not expected.

Notes

1 I am particularly grateful to Anne Elene Delavigne, Anne Murcott and Arounda Ouedraogo for helpful suggestions. I also thank Ken, my partner, who helped me to translate this text.
2 The exogamy is possible only for Muslim males.
3 i.e. Jews and Christians.
4 This phrase can be translated from Arabic as 'Islam home'.
5 Benkheira (1995) suggests that 'halal meat' in the Maghreb is meaningless because there is no need to identify it as 'halal'.
6 In order to meet standards of safety, hygiene and animal welfare in the case of ritual slaughter, EC Directive 93/119/EC requires the use of a restraining pen or casting pen.
7 In the kosher case, after ritual examination by a religious specialist (the *chokhatim*), the carcasses are declared either to conform, in which case they are sent to the kosher circuit, or not to conform, in which case they are rejected and sent to the ordinary circuit. All the backs of the carcasses are sent out of the kosher circuit.
8 What I refer to as 'non-halal' meat of 'ordinary' butchers excludes kosher butchers.
9 The analysis presented here has been built on data collected in Aquitaine where I undertook a study on the production and consumption of halal meat. The survey on consumption included interviews with ninety-seven Maghrebi families (mainly Moroccan and Algerian, and a minority of Tunisian) and systematic investigation of web forums (Oumma and Islamie). The survey included investigations of the 5 abattoirs in Aquitaine used for ritual slaughter and systematic interviews in all the butchers' shops (49 in total) found in the 5 departments of Aquitaine: Gironde, Lades, Pyrénées, Atlantiques and Dordogne. This study, which started in January 2000 and ended in October 2001 with the delivery of the final report, was funded by Aquibev, DRAF Aquitaine and DGAL Ministry of Agriculture.
10 *Haram* is an antonym of halal.
11 At the time of the survey of the Islamic butcheries in Bordeaux, the director of vetinarian services knew of the existence of 5 halal butchers' retailers, whereas I found 20.
12 The publication of Salman Rushdie's *The Satanic Verses* provoked numerous protests by Muslims in Europe and throughout the world, calling for his condemnation as a blasphemer.
13 Three young Muslims were excluded from school classes because they wore a *hijab* (Islamic headscarf). For the first time Muslim associations openly took a stand to support them.
14 Exemptions were accorded to very small businesses during the first two years, and for longer for those set up in 'sensitive' zones.
15 Bovine Spongiform Encephalopathy (BSE, or mad-cow disease), poultry dioxin, foot-and-mouth disease.
16 The longer a piece of meat is refrigerated the more it coagulates and easier it becomes to cut. Conversely, when it is very fresh, the meat fibres are more flexible and the more difficult it is to cut it into regular slices.
17 According to Beardsworth and Keil (1997: 154), the 'flavour principle', an expression developed by Rozin and Rozin (1981) consists of 'specific combinations of flavouring elements which provide each cuisine system with its own characteristic gustatory identity'. It characterises the traditional cuisine and one of its functions is to 'sustain a sense of familiarity and confidence.'

18 To give a Tunisian example, the ratio of consumption of meat between the poor and the rich has been found to be 1:7 (Tahar Jaouadi 2000).
19 The animal becomes the focus of the controversies because it raises more than ever the question of animal slaughter and mobilises animal welfare organisations.
20 'The dead animal, the blood, and the flesh of pork are forbidden, and any [food] over which the name of other than Allah has been invoked' (Holy Koran, excerpted from 5:3). For a list of noteworthy exceptions see Simoons (1994: 35–6).
21 In the domestic convention 'the risk for the customer to be disappointed by the characteristics of a product is minimised by the establishment of repeated relations between the seller and the customer' (Nefussi 1995b: 3).
22 'Les euphémisms pratiques sont des espèces d'hommages que l'on rend à l'ordre social et aux valeurs que l'ordre social exalte, tout en sachant qu'elles sont vouées à être bafouées' (Bourdieu 1994: 185).
23 For a broader view read *Halal Food Products Market Report* by Agriculture and Agri-Food Canada (2002). A copy can be found on the Canadian Government's official website at http://sea.agr.ca/africa/e3281.htm.
24 Document of MATRADE (Malaysian External Trade Development Corporation), the national trade promotion agency of Malaysia, available: www.matrade.gov.my.

References

Agriculture and Agri-Food Canada (2002), *Halal Food Products Market Report*, Ottowa, AAFC.
Agulhon, M. (1981), 'Le sang des bêtes: le problème de la protection des animaux en France aux XIXme siècle', *Romantisme*, 31, pp. 81–109.
Beardsworth, A. and Keil, T. (1997), *Sociology on the Menu*, London, Routledge.
Benkheira, M. H. (1995), 'La nourriture carnée comme frontière rituelle: les boucheries musulmanes en France', *Archives de Sciences Sociales des Religions*, 92, pp. 67–87.
Benkheira, M. H. (1998), 'Sanglant mais juste: l'abattage en Islam, *Etudes Rurales*, 147–8, Paris, Editions de l'Ecole des Hautes Etudes en Sciences Sociales.
Benkheira, M. H. (2000), *Islam et Interdits Alimentaires: Juguler l'Animalité*, Paris, Presses Universitaires de France.
Bergeaud, F. (1999), 'L'institutionnalisation de l'Islam à Bordeaux: enjeux sociaux, politiques et économiques de l'implantation du culte Musulman dans un espace urbain', PhD thesis, University of Bordeaux.
Bergeaud-Blackler, F. (2000), 'Le goût de la viande halal: viande de boucherie française et viande de boucherie marocaine', *Bastidiana*, 31–2, pp. 147–58.
Bergeaud-Blackler, F. (2001), 'Enquête sur la consommation maghrébine de viande halal et sur les marchés de viande de boucherie halal en Aquitaine, rapport pour Aquibev', Report financed by Aquibev, DRAF Aquitaine, Ministère de l'Agriculture DGAL.
Berque, J. (1993), *Relire le Coran*, Paris, Albin Michel.
Bonte, O., Brisebarre, A. M. and Gokalp, A. (1999), *Sacrifices en Islam: Espaces et Temps d'un Rituel*, Paris, CNRS Editions.
Bourdieu, P. (1994), *Raisons Pratiques: Sur la Théorie de l'Action*, Paris, Seuil.
Brisebarre, A. M. (1998), *La Fête du Mouton: Un Sacrifice Musulman dans l'Espace Urbain*, Paris, CNRS Editions.

Dasseto, F. and Bastenier, A. (1980), *L'Islam Transplanté: Vie et Organisation des Minorités Musulmanes en Belgique*, Anvers.

Détienne, M. (1979), 'Pratiques culinaires et esprit de sacrifice', in Détienne M., and Vernant J. P. (eds), *La Cuisine du Sacrifice en Pays Grec*, Paris, Gallimard.

Douglas, M. (1971), *De la Souillure: Essai sur les Notions de Pollution et de Tabou*, trans. from the English by Guérin, A., Preface by Heusch, L. de, Paris, F. Maspéro.

Hal, F. (1996), *Les Saveurs et les Gestes: Cuisines et Traditions du Maroc*, Preface by Ben Jelloun, T., Paris, Stock.

Jaouadi, T. (2000), 'Evolution du comportement alimentaire tunisien', in Padilla, M. and Oberti, B. (eds), *Alimentation et Nourritures Autour de la Méditerranée*, Karthala, CIHEAM.

MATRADE (Malaysia External Trade Development Corporation), accessible online: www.matrade.gov.my.

Nefussi, J. (1995a), *Le Marché de la Viande Halal en France*, Report of the Mission Agro Développement (MAD) for the Director General of Food, Ministry of Agriculture, vol. 1.

Nefussi, J. (1995b), *Convention de Qualité dans la Filière Halal*, Report of the Mission Agro Développement (MAD) for the Director General of Food, Ministry of Agriculture, vol. 2.

Nizard-Benchimol, S. (1997), 'L'économie du croire: une anthropologie des pratiques alimentaires juives en modernité', PhD thesis, Ecole des Hautes Etudes en Sciences Sociales.

Oubrou, T. (2001), Entretien conduit par Florence Bergeaud-Blackler: 'La viande halal, la face cachée', *La Medina*, 5 (special issue).

Roy, O. (2002), *L'Islam Mondialisé*, Paris, Seuil.

Rozin, E. and Rozin, P. (1981), 'Some surprisingly unique characteristics of human food preferences', in Fenton, A. and Owen, T. M. (eds), *Food in Perspective: Proceedings of the 34th International Conference on Ethnological Food Research, Cardiff, Wales*, Edinburgh, John Donal.

Simoons, F. J. (1994), *Eat Not this Flesh*, Wisconsin, University of Wisconsin Press.

Sylvander, B. and Melet, I. (1992), *Marchés des Produits de Qualité Spécifique et Conventions de Qualité dans Quatre Pays de la CEE*, INRA–MAP–MESR, Série P, no. 92–102.

Vialles, N. (1987), *Le Sang et la Chair: Les Abattoirs des Pays de l'Adour*, Paris, Maison des Sciences de l'Homme, Mission du Patrimoine Ethnologique.

5

Food agencies as an institutional response to policy failure by the UK and the EU

David Barling

Introduction

The UK public's confidence in the quality of the modern food supply, and in the governance of that supply, took a buffeting through a series of food safety crises in the 1980s and 1990s. The much-quoted list ranged from pesticide residues to salmonella in eggs, to BSE (which was estimated as a cost of over £4 billion to the public purse) and E.coli 0157. The internal market of the EU shared in some of those incidents, notably that of BSE, and added others such as dioxin contamination and nitrofurans in feed and poultry in the 1990s and into the early 2000s.

At both the UK and the EU level of governance there was a perception of policy failure over the safety of the final food product emerging from the supply chain. The safety concerns reached back along the food chain to the production inputs on the farm, such as animal feed, and to processing and manufacturing practices. The response at both EU and national levels has been to bring forward a phase of institutional change and reordering with regard to food safety and standards with an emphasis on the safety and health of the consumer. The EC rearranged its food safety responsibilities, putting them under the newly constituted Directorate General for Health and Consumer Protection, and began a process of revising and rationalising EU food laws and regulation. An independent European Food Safety Authority (EFSA) was also created. The UK introduced its own independent Food Standards Agency (FSA) in 1999, hiving off responsibilities from the Ministry of Agriculture, Fisheries and Food (MAFF). The final break-up of MAFF took place in June 2001, with its remaining responsibilities being reconstructed within a new Department for Environment, Food and Rural Affairs (DEFRA), in the wake of the foot-and-mouth crisis. The political resonance of foot-and-mouth as a bio-security threat lay in its impact on the perception of the food quality and economic value of UK and European meat rather than in its animal health implications alone.

A further product of the response to policy failure in the UK was a review of the future of farming and food in the UK, called the Curry Commission, which led in turn to DEFRA's *Strategy for Sustainable Farming and Food*

(2002) laying out a reordering of policy. At the EU level the hitherto largely autonomous agricultural policy process, as enshrined in the Common Agricultural Policy (CAP), is also evolving through a long and ongoing period of policy adaptation. The signalled intention of the next phase of CAP reform is to shift supports more substantially away from production subsidies to the (largely non-production) rural development pillar supports, part of the move to a so-called multifunctional model for agriculture. This shift incorporates an agricultural subsidy system, based not only on quantitative measures of production or acreage and livestock head-count but on qualitative measures such as wildlife, plant and landscape conservation, animal welfare, rural business diversification and food quality and diversity. The UK has endorsed this approach, and it is evident in the details of the *Strategy for Sustainable Farming and Food* (DEFRA 2002).

The EC depicted the introduction of EFSA as a part of a comprehensive 'farm to fork' recasting of food safety, including the aforementioned reorganisation and recasting of European food laws. In addition, the EC is beginning to frame a policy link between food safety and standards and in turn food production supports in terms of food quality, connecting food production with consumption and vice-versa. The role of food provenance, as an indicator of quality and market value, is a feature of the linking of production to consumption. The importance of the competitiveness of UK farming and food is another key theme of DEFRA's *Strategy for Sustainable Farming and Food*, and is addressed, in part, in the value-added aspects of food quality from the UK and its regions.

The food agencies introduced in the UK and at the EU level are located within these wider policy configurations. They are part of the authorities' response to policy failure in agri-food governance. The key issues here are to examine the ways in which these food agencies, through their remits and scope (and subsequent action), represent institutional responses to wider food quality concerns. How are those concerns being portrayed and interpreted through the particular institutional configurations of these agencies? Where do the agencies fit within the differing, but linked, policy responses to perceived failures at UK and EU levels? To what extent do they differ in terms of their remit and scope, and in their relationship with other (and the new) political institutions? How has the establishing of the agencies addressed the problems of food quality? Given that the FSA pre-dated EFSA, what can be gleaned from the first three years of the FSA's operation? What is the likely relationship between the FSA (an institution of a member state) and EFSA (an EU institution)? How are the linkages between the policy developments at EU and UK levels to be understood?

The analysis here presented is framed by an institutionalist approach that draws on the emerging literature on the interlinking of multiple levels of governance in the explanation of the shaping of agri-food policy decisions in national and international arenas. The juxtaposition of national level change and of EU level reform allows the multilevel governance dimension to be incorporated and more fully articulated, particularly as it has impacted on UK policy formulation and institutional reform. An explanation of EU level reform is a necessity, in any case, as it sets a framework for response at the national level and points to possible future policy-making dynamics between the distinct levels. Equally, it allows for the diverse (albeit linked) circumstances and influences shaping the two agencies to be explored and for the approaches to food safety and food quality to be compared and contrasted. In the case of the UK, the FSA has set up devolved management boards for Scotland, Wales and Northern Ireland under its sub-national devolution of government. Multilevel governance incorporates those levels, though the focus of the analysis presented here remains the national UK–EU interaction, within the context of the evolving international governance of food and agriculture.

Multilevel governance and strategic policy decisions

The determination of some key decisions by the EU and its member states has been explained within a framework of multilevel governance, in the form of two-level or multilevel strategic bargaining and decision-making (Moravcsik 1993; Marks et al. 1996; Scharpf 1997). Domestic considerations impact on international decisions, but international decisions also catalyse domestic considerations (Putnam 1988). There may be a range of decisions taking place simultaneously, according to different institutional rules and in slightly different domestic policy contexts, each of which is shaping the others to some extent. In agriculture, the negotiation of the GATT Uruguay Round agreements and the so-called McSharry reforms of the CAP (achieved in 1992) took place simultaneously and involved international (including the USA and the Cairns group of commodity exporting countries), EU and national level bargaining games (Paarlberg 1997; Moyer and Josling 2002).

The Agenda 2000 reforms of the CAP were shaped, at least in part, by the terms of the trade rules laid out in the General Agreement on Trade and Tariffs (GATT) Uruguay Round's Agreement on Agriculture (hereafter, AoA; Moyer and Josling 2002; Barling 2003). The AoA was designed to begin the liberalising of domestic agricultural supports. The different types of domestic support were subject to distinct arrangements under the AoA. These differing arrangements are known as 'boxes' and are colour-coded. The agreement allowed for government supports for agriculture that have 'no, or at most minimal, trade distorting effects or effects on production' and that lacked 'the effect of providing price support to producers'. Such supports were seen as truly decoupled from production and so were put into the so-called 'green box'. Direct payments to farmers that seek to reduce production under Agenda 2000, such as arable area and livestock headage payments, are also allowed under the AoA. However, such supports are supposed to be phased out over a period of time and were put in the 'blue box'. There were several ambiguities in the wording of the AoA, reflecting the fraught diplomatic negotiations and compromises that produced it, and a review was built in from 2000 which was to be undertaken by 2003. That review was still incomplete by mid-2003. Its completion was seen as being contingent, in part, on the mid-term review of the Agenda 2000 reform of CAP and, with it, the agreement of a common EU position for the AoA's review (Barling 2003). Progress in further liberalising developed countries' agricultural subsidies is seen as essential for the completion of the so-called Doha, or development round of the WTO trade liberalisation negotiations. This process of mutually contingent regime reviews is illustrative of the context within which multilevel governance leads to strategic policy choices, and multilevel bargaining and game-playing, by states and other participants (such as international organisations).

In the case of the CAP Agenda 2000 mid-term review the EC has signalled a further shift away from production subsidies, a process termed 'decoupling', towards more qualitative supports. The EU has sought to frame those supports as 'green box'-compliant and non- or minimally trade-distorting under the AoA. The EC has described these supports as reflecting a multifunctional model of agriculture, one that 'covers the protection of the environment, and the sustained vitality of rural communities, food safety and other consumer concerns' (WTO 2000: 1).

The UK Government has supported the EC's policy direction on CAP reform. The introduction of DEFRA as a governmental department merging environment with agriculture and rural affairs marked an institutional affirmation of this policy approach of wider agri-environment and rural development supports for British agriculture. Hence, an important area of strategy calculation informing the UK's response to policy failure over food quality (from BSE and its antecedents to foot-and-mouth disease), was shaped by calculations derived from the directions of trade liberalisation agreements and CAP reform.

Strategic decision-making, of course, is just that. It is highly contingent on calculations of the policy directions at other levels playing out in certain directions. The momentum-shifting permissible state supports towards rural development under the mid-term review of CAP have had their momentum jarred by an initial Franco-German agreement to slow down the pace of such transfers to beyond the mid-term review (Grant 2003). Similarly, exactly which kinds of supports are indeed green box-compliant is still open to interpretation – for example, organic farming supports (Barling 2003). The subsequent institutional reforms at EU and UK levels are located within these broader strategic policy calculations and directions.

New institutionalist approaches to analysing policy response and food quality

The new institutionalist schools of analysis place an emphasis on the influence of institutions, their operating procedures and practices as shaping factors of public policy. Policy network formations and the pressures applied by external interests are not seen as the only determinants of the final shape of policy outcome. The norms and operating procedures of institutions can also shape the final nature of policy. Within new institutionalist theory, historical institutionalism stresses that certain path dependencies may be put in place during periods of institutional creation. That is, there are critical junctures in the historical development of policy where policy moves in a different direction, creating a path dependence that subsequently is difficult and costly to reverse. The creation of new institutions can be a key component in setting forward a new path for policy consideration – such institutions becoming the part of the new framework setting the boundaries within which policy will be made. Institutions become the '"carriers of history", with the ideas behind early policy choices continuing to serve as parameters in which actors respond to new socio-economic challenges' (Jones and Clark 2001: 7). At this relatively early stage we might consider the extent to which the enabling legislation of the agencies reflect policy choices that are likely to endure. In the case of the FSA, moreover, we can take the first three years of the institution's operation and consider the extent to which such policy choices have evolved and the paths they have taken.

The creation, respectively, of the FSA and the EFSA occurred at a juncture when perceptions of policy failure were acknowledged at UK and EU governmental levels. My analysis seeks to explore more fully this period of institutional reform and the rationales behind the setting in place of these new institutions and the other institutional and policy reforms that have occurred alongside them. The institutional configurations set up during this period will play a role in shaping policy in the near to mid-term future, at least. The policy ideas that have shaped the introduction of these institutions can begin to be unravelled.

The reform period that was embarked on at the turn of the millennium is in certain ways a significant departure, yet one which remains (at this stage) a hesitant and variable approach to food quality in policy terms. The immediate, or priority, policy concern regarding food quality has been one of food safety, notably microbial food safety, for the consumer. Beyond that, there are distinctions to be found at the UK and EU levels, but there is some commonality also. Food authenticity and provenance are emerging issues. The value-added aspects of food quality within a liberalising (but still far from perfectly competitive) international trade are recognised, as part of a linking of food production to its consumption. Such recognition is framed within an adherence to the liberal trade paradigm, where national (or regionally integrated) economic areas seek competitive advantage through the realisation of such added value. The environmental and cultural aspects of food production have been partially integrated into this notion of food quality also, as the CAP reform process indicates. The public health consequences of nutrition and diet are beginning to be addressed in a cautious fashion in the UK, and there are signs of policy movement on an area that has lacked any clear strategic vision in the recent past (Lang and Rayner 2003). The picture on nutrition and diet remains somewhat fragmented at the EU level, although there have been initiatives, notably from the French presidency of the EU in 2000 (CEC 2000a). The nutrition remit of EFSA is, however, weak.

EFSA does have a remit to look right along the food supply chain. The FSA's remit is less extensive, as it starts after the farm gate; but ambiguities have become evident in this regard. In the case of the EU, the imperatives of managing the single market and underpinning the legitimacy of the integrationist project are drivers for the policy and institutional responses to the failures over food safety and quality. The setting up of the agencies and an assessment of their early inception are presented below in the context of the wider reforms taking place in food safety and food policy in the UK and at the EU level, respectively.

Food safety regulation in the 1990s: setting private and public sector food standards

The creation of the FSA was the first significant stage in a revision of the institutions of food governance in the UK. A previous response under the Conservative Governments had been to endorse self-regulation by the food industry with the 1990 Food Safety Act. That Act emphasised the 'due diligence' defence which requires a person to have taken 'all reasonable precautions and exercised all due diligence'. Food safety became more process-driven with the introduction of workplace regimes centred on hazards analysis critical control point (HACCP) practices. These instruments placed the onus on the supply chain to self-improve and to show that it was doing so.

This approach has been reinforced by the commercial realities of modern food supply chains, especially increased corporate concentration along the supply chain, notably in retailing but also in manufacturing and, increasingly, catering. These developments have brought what might be broadly described as a dual regulation to the agri-food system. Private forms of regulation through grading, standards and contract specifications have rapidly evolved with the increased international sourcing of foods and food and feed ingredients. The private sector has led the way in consumption-end-led regulation of the food supply chain, often in the absence of adequate public regulation (Reardon and Farina 2001; Reardon and Berdegué 2002). The main form of private (or quasi-)regulation from the public and private sectors has been process-based around systems, such as 'good manufacturing practice' (GMP) and HACCP. Large multinational companies have introduced HACCP in the sourcing of food ingredients, as Unilever has for its coconut production suppliers in Brazil (Reardon and Farina 2001). Indeed, internationally, governments beyond the UK have rapidly adopted HACCP as a self-regulatory instrument, for example in the fisheries sector (Lazer 2001). The other form has been product characteristics such as grading and standards, or maximum residue levels (MRLs) often validated by the State.

Dual regulation, public and private, has crossfertilised, leading to a degree of hybridisation. This has occurred through a mix of state cooption of the private sector and state adaptation of private sector standards or instruments. An example of the former is the application of the Home Authority Principle for the food safety regulation of corporate supermarkets in the UK (Flynn et al. 1999). The private sector has led the way in a range of food quality controls through the setting of standards, such as organic farming and food standards, the development of new quality systems such as farm assurance schemes and product-tracing, or traceability, systems. The rapid development of private sector standard-setting has left public sector regulation in its wake, and has led to a catch-up process of the overseeing and review of such standards for new institutions such as the FSA.

The Labour Party's manifesto in 1997 made two main food-specific electoral promises. The first was to reform MAFF by setting up a food standards body. The second promise was to reform the CAP. The Labour Party under the Atlee Government had introduced in 1947 the Agriculture Act that established the framework for state support of and subsidy for farming over the next half-century. In its long period in opposition from 1979 Labour promised to reduce that support. Also, Labour in opposition had learned to embarrass the Conservative Government for its poor food governance but was slow to formulate its own policy solutions in terms of a food agency. The Wishaw E.coli 0157 case in February 1997 spurred Labour to develop more detailed policy proposals (HMSO 1997). The Wishaw example showed that regulatory incompetence accompanied by appalling standards of hygiene in a butcher's shop (where a *de facto* meat factory also functioned) could have disastrous public heath consequences, as well as political fall-out. Tony Blair, as leader of the Opposition, commissioned Professor Phil James, then of the Rowett Research Institute, to produce a draft plan for a food agency, which was published the day before Labour's election to government (James 1997). A ministerial group on food safety was set up, followed by a white paper from MAFF in January 1998, the Food Standards Act in 1999, with the FSA coming into being in 2000.

The FSA and policy reform in the UK

The main aim of the FSA as set out in the Food Standards Act (HMSO 1999: 1) was 'to protect public health from risks which may arise in connection with the consumption of food (including risks caused by the way in which it is produced or supplied) and otherwise protect the interests of consumers in relation to food'. Its key task was to 'rebuild public trust' in the Government's handling of food safety (Krebs 2003a). The FSA was made accountable to the secretary of state at the Department of Health (DH). The close relationship between food producer and government department, where MAFF was both sponsor and regulator of the farming and agricultural supply industries, was broken. The FSA could claim to be free from the direct sponsorship of any sector of the food industry. It was established as an agency of the crown, with an arm's length independence of the sponsoring government department, similar to the Health and Safety Executive. Sir John Krebs (an Oxford University zoologist) was appointed chair of the FSA, with the chief executive appointed from the DH and its initial membership drawn largely from the Food Standards and Safety section of MAFF.

On matters connected with 'food safety or other interests of consumers in relation to food', the FSA had both an advisory and an informative function, and a responsibility for 'developing policies (or assisting in the development by any public authority of policies)' (HMSO 1999: 3). These responsibilities extended also to animal feed. In addition, the FSA was given the executive tasks of monitoring the enforcement of food and feed safety, which included absorbing the Meat Hygiene Service. The functions of risk assessment and risk management were combined, with the FSA seeking to act as an authoritative voice. Risk assessment was to be provided by the network of scientific advisory committees concerned with food that had been moved from MAFF and the DH to be under the sponsorship of the FSA. In short, the FSA was given a policy-making role as well as policy advice and enforcement roles.

The FSA's other key function of protecting 'other interests of consumers in relation to food' was defined in the white paper as encompassing 'issues relating to the compositional quality of food, the choice of foods available and the information on which choices can be made' (MAFF 1998: 8). This remit has allowed it to undertake a range of policy reviews and consultations in areas such as food authenticity and labelling where the private sector is already well advanced. Reviews of farm assurance schemes, advertising claims and quality claims (such as on 'freshness' of food), and policy advice on traceability and authenticity, have been undertaken by the FSA.

In relation to the food chain the remit covers risks in how food (and feed) is produced or supplied. The white paper offered the qualification that in 'some areas such as nutrition policy and food safety issues which relate to farming practices, Health, Agriculture and Environment Departments will retain important policy and statutory responsibilities' (MAFF 1998: 8). A senior civil servant from the old MAFF who had been involved in the drafting of the legislation felt the intention was for the role of the FSA to stop at the farm gate. The white paper gave the example of BSE controls where the FSA would be responsible for controls on the human food chain from the slaughterhouse onwards (MAFF 1998: 19). Areas such as veterinary medicines and pesticides remained under the purview of MAFF, not of the FSA. The hand of MAFF was clearly visible here, contradicting the recommendation of James that the remit should be right along the food chain, from farm to fork, to include these responsibilities (James 1997; Lang et al. 1997). The white paper felt that responsibilities for pesticides and veterinary medicines would 'risk diverting it from its essential role of protecting public health'. MAFF felt that the proposals nevertheless allowed the FSA to intervene 'where farming practices impact on the safety of food' (MAFF 1998: 17).

In practice, the FSA has been able to articulate on food safety and quality where production and process methods are a defining characteristic of the food, while absolving itself of the need to consider other production-related factors such as environmental or animal welfare impacts of production. This has been illustrated by the FSA's stances on, respectively, organic farming and food, and GM crops and food, issues considered in more detail below.

The FSA has prioritised its food safety function during its first three years with a particular focus on micro-organisms and microbiological safety. As Krebs has acknowledged: '[in] the past three years we have focused very much on what might be described as "traditional" issues of food safety: chemical contaminants, BSE, food poisoning, and so on' (Krebs 2003a). The FSA was given increased funding by the Treasury, having set itself the target of reducing food-borne illness by 20 per cent over 5 years (i.e. by 2006). This was an ambitious target, as after three years the spread of Campylobacter in UK poultry was reported to be on the rise (*Environmental Health News* 2003). James (1997) had described policy over chemical contaminants as chaotic, and retail industry insiders have complained that there is still a lack of prioritisation on chemical contaminants by the FSA, such as a listing of their importance in safety terms and prioritising those that should be minimised or eliminated.

The FSA was given a role in nutrition policy. James (p. 33) had given this role a very high priority, suggesting that the FSA should be called the Food and Health Commission to emphasise the importance of integrating nutrition and diet policy within its remit. The white paper was more circumspect, dividing nutrition policy responsibilities between the DH and the FSA. The DH retained the public health functions, such as the links between diet and health, including behavioural and lifestyle issues where nutrition is an important factor; while the FSA was ascribed functions relating to food information needed by the public. The responsibility for the interface between these two areas was shared.

The DH has retained pre-eminence on nutrition and diet policy, and has overseen a range of initiatives on food and diet, although this has led to little in the way of grand or strategic thinking and action (Lang and Rayner 2003). The FSA board approved a joint DH–FSA Nutrition Forum in March 2001 as part of its nutrition strategic framework (FSA 2001a). This stakeholder body has remained a discussion and information exchange forum. It does not have an advisory role and has not put forward policy recommendations, unlike its predecessor under the DH – the Nutrition Taskforce. During its first three years, it remained unclear where and how the FSA's remit would integrate with health strategies at the DH and at regional, local and community levels (Lang and Rayner 2003).

The policy review undertaken by the Curry Commission and the subsequent *Strategy for Sustainable Farming and Food* (DEFRA 2002) did address food and health issues, with a focus on England. At the devolved levels of Scotland and Wales, nutrition and dietary strategies were formulated by 2003, leaving England without an equivalent and, more confusingly, no overall plan for the UK. A cross-departmental food and health action plan was set in motion by DEFRA's strategy document. The plan was to be coordinated under a DH steering group chaired by the deputy-chief medical officer and included a range of other departmental and agency representatives (DEFRA 2002: 39). The outcome of this process in terms of the content and impact of the plan will be important and will reflect the extent to which pubic health becomes a component of the policy reformulation of food quality.

Krebs (2003a) signalled a change in emphasis on diet and nutrition policy in a speech to mark the FSA's three-year anniversary in April 2003: 'we will pay more attention than we have in the past to issues of diet and health'. The diet-related causes of mortality and morbidity through cardio-vascular disease and cancers, the problems of obesity and the evidence from the national diet and nutrition surveys were cited. The speech left unclear the extent of the FSA's intervention in this policy area: 'there is a fundamental question about how much of this area is down to individual choice, how much is down to the responsibility of industry and how much of it is down to the Government to legislate' (Krebs 2003a). Nonetheless, a coronary heart disease policy specialist described the speech as expressing an 'almost Damascene conversion' on the part of the FSA's chair. The FSA launched at the same time a high-profile campaign to reduce salt levels in the diet, focusing on getting the food industry to reduce the amount of salt in manufactured and prepared foods sold at retail and catering outlets, much to the industry's discomfort. However, the extent to which the FSA adopts a more interventionist role in diet and health remains to be seen. During its first three years the FSA has adopted a consumerist, market-based, approach to many issues of food safety advice, often stressing the role of individual preference and choice as opposed to a more fundamentally structural assessment of food safety and the food system. The ways in which the FSA and the DH address the interaction of individual choice, industry responsibility and government regulation will play a key role in determining the dietary health of the UK's population.

The new agency made a conscious attempt to change the culture and embrace consumer organisations and wider public consultation, in an effort to overcome perceived faults and bias in MAFF's operation and as part of the long task of rebuilding public trust. The goal was to restore consumers' confidence in food. To that extent there has been a transparent and consultative approach embracing a wide range of interests, including consumer groups, as the FSA has sought to pacify and incorporate consumer concerns. NGOs complain privately of 'consultationitis', being drowned by endless consultation after the main parameters of policy have been set. Industry groups have also expressed private frustrations at the lack of genuine openness in the policy formulation stage or, as one characterised it, 'transparency without openness'. Both consumer and industry groups are aware that the key to policy influence is to have inputs in the initial drafting stages of the process. To that extent the FSA has underlined its independence.

One area where there are signs that the FSA is considering a more transparent approach is in the processes for risk-assessment advice to allow for a clearer presentation of scientific uncertainties. The review of the expert committees suggested that meetings should be held in the open and that contrary scientific views should be considered. The scientific committees should provide a record of differences of opinion, of how and why decisions were reached, and of where inherent assumptions helped frame decisions. This could allow both for the uncertainties and for the framing assumptions around risk assessment to be more clearly acknowledged, leading to a more transparent and open risk-analysis process (Millstone and van Zwanenberg 2002).

Transparency turned to opacity in the FSA's consideration of the deeper implications of consumers' concerns regarding food safety and quality. The FSA's consumerist approach was reflected in the submission it made to the DEFRA-sponsored Curry Commission on the future of food and farming. Using its own 'Consumer attitudes to food safety' survey evidence (see FSA 2000a), it grouped consumer concerns on shopping for food into primary concerns (price, time and convenience) and secondary and more complex concerns (intensity of production, animal welfare and the environment) (FSA 2001b). The survey (FSA 2000a) also showed that a significant proportion of consumers had concerns, when prompted, about food-poisoning (59 per cent), BSE (55 per cent) and the use of pesticides on food (50 per cent). However, there was no discussion of the implications of the secondary concerns (which go beyond the moment of shopping) for the nature of the food system and consumers' concerns regarding the dominant production methods of conventional agriculture. Instead, the importance of maintaining regulatory control systems through the food chain was seen as the key to addressing these 'secondary concerns'.

The FSA's potential for performing an advisory role that examines the deeper-rooted links between the systems of food production, manufacture, trade, safety and consumption have not been taken up. Rather it has adopted a conservative and relatively narrow approach to its remit of protecting the consumer against 'risks caused by the way in which [food] is produced or supplied', effecting a defence of conventional or industrial agriculture and food production. To that extent it has been willing to take a more activist role: not exactly policy-making, but certainly effective policy promotion. For example, in the wake of an Advertising Standards Authority ruling on the accuracy of health claims made by organic food producers in 2000, the FSA issued a hostile position paper on organic foods. This stated that the FSA 'considers that there is not enough information available at present to be able to say that organic foods are significantly different in terms of their safety and nutritional content to those produced by conventional farming' (FSA 2000b: 1). The FSA, despite an enlarged research budget, initially declined to fund, entirely or in part, such work from its own research budget. Criticism of its stance led the FSA to hold a subsequent seminar to discuss research needs regarding organic foods.

DEFRA had begun to address the market potential (as well as the environmental benefits) of organic food and farming through increased subsidy and research support at the national level within the space afforded under the CAP. That support included the drafting of an organic action plan. In late 2002 and early 2003 Minister for the Environment Michael Meacher corresponded with Sir John Krebs seeking a declaration from the latter concerning the environmental benefits of organic food production over conventional agricultural methods. Krebs's initial response was to say that environmental issues were not part of the FSA's remit and that there were no discernible benefits regarding the final food product; also, that it was not the role of the FSA to promote organic food – thus maintaining the FSA's independence. By June 2003 this stance had been ameliorated somewhat, with the concession that organic food was relatively free from pesticides (Krebs 2003b).

The critical stance taken on organics was in contrast to a much more benign approach to the safety of GM food and consumers' needs. For example, the FSA adopted an oppositional stance to the wishes of consumer groups and the retail industry on the EC's proposal of regulation for the full traceability of GMOs in food and feed along the food chain. The FSA advised the UK Government to oppose the EC's proposals as unworkable, siding with some manufacturers and processors (notably in animal feed) and with the large-scale commodity exporters (such as the American Soybean Association, which had the backing of the US government). Conversely, the large-scale retailers had endorsed traceability of GM food and feed along the food chain, drawing up their own code of conduct and putting it into practice (Barling and Lang 2003a). The Consumers' Association food policy officer saw the FSA and its chair as 'having a complete blind spot on GM issues' (personal communication to the author). In part, the FSA was following the line of the Labour Government and endorsing its desire to promote biotechnology in the interests of national economic competitiveness (Barling and Henderson 2000). The FSA's chair is a member of the Cabinet Sub-Committee on Biotechnology for which the promotion of biotechnology is a key goal, according to a former minister and member of the panel (Hall and Vidal 2003). Yet, the Government's overriding desire to be able to endorse GM crops and ease their entry into the European market is running into the obstacles generated by the complexities of realising consumer preferences through management of the food supply chain. While the FSA and the Government have sought to block traceability of food and feed derived from GM sources, the large retailers have been left to fill the regulatory vacuum and provide this food quality control on behalf of their customers.

To some extent, the FSA was able to operate in the first 2–3 years in a relative policy vacuum. This vacuum was subsequently filled with the creation of DEFRA in June 2001 and with the completion of the policy review and the prime minister's endorsement of DEFRA's *Strategy for Sustainable Farming and Food* at the end of 2002. The policy review's remit had been bounded within the international trade paradigm, to advise the Government in a manner 'consistent with . . . increased trade liberalisation' (PCFFF 2002: 2). DEFRA sought to merge strategies for the efficiency of the UK agri-food sector and its economic competitiveness with the rural development and multifunctional agriculture agenda that the UK had endorsed under the terms of the AoA and the Agenda 2000 reform of CAP.

A Food Chain Centre was set up under the industry-sponsored Institute of Grocery Distribution, with initial priority given to the red meat supply chain and its export promotion and benchmarking along the supply chain. There was an emphasis on reconnecting with the market and 'that a drive for added value is likely to go hand in hand with the pursuit of higher quality and that quality will need to be recognised and verified to assured standards' (DEFRA 2002: 15). Local and regional foods were to be promoted by encouraging increased local supply to large retailers and caterers as well as through more innovative outlets such as public sector procurement and farmers' markets. Small local and regional producers of foods were to be supported by Food for Britain, a government–industry sponsored export promotion body. Assurance schemes, already prevalent in the private sector, were identified as important in re-establishing public confidence. The organic action plan was seen as a competitive move designed to reverse, over a period of time, the 70 per cent imported–30 per cent domestically produced organic food share in the UK market to 70 per cent home produced. The importance of harnessing new technology to the agri-food sector, including GM within a robust risk-assessment regime, was also stressed. The economic and farm and supply management difficulties of ensuring coexistence of GM crops and seeds with their organic and conventional equivalents were not discussed.

The support for a decoupling of state supports through the CAP from production subsidies to rural development and wider agri-environment supports were emphasised. Also, DEFRA addressed the importance of nutrition (see above), animal welfare (on food safety and economic grounds) and food safety (with reference to some of the main initiatives of the FSA). The overall scope of the strategy will demand a far more coordinated and integrated approach to food policy than shown previously by the UK Government (Barling et al. 2002). The FSA will be only one of the institutional players. There are gaps in the strategy and, of course, many intentions are yet to be realised. The tensions within the contemporary food system are many and their resolution may not be achieved by policies formulated within the trade liberalisation–economic competitiveness paradigm and multilevel governance boundaries set by the AoA–CAP reforms (Lang 1999; Barling and Lang 2003a). The response at the international level of the EU was to introduce institutional reforms also, including an international food agency in the form of EFSA that came into operation some three years after the FSA, alongside a significant policy review.

Food safety reform at the international level: the EU and the creation of EFSA

The reform of food safety in the EU has had a high a place on the policy agenda of the EC since the mishandling of the BSE crisis during the mid–late

1990s. The European Parliament found the EC guilty of serious maladministration and threatened it with censure should it fail to act. Responding in 1997 the European Commissioner Jacques Santer acknowledged shortcomings in the protection of consumer health and promised radical reform of the EC's machinery. He called for 'nothing short of a revolution in our way of looking at food and agriculture' (Santer 1997). This set in train organisational reforms. In 1997 the EC's scientific committees were moved to the Consumer Protection DG, and two green papers were issued laying out plans for food safety reform and for a revision of EU food law (Barling 1998).

After the collapse of the Santer Commission in 1999, the new Prodi Commission kept food safety as a priority and furthered the reform process, including a reorganisation of the EC's DGs. The Consumer Protection DG was renamed Health and Consumer Protection (DG SANCO), taking over food safety and food law policy-making responsibilities previously housed in the DGs for, respectively, Industry and Agriculture. These services had also been responsible for promotion of the agri-food industries. A white paper on food safety, released early in 2000, spelt out more clearly the introduction of a wide-ranging consolidation and revision of European food law. It enumerated over eighty legislative revisions and actions to the body of EU food law. It also proposed the new EFSA that was created with a regulation in January 2002, leading to the establishment of the agency in 2003. Continuing food scandals and controversies (e.g. dioxin contamination and GM foods) reinforced the importance given by the Prodi EC to food safety reform. This institutional reorganisation and renewed legislative agenda were part of a strategy by the EC to work towards the restoration of citizen confidence in the safety of the food supply in the EU. The ability of the single market to deliver safe food was seen as particularly important to the legitimacy of the European integration project, at a time when the next wave of EU enlargement was pending and the revision of EU governance was being formulated. European Commissioner for DG SANCO David Byrne described the EC's policy response as a three-pillared approach: the first pillar was an effective range of food safety legislation; the second pillar was creating EFSA to identify risk and communicate with the public; and the third, a more effective approach to official enforcement controls. Elsewhere in the speech EFSA was described as the 'cornerstone in our strategy' (Byrne 2002).

EFSA's mission, as laid out in the regulation (CEC 2002: L 31/12), is to 'provide scientific advice and scientific and technical support for the Community's legislation and policy in all fields which have a direct or indirect impact on food and feed safety. It shall provide independent information . . . and communicate on risks.' The remit reaches along the whole food and feed supply chains, but the scientific opinions are limited to food safety only. The scope of EFSA does include scientific advice on human nutrition in relation to EC legislation, and assistance, at the EC's request, with communication on nutritional issues within its health programme. The original name for the body was European Food Agency, but 'Safety' was added to reflect a down-playing of the nutritional and dietary responsibilities that were previously accentuated to meet the desires of France during its tenure of the EU presidency in the latter half of 2000.

The scientific committees from SANCO were transferred to EFSA, being reconstituted and newly appointed as eight committees, coordinated by a scientific committee of the chairs plus six other members, a process completed by May 2003. A concern voiced by some of the members of the EC's scientific steering committee is that EFSA's scientific committees will become segregated from non-food scientific advice, prohibiting a holistic approach to food safety issues, where safety has been compromised due to external factors (*EU Food Law Monthly* 2003a). A DG SANCO official was quoted as expecting EFSA 'to be independent but not out of control' (van Zwanenberg and Millstone 2003: 36). While EFSA is responsible for risk assessment, risk management is seen as residing with the EC in DG SANCO and with the other elected political bodies of the EU, the European Parliament and the Council of Ministers. This is a crucial distinction in the EC's strategy to renew consumer faith in the EU's food safety institutions.

The strategy adopted by the EC with the creation of EFSA is not without potential flaws. The attempt to make a demarcation between risk assessment and risk management is difficult as the boundaries between the two are by no means clear. There are often inherent management decisions in the framing of the ways that risks are assessed, and the extent to which uncertainties are acknowledged. The FSA has suggested a more transparent and open process of acknowledging framing and assumptions and uncertainties. The danger is that EFSA and SANCO will not be significantly transparent, and that this will undermine the authority of the new body. Similarly, the role of risk communication, given to EFSA, but in management terms shared with DG SANCO (that is, shared by the assessors and the managers) could be problematical (van Zwanenberg and Millstone 2003).

The creation of EFSA comes at a time when most of the EU member states have either created or reformed their national food agencies. Co-ordination between and across national bodies will be a key issue. In some cases (e.g. the UK's FSA) these food agencies embody both the risk assessment function with risk management, while in others (France's AFSSA) they follow EFSA role. The task of coordinating national viewpoints is the Advisory Forum's, the intergovernmental arena for resolving differences which will bring the competent national authorities together at EFSA. This is a potentially important forum and will almost inevitably see interplay between risk-assessment and risk-management issues. At the outset, EFSA's executive director (the former chief executive of the FSA) has sought to have the agenda of the Advisory Forum's meeting kept secret, offering publication of the minutes at a later date (*EU Food Law Monthly* 2003b). The cross-over between risk assessment and risk management may well become evident in the debates arising within this forum.

Its management board may assist EFSA to establish its independence from the EC over time. The national or inter-governmental dimension of EU policy has also appeared in the appointment of the fifteen-person board of EFSA, each drawn from a different member state, described by one insider as an inter-governmental 'carve-up' (Barling and Lang 2003b). The board members also represent different categories of stakeholder, to some extent. There are seven civil servants, two farming representatives and two manufacturing industry representatives, with one representative from each of medicine, retail, and consumer interests.

The reform of EU food legislation, as laid out in the white paper, covered a wide range of regulatory initiatives and revisions. In particular, food and feed hygiene legislation and food control enforcement were prioritised, as were labelling reforms (allowing nutritional and health claims to be made) to enhance consumer choice. The general principles and requirements of European Food Law Regulation 178/2002 laid down the key principles for legislative reform. Two related principles are the adoption of a 'farm to table', or whole-food chain, approach, and that food business operators should bear primary responsibility for food at all stages along the chain. Food operators have the responsibility to inform the relevant authorities of any safety concerns they may have over foodstuffs. Such concerns should be scientifically based. Consumer protection is supported by the adoption (as a new principle in food safety law) of the principle of traceability right along the food chain with responsibility again being held by the operator at each stage. The effectiveness of this legislation is hard to predict, as it might be difficult for food operators to be always clear about the safety of some product they are handling. To be effective, the regulation may need to be buttressed by further laws that detail safe levels for additives, contaminants and residues in food composition and it will contain the same food operator responsibilities (Hagenmeyer 2002).

The EC is seeking to strengthen its overseeing of food law enforcement and control at national levels. Commissioner Byrne announced a new regulation on Official Food and Feed Controls legislation (COM 2003: 52) in February 2003 that will strengthen the role of the EC and the Food and Veterinary Office in inspection control. It is due to be implemented in 2005. The most telling issue here is of the burden of the cost for these controls, as anything over and above normal inspection will be charged to the companies. The enlargement of the EU to include new member states from central and eastern Europe will place a further burden on the effective implementation of the rapidly evolving EU food laws.

Within these centralising trends in EU food safety, there are caveats being made that reflect a wider conception of food quality beyond the science-based hygiene enforcement approach. This wider conception is emerging in different areas of EU agri-food policy like scattered pieces of a yet to be completed jigsaw. The multifunctional model of agriculture embraces a greater diversity of farm activity as well as the public utility of traditional food production practices. A caveat that the EC has entered within its food standard-setting agenda is to allow for flexibility of standards on traditional foodstuffs. This reflects sensitivity regarding traditional foods on the part of Europe's rural peripheries. The revision of EU food law allows for specific rules for traditional foodstuffs to preserve their special methods of production. The CAP reforms intend to shift supports to rural development, and DG SANCO has stressed the need for rural development and sustainable agricultural programmes to support traditional food production. The EU has long sought the recognition of European legislation on the geographical indication of food within world trade rules, despite attempts by Australia and the USA to undermine their viability by challenging their applicability under the WTO's disputes procedure (*Agra-Europe Weekly* 2003). A discourse illustrative of attempts to link these policy streams was the *Food Quality Dialogue* overseen by the European commissioners for Agriculture and for Consumer Health and Consumer Protection. The dialogue took place both digitally and through a series of roundtable discussions held during 2001–2 in Brussels and member states. The dialogue served to link CAP reform to reform of standards-setting for food and for consumer desires for quality, while asserting food safety as the 'bedrock of quality' (EC 2002).

Conclusions

The multilevel governance approach has helped to delineate the parameters within which the perceived policy failures in agri-food governance in the UK and at the EU level have been addressed. The responses to policy failure in agri-food governance have been to overhaul the institutional arrangements and engage in processes of policy review. The introduction of food agencies has been a key element of the new institutional arrangements. The prime focus of the agencies has been on food safety. There has been differentiation between the UK and the EU in the remit and role of the agencies, as with differences in the division between risk-assessment and management functions, the scope of remit along the food chain and the extent of responsibilities beyond food safety. The food safety concerns of the public arising from the succession of food crises of the 1980s onwards have led to politicians scrambling to regain consumers confidence and trust. Consumers have become increasingly literate about the modern food supply chain and increasingly vocal about practices in that chain. The modern food system has thrown up some fundamental challenges for governance. Food at the point of consumption has become increasingly politicised. New production–consumption links are being demanded of policy makers. Yet there remains a reaction among policy makers to frame solutions in overridingly consumerist and individual choice terms and according to voluntary agreements. The deeper lying forces in the food system, corporate concentration, branding focused advertising, technological fixes, end of the chain value-adding, and so on, are not directly confronted.

The consumer choice metaphor has led to a tentative widening of the policy focus beyond core food safety issues to consider quality in terms of its market value, as witnessed by DEFRA's response to the strategy review of UK food and farming. There are signs that EU policy makers are making links between traditional food production practices in the rural periphery and market demand for quality and authenticity, with the multifunctional model of agriculture accommodating these notions of food quality. Yet the CAP is highly resilient. Its heritage is rooted in the defence of rural employment, a task it has managed as a desperate rearguard action against the advances of industrialised agriculture. The current reformulation contains echoes of past policies and a continued defence of the rural periphery, not withstanding the advance of the agri-environment agenda. In any case, food safety remains the 'bedrock', that is, the priority of the current policy response.

The impact of food nutrition and diet on health is a rapidly emerging issue on the policy horizon. This is an issue of public health demanding an approach based on populations. The agencies are struggling to find a response within their differing remits, cast in the role of support players. EFSA remains in the lay-by while DG SANCO seeks to re-engineer labelling messages and introduce effective traceability along the supply chain. The FSA is caught in the headlights between the triangle of individual choice, industry responsibility and government legislation. The FSA's chair has begun to use his advisory capacity to challenge industry over salt content in foods, but he may find his policy-making powers more persuasive if the FSA's institutional partners allow such interventionist gestures. Diet- and nutrition-related health may become the consumer issue of the future, replacing the current discontent over food safety with a food quality issue of much greater consequence in morbidity and mortality terms (Lang and Rayner 2001). The policy landscape that is being shaped within the trade liberalisation–economic competitiveness paradigm and multilevel governance boundaries set by the AoA–CAP reforms looks an incomplete patchwork. The institutional paths for agri-food governance created at the beginning of the new millennium look unsuitable and in need of fresh construction, shaped by a new set of policy ideas for the longer haul.

References

Agra-Europe Weekly (2003), 'Analysis: what's in a name? The mounting row over geographical indications', 2051, 25 April, pp. A1–2.
Barling, D. (1998), 'In or out through the policy window? The European Commission and the reform of food safety', in Dobson, A. and Stanyer. J. (eds), *Contemporary Political Studies 1998*, Nottingham, Political Studies Association of the UK.
Barling, D. (2003), 'Impact of international policies (CAP) and agreements (WTO) on the development of organic farming', in den Hond, F., Groenewegen, P. and Straalen, N. van (eds), *Pesticides: Problems, Improvements, Alternatives*, Oxford, Blackwell Science.
Barling, D. and Henderson, R. (2000), 'Safety first? A map of public sector research into GM food and food crops in the UK', Centre for Food Policy Discussion Paper 12, London, Thames Valley University.

Barling, D. and Lang, T. (2003a), 'A reluctant food policy? The first five years of food policy under Labour', *Political Quarterly*, 74(1), pp. 8–18.

Barling, D. and Lang, T. (2003b), 'Codex, the European Union and developing countries: an analysis of developments in international food standards setting', Report for the Rural Livelihoods Department of the UK Department for International Development, May, London, DfID.

Barling, D., Lang, T. and Caraher, M. (2002), 'Joined up food policy? The trials of governance, public policy and food systems', *Social Policy & Administration*, 36(6), pp. 556–74.

Byrne, D. (2002), 'European quality policy for foodstuffs', Speech /02/55 at the Winter Meeting, Vienna, 11 February 2002, Brussels, European Commission.

CEC (2000a), Council Resolution on Health and Nutrition, 8 December, 14274/00, Brussels, Commission of the European Communities.

CEC (2000b), White Paper on Food Safety, COM (1999) 719 final, 12 January, Brussels, Commission of the European Communities.

CEC (2002), Regulation (EC) No. 178/2002 of the European Parliament and of the Council of 28 January 2002 laying down the general principles and requirements of food law, establishing the European Food Safety Authority and laying down procedures in matters of food safety, *Official Journal of the European Communities*, 1 February, L31/1–24.

DEFRA (2002), *The Strategy for Sustainable Farming and Food: Facing the Future*, London, HMSO.

EC (2002), Fischler and Byrne Final Round Table on Agriculture and Food, EU Institutions Press Release IP/02/700, 13 May, Brussels, European Commission.

Environmental Health News (2003), 'Chicken illness threatens FSA safety targets', 18(23), 20 June, p. 3.

EU Food Law Monthly (2003a), 'SSC warns that FSA could have a negative impact', 133 (January), pp. 5–8.

EU Food Law Monthly (2003b) 'EFSA's secret agenda', 137 (May), pp. 3–4.

Flynn, A., Marsden, T. and Harrison, M. (1999), 'The regulation of food in Britain in the 1990s', *Policy & Politics*, 27(4), pp. 435–46.

FSA (2000a), 'Consumer attitudes to food standards – United Kingdom', February, London, Food Standards Agency.

FSA (2000b), 'The Food Standards Agency's view on organic food – a position paper', August, London, Food Standards Agency.

FSA (2001a), 'Nutrition strategic framework: proposed action plan', Paper FSA 01/08/02, London, Food Standards Agency.

FSA (2001b), 'Submission from the Food Standards Agency to the Policy Commission on Farming and Food for England', London, Food Standards Agency.

Grant, W. (2003), 'Prospects for CAP reform', *Political Quarterly*, 74(1), pp. 19–26.

Hagenmeyer, M. (2002), 'Modern food safety requirements – according to EC Regulation No. 178/2002', *Zeitschrift für das gesamate Lebensmittelrecht*, 4, pp. 443–59.

Hall, S. and Vidal, J. (2003), 'Meacher says health risks were played down', *Guardian*, 23 June.

HMSO (1997), *Report on the Circumstances Leading to the 1996 Outbreak of Infection with E.coli 0157 in Central Scotland, the Implications for Food Safety and the Lessons to Be Learned*, April, Edinburgh, HMSO.

HMSO (1999), *Food Standards Act 1999*, London, HMSO, chapter 28.

James, P. (1997), *Food Standards Agency: An Interim Proposal*, 30 April, London, Department of Health.

Jones, A. and Clark, J. (2001), *The Modalities of European Union Governance: New Institutionalist Explanations of Agri-Environment Policy*, Oxford, Oxford University Press.

Krebs, J. (2003a), Speech to Westminster Diet and Health Forum Seminar, 3 April, London, Food Standards Agency.

Krebs, J. (2003b), 'Is organic food better for you?', speech given by Food Standards Agency Chair Sir John Krebs at the Cheltenham Science Festival, 4 June, London, Food Standards Agency.

Lang, T. (1999), 'The complexities of globalization: the UK as a case study of tensions within the food system and the challenge to food policy', *Agriculture & Human Values*, 16(2), pp. 169–85.

Lang, T., Millstone, E. and Rayner, M. (1997), 'Food standards and the State: a fresh start', Centre for Food Policy Discussion Paper 3, London, Thames Valley University.

Lang, T. and Rayner, G. (eds) (2001), *Why Health Is the Key to Farming and Food*, Report to the Chartered Institute of Health, Faculty of Public Health Medicine, UK Public Health Association, National Heart Forum, London, Centre for Food Policy–UK Public Health Association.

Lang, T. and Rayner, G. (2003), 'Food and health strategy in the UK: a policy impact analysis', *Political Quarterly*, 74(1), pp. 66–75.

Lazer, D. (2001), 'Regulatory interdependence and international governance', *Journal of European Public Policy*, 8(3), pp. 474–92.

MAFF (1998), *The Food Standards Agency: A Force for Change*, Cm 3830, London, HMSO.

Marks, G., Hooghe, L. and Blank, K. (1996), 'European integration since the 1980s: state-centric versus multi-level governance', *Journal of Common Market Studies*, 34(3), pp. 341–78.

Millstone, E. and Zwanenberg, P. van (2002), 'The evolution of food safety policy-making institutions in the UK, EU and Codex Alimentarius', *Social Policy & Administration*, 36(6), pp. 593–609.

Moravcsik, A. (1993), 'Preferences and power in the European Community', *Journal of Common Market Studies*, 31, pp. 473–524.

Moyer, W. and Josling, T. (2002), *Agricultural Policy Reform: Politics and Process in the EU and US in the 1990s*, Aldershot, Ashgate.

Paarlberg, R. (1997), 'Agricultural policy reform and the Uruguay Round: synergistic linkeage in a two-level game?', *International Organisation*, 51(3), pp. 413–44.

PCFFF (2002), *Farming and Food: A Sustainable Future*, London, HMSO.

Putnam, R. (1988), 'Diplomacy and domestic politics: the logic of two-level games', *International Organisation*, 42(3), pp. 427–60.

Reardon, T. and Berdegué, J. A. (2002), 'The rapid rise of supermarkets in Latin America: challenges and opportunities for development', *Development Policy Review*, 20(4), pp. 371–88.

Reardon, T. and Farina, E. (2001), 'The rise of private food quality and safety standards: illustrations from Brazil', *International Food & Agribusiness Management Review*, 4(4), pp. 413–21.

Santer, J. (1997), Speech by the President of the European Commission in the debate on the report by the Committee of Inquiry into BSE, 18 February, Speech 97/39, European Parliament, Strasbourg, Brussels, European Commission.

Scharpf, F. (1997), 'Introduction: the problem-solving capacity of multi-level governance', *Journal of European Public Policy*, 4(4), pp. 520–38.

World Trade Organisation (2000), EC comprehensive negotiating proposal, Committee on Agriculture Special Session, G/AG/NG/W/90, 14 December, Geneva, WTO.

Zwanenberg, P. van and Millstone, E. (2003), 'BSE: a paradigm for policy failure', *Political Quarterly*, 74(1), pp. 27–37.

6

Theorising food quality: some key issues in understanding its competitive production and regulation

Terry Marsden

Introduction

Recent debates concerning food quality offer an important window on the changing nature of broader social, political and economic relations. Not least, this has reinforced a more serious concern with understanding food consumption processes; through more theorisation and conceptualisation of social and natural factors in the context of wider consumption trends and processes (see Goodman 2002). In this chapter my aim is to re-examine some of the key issues associated with the production and regulation of food *quality*. These are, as will become clear, highly influenced by consumption dynamics; but, for the moment, I regard it as important to analytically separate these spheres in order to attain the requisite depth of treatment of the ways in which quality foods are constructed and regulated – albeit in the consumers' interest.

I examine ideas of quality in the context of the development and regulation of food supply chains with reference to some European research and some further examination of the current British experience. These research experiences demonstrate how, in recent years, contestations over aspects of food quality and assurance have come to play a key role in both preserving and reallocating power relations within particular types of food supply chain. In particular, evidence and arguments are drawn here between, first, the uneven emergence of what are increasingly called 'alternative' food supply chains and networks which are developing within the interstices of the (more conventional) retailer-led supply chains. I represent this dichotomy as a battle for knowledge, authority and regulation between food chain actors and their consumers. This is competitively fought around distinct conventions, and social and technical definitions of quality; the outcome is to empower, or disempower particular sets of supply chains actors. Put simply, the strict and hygienic quality definitions in conventional supply chains, for instance, have tended to empower corporate retailers over and above primary producers. Alternatively, the uneven development of ecological and regional quality conventions are put in place partly in order to re-empower the latter over the former. One important theorisation of food quality thus becomes associated with the ways in which different supply chain actors compete for the authority and legitimacy of defining its particular character. As this chapter shows, this is becoming a highly competitive and contested process; one which is shaping not only consumer decisions, but the competitive 'spaces', boundaries and markets themselves in which both established conventional players and 'alternative' food actors are situated.

A growing aspect of these competitive relations in supply chains concerns the actual *use* of quality conventions and how these begin to reshape the allocation of economic and political power in food supply chains. Usage can then, in turn, affect aspects of rural development at the level of food production and aspects of food consumption in the urban realm. Quality definitions and conventions can therefore reflect and redistribute aspects of economic and social power (Marsden 2003). It becomes necessary, therefore, to examine how notions of quality are constructed and used by the different actors in supply chains and how these notions then have both rural development and food consumption effects. The chapter starts by examining the growing significance of 'short supply chains', with reference to some Europe-wide evidence. These are developing apace in some member states, but remain marginal in others (especially the UK). Thus far, the literature documenting this process has tended to concentrate on the success stories, sometimes underestimating both the obstacles to and the potential vulnerability of these new ventures.

The second part of the chapter – the case study of the retailer-led conventional chains in the UK, even during a severe crisis of confidence in them on the part of the British consumer during the BSE and foot-and-mouth disease affairs – examines how different 'quality logics' actually *collide* in the competitive world of food consumption and production. In particular, I argue that it is necessary to examine the wider context of governance and consumer relations within which corporate retailers are engaged.[1] This is associated not only with food quality regulation: it is bound up with engaging in the politics and regulation of economic competition itself. In conclusion, this preliminary analysis leads on to identify a need to define the theoretical implications for understanding food quality in relation specifically to rural development policy.

First, however, I explore and attempt to conceptualise the diversity and impacts of short food supply chains (SFSCs). These are bounded, as the second part of the chapter indicates, by the competing private sector and regulatory forces associated with retailer-led food governance. This competitive dialectic, played out in EU member states like the UK, is in part centred on the battleground of 'quality'.

Short-circuiting for quality: the morphology and dynamics of SFSCs

Throughout Europe new rural development practices are emerging which could represent important building-blocks for new ways to sustain farming and food production. These can be seen as counter-movements, in the sense that they are constructing and articulating new strategies which confront the more conventional extended retailer-led supply chains. It is still too early to judge their viability and efficiency in delivering goals of sustainable agriculture and rural development. This is due partly to the lack of empirical data of sufficient reach and quality, but also to the relatively early developmental stage of many of these practices. Nevertheless, it is important to seek an improved insight to their potential. In particular, it is necessary to go beyond the particularities of individual cases and gain a wider overview and comparative analysis of their reach and impact. How many farms are involved in various activities? Does this involvement generate extra income and employment? And what factors condition their successful evolution and continuity?

The reconfiguration of supply chains is an important mechanism underlying the emergence of new rural development practices. For producers, the involvement in new forms of supply chain offers possibilities of retaining more added value on farms and in rural areas. It holds potential for shifting food production out of its 'industrial mode' and for breaking out of the long, complex and rationally organised industrial chains (Marsden et al. 2000) within which primary producers capture a decreasing proportion of total added value. At the same time, new food supply chains could be an important vehicle for creating more effective linkages between agriculture and society. They bring consumers closer to the origins of their food and in many cases involve a more direct contact between farmers and the end-users of their products. A key characteristic of emerging supply chains is their potential capacity to re-socialise, or re-spatialise, food, thereby allowing the consumer to make different value judgements about the relative desirability and quality of foods on the basis of their own knowledge, experience or perceived imagery. Commonly such foods are defined by the locality or even the specific farm where they are produced; and they serve to draw on an image of the farm and/or the region as a source of quality. In this, often more direct linkages emerge between farming on the one hand and rural nature, cultural landscapes and local resources on the other – what the French call the 'terroir' of agricultural production (see Allaire and Sylvander 1995).

For these reasons, rather than the unspecific adjectives 'new' and 'alternative', I prefer the term 'short' as a common denominator for the types of food supply chain that are emerging within rural development. On the one hand, SFSCs short-circuit the more anonymous and closed long supply chains characteristic of the industrial and retailer-led mode of food production. On the other hand, producer–consumer relations are 'shortened' and redefined by giving clear signals on the provenance and quality attributes of food, potentially constructing more transparent chains in which products reach the consumer with a significant degree of value-laden information. Also, SFSCs can be an important carrier for the 'shortening' of relations between food production and locality, possibly enhancing a re-embedding of farming towards more environmentally sustainable modes of production (see van der Ploeg et al. 2002).

The unexpected emergence of SFSCs demonstrates that we urgently need better conceptualisations of the ways in which such 'quality' and alternative markets are socially constructed. In neo-classical economics 'the market' appears merely as external to the social world and its outcome is thought to correspond to a singular distinctive logic or 'magic hand'. The emergence of new food markets, however, indicates that SFSCs are not simply the result of some kind of external, elusive 'free market'. They result, rather, from the active construction of networks by various actors in the agro-food chain, such as farmers, food processors, wholesalers, retailers and consumers. To understand developments on food markets we therefore need to explore a 'sociology of the market and competition' (Marsden and Arce 1995) that attempts to unravel the distinct patterns of social interaction between different actors in the agro-food chain. This is in line with the approach proposed by van der Ploeg and Frouws (1999) who, following some elements of actor network theory, analyse food supply chains as *arrangements of interlocking projects* of different actors in the agro-food chain.

The dimensions of SFSCs

A first step concerns the development of a better understanding of the morphology and dynamics of SFSCs and to come to grips with the empirical variety of SFSCs throughout the European countryside. How can we understand the different ways in which consumer demands and producer supplies are articulated to specific (organic, regional, artisanal, etc.) production 'codes'? And why is this in many cases accompanied with new market structures, while in others supply and demand are articulated by conventional and more intermediated market mechanisms? In addressing these issues it is important to go beyond a simple description of product flows and focus our analysis of SFSCs on the *type* of relationship between producers and consumers in these supply chains, and the role of that relationship in constructing value and meaning, rather than solely on the type of product itself.

On the basis of an inventory of SFSCs in Europe for the IMPACT research programme two interrelated dimensions were found useful for describing the empirical variety of producer–consumer relations within SFSCs. A first dimension concerns their organisational structure and the specific *mechanisms* involved in these to variably extend relations in time and space. A second dimension concerns the different *quality definitions* and *conventions* involved in the construction and operation of SFSCs. In the first dimension three positions are distinguished, corresponding to different mechanisms for extending SFSCs across longer distances in time and space (see figure 6.1). It is important to note that a single farm business might be involved in supplying one or more of these distinct supply chains.

The first category of SFSCs is essentially based on *face-to-face* interaction, as a mechanism for aligning producer–consumers networks. Consumers purchase products directly from the producer/processor, and authenticity and trust are mediated through personal interaction. This category coincides largely with a narrow definition of direct sales, be it through roadside sales, 'pick your own', farmers markets or farm shops. Marketing concepts like box

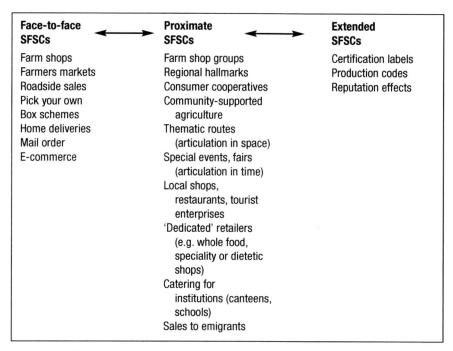

Face-to-face SFSCs	Proximate SFSCs	Extended SFSCs
Farm shops	Farm shop groups	Certification labels
Farmers markets	Regional hallmarks	Production codes
Roadside sales	Consumer cooperatives	Reputation effects
Pick your own	Community-supported	
Box schemes	agriculture	
Home deliveries	Thematic routes	
Mail order	(articulation in space)	
E-commerce	Special events, fairs	
	(articulation in time)	
	Local shops,	
	restaurants, tourist	
	enterprises	
	'Dedicated' retailers	
	(e.g. whole food,	
	speciality or dietetic	
	shops)	
	Catering for	
	institutions (canteens,	
	schools)	
	Sales to emigrants	

Figure 6.1 Different mechanisms for extending SFSCs in time and space

schemes, mail order and home deliveries offer some possibilities to extend the reach of this form of SFSC, but mostly these remain restricted to individual farms. The internet now provides opportunities for new variants of face-to-face contact through online trading and e-commerce.

A second category of SFSCs extends its reach beyond direct interaction and is essentially based on relations of *proximity*. Obviously, extending SFSCs over longer distances in time and space supposes the creation of new institutional arrangements. Most common is the cooperation between producers, who, for example, widen their product range by exchanging products between farm shops or combining individual products under a regional quality hallmark (Banks 2001; Roep 2001). Consumer cooperatives and 'community supported agriculture' are examples of consumers combining their buying power to facilitate the extension of SFSCs (Alonso Mielgo et al. 2001; Mormont and van Huylenbroeck 2001). Networks are based mainly on *spatial* proximity, so that products are sold in the region (or place) of production, and consumers (e.g. tourists) are made aware of the 'local' status of the product at the point of retail. The articulation of activities in space and time by organising specific events, fairs or thematic routes (Brunori and Rossi 2000) may contribute to the regional identity of products, attracting customers and thereby enhancing a further stretching out of SFSCs. Producer–consumer networks may also be based on *cultural* proximity, as exemplified by the sale of regional specialities to emigrants (LEADER 2000). Proximate SFSCs often include intermediate actors in the agro-food chain, who then take over the role of guaranteeing product authenticity. Examples are local shops and restaurants (for regional products), but also specialist retailers like 'whole food' and dietetic shops that play an important role in the marketing of organic products.

A third category further enlarges the reach of SFSCs to *extended* relations in time and space. Here products are sold outside of the region of production to consumers who may have no personal experience of the locality. In most cases products are exported from the region to national markets, but some extended SFSCs may span large distances covering the globe. Examples of these are well-known regional specialities like Champagne wine or Parmigiano-Reggiano cheese (de Roest and Menghi 2000), but also 'fair trade' products like coffee and tea. These global networks are still distinctively 'short' FSCs in that, despite the large distances travelled, they reach the consumer embedded with a special sort of value-laden information which is, for example, printed on packaging or communicated at the point of retail. This enables the consumer to make local connections with the place/space of production and, potentially, the values of the people involved and the production methods employed. This successful transmission of information allows products to be differentiated from more anonymous and standardised commodities, commanding a premium price if the accompanying information is considered valuable by consumers.

Such extended SFSCs depend critically on institutionalised conventions, codes and mediators enabling a lengthening of producer–consumer networks which may be 'acting at a distance'. Sometimes networks are aligned on the basis of 'reputation effects' (Shapiro 1983), but here it is difficult to safeguard the exclusivity of the product, and markets become prone to imitations, substitutions and potential downward pressure on prices. Extended SFSCs tend, therefore, to involve the creation of more formalised institutional codes (e.g. labels), which specify regulations for production, processing and other stages of the agro-food chain. The authenticity of products, rather than being founded in networks of trust and confidence, is backed up by securing a formal juridical basis for brands and labels, involving independent external bodies for control and certification. The rising transaction costs resulting from this, together with the relatively high transport costs, accentuate the importance of economies of scale and may turn larger (conventional) market parties into 'obligatory passage points' within extended SFSC networks. It is important to recognise, however, that the new production codes and certification procedures are largely independently created, that is, they fall outside of the more conventional hygienic quality regulation implemented by governments and corporate retailers. Yet, once developed, they may come into direct competition with the conventional sector.

The specific quality definitions and conventions involved in the operation of new food networks represent a second dimension which differentiates

empirical expressions of SFSCs. This dimension relates to the quality definitions (by the producer and the consumer) of the product rather than the spatial definition of the chain. All SFSCs operate, in part at least, on the
principle that the more embedded and differentiated a product becomes, the
scarcer its presence in the market. Product differentiation implies the construction of transparent market relations around specific sets of quality definitions that are shared by all parties involved, and are sufficiently translated
to convince consumers to pay premium prices. When looking at the empirical variety of SFSCs, two main categories of quality definitions may be distinguished, as shown in figure 6.2.

The first category of SFSCs stresses mainly the link between quality attributes of the product and its *place* of production or producer. Specific characteristics of the place of production (natural conditions, cultural and
gastronomic traditions, etc.) or the production process (artisanal, traditional,
farm-based, etc.) are crucial parameters to the definition of the product's
quality, and in many cases are claimed to result in distinctive and typical
tastes or appearances. The clearest examples are regional speciality foods
with EU protected origin indications. Farm/cottage foods tend to stress the
artisanal nature of the production process and the experience and capacities
of the producer, but in many cases they tacitly refer also to cultural heritage
and (local) traditions. Quality definitions based on 'fair trade' are also
included for their emphasis on links with producers, where considerations of
ethics and justice are paramount.

The second group of SFCSs defines quality in terms of the links of food
production and consumption with *bio-processes*. This group includes, first of
all, products that, in response to public concerns over ecology, distinguish
themselves with environmentally sound production methods like organic
and integrated production. Apart from clearly specified labels, there is a vast
range of products with more general claims to being 'natural'. These draw in
part on romantic images of traditional farming, but they also express a tendency towards the valorisation of multifunctional forms of agriculture, for
example, for their contribution to rural nature and landscapes. This category

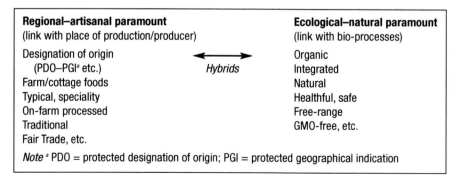

Regional–artisanal paramount (link with place of production/producer)		Ecological–natural paramount (link with bio-processes)
Designation of origin (PDO–PGI[a] etc.)	Hybrids	Organic Integrated
Farm/cottage foods		Natural
Typical, speciality		Healthful, safe
On-farm processed		Free-range
Traditional		GMO-free, etc.
Fair Trade, etc.		

Note [a] PDO = protected designation of origin; PGI = protected geographical indication

Figure 6.2 Different quality definitions employed within SFSCs

also includes products conceived as more healthful and safe. While such claims are rarely made explicit, there appears to be a widespread common-sense idea among consumers that products with less chemical substances (or that are free of GMOs) are more healthful (Nygard and Storstad 1998). The third type of quality definition included here concerns 'free-range' products, which are distinguished by their production's respect for the natural behaviour and welfare of animals.

It should be stressed that in reality clear distinctions between various quality definitions often are unavailable and boundaries between categories become blurred. This results from associations made by consumers, but also because several SFSCs actively create interlinkages between distinct quality aspects. This is, for example, the case with some regional products. For instance, as a part of product imagery they can stress the role of farming in safeguarding rural landscapes; conversely, they can stress environmentally sustainable products as part of their marketing strategies, thus extending product identity with a regional dimension. Quality conventions involve, therefore, more than merely the language of production regulations: they refer also to the perceptions and discourses of the actors involved and are influenced by their personal (lay-)knowledge, interests and cultural backgrounds. However, important struggles occur between actors – not least around quality conventions involved in SFSCs, but also in attempts to construct compromises and coalitions.

Clearly, while both the scale and the quality dimensions give some framework for mapping the diversity of SFSCs, neither dimension maps onto the other directly. Figure 6.3 exposes the relationships between the scale (figure 6.1) and quality dimensions (figure 6.2). This further demonstrates the 'quality battle' occurring between the more highly intermediated and extended quality supply chains (often retailer-led), and the local face-to-face, or proximate, regional and ecological product chains. This multidimensional matrix demonstrates two important tensions for the development and evolution of SFSC's. First, and possibly increasingly, regional–artisanal or ecological–natural quality product definitions can be adopted by distinct types of supply chain. Organics sales in the UK, for instance, are dominated by corporate retailer sales (70 per cent plus), and overseas (extended) procurement (c. 70 per cent of all retailer supplies (see Smith and Marsden forthcoming). The implication of this is that regional and ecological quality definitions are vulnerable to substitution, duplication and intense competition between extended, proximate and face-to-face chains.

Second, this multidimensional SFSC matrix suggests, perhaps more positively for smaller and local producer interests, that attempts and struggles to capture more value in SFSCs through shortened chains, and in redefining the quality of products around local–ecological criteria, represents a growing process of *social and economic diversity and fission* in producer–consumer relations. This is diametrically in contrast to the (more post-Fordist) process of retailer-led standardised differentiation associated with conventional

	Quality parameters	
SFSCs scale	**Regional–artisanal paramount**	**Ecological–natural paramount**
face-to-face (direct producers–consumers)	typical products (e.g. speciality cheeses) on-farm processing farm shops farm producer	organic box schemes farmers markets organics
proximate (some intermediation)	farm–cottage foods regional labels wine routes special events local–cuisine restaurants new cooperative marketing arrangements	free-range GMO free
extended (high intermediation)	designation of signs (CPDO–PGI) fair trade products ethical products regional brands in supermarkets	retailer organics (+70% in UK) integrated pest management systems free range GMO free 'slow food products'

Figure 6.3 Opening up the quality food spectrum: the SFSC battleground

chains. In the latter, it is not that quality criteria are irrelevant, rather it is that they are standardised and conventionalised *outside* of the local and ecological context in which they are produced and processed. In the context of the overall finite nature of the food markets, one point of vulnerability for these conventional chains, as I show, becomes the degree to which the actors and institutions involved in developing SFSCs are given the agency and support to exploit their new found diversity. As I indicate with reference to the UK case, these vulnerabilities for the conventional system play an important part in shaping contemporary food regulation more broadly.

Some empirical evidence on the incidence and impact of SFSCs in Europe

It is important to recognise that the typologies developed here have been constructed from a detailed and largely qualitative analysis of comparative case studies from across the seven European countries. This enables a better understanding of the underlying mechanisms and evolutionary dynamics of

SFSCs. However, any attempt to obtain a wider overview is seriously hampered by the lack of official quantitative data of sufficient reach and quality (Knickel and Renting 2000), and therefore necessarily has to remain exploratory. In fact, the only type of SFSC for which in recent years some more standardised data are emerging concerns organic farming. For all other fields, any comprehensive overview is lacking, which obviously represents a major obstacle for an appropriate monitoring and analysis of new rural developments.

In spite of this limitation, the IMPACT project[2] attempted to obtain an overview of the spread and impact of SFSCs in seven European countries, altogether representing some 75–85 per cent of farming in the EU-15. Where possible, data were used from official (national) statistics and secondary sources, but to obtain an overview of SFSCs a wide range of methods (including surveys, expert consultation and 'grey' data) had to be applied (Renting et al. 2002). Table 6.1 gives an overview of the incidence of different types of SFSC as obtained through the application of this 'toolbox'. The figures give an impression of the range and diversity of SFSCs throughout Europe, both with respect to their incidence and the types of activity in different national settings. We need to keep in mind that there are probably still various 'blind gaps', and therefore actual numbers might still be considerably higher. Also, for reasons of data availability, the year 1998 was taken as the reference point, and since then SFSCs appear to have expanded significantly. In view of the lack of sufficient data, a differentiated typology of SFSCs, such as that set out above, could not be applied. Rather, data were collected according to three much broader categories in different, empirically defined, fields of activity: organic farming; quality production; and direct selling. As a result, while the category of direct selling largely coincides with face-to-face SFSCs, organic farming and quality production may cover all three types of SFSC and are defined mainly by the type of quality definition employed.

Nevertheless, despite these inconsistencies between the qualitative and the quantitative analysis, on the basis of these provisional estimates of the incidence of SFSCs, a range of indicators for their socio-economic impact were calculated (see table 6.2). The number of farms involved in SFSCs were first of all related to the total number of farms (Eurostat data for 1997) so as to compare the degree of dissemination of the activity. The same figures were also related to the number of farms above a minimum of two ESUs (economic size units), in order to correct for (the sometimes substantial) number of 'farms' that only involve hobby activities. The impression is that SFSCs are taken up mainly by medium-sized farm businesses; a minimum production level is often necessary to make the activity viable and finance investments, while large volumes are sometimes at odds with the specific and differentiated processing and marketing structures involved.

To explore the national economic importance of SFSCs, their socio-economic impact was also expressed in terms of the net value-added generated. This was the most appropriate measure for socio-economic impact, because it covers both family labour and employed labour remunerated by the activity. It therefore expresses rural development benefits, at both farm and regional levels. The *additional* net value-added generated on top of conventional agricultural production (ΔNVA) was used to express the rural development gains of SFSCs in comparison to more conventional productivist development trajectories. Even more than for estimates of the incidence of SFSCs, impact figures have the character of 'best educated guesses' and are strictly exploratory. Again this is the result of the unavailability of adequate data. The data presented have been elaborated on the basis of farm economic studies, representative sets of farm accounts and expert opinion. While their accuracy can certainly be further improved, the data do give us a sufficient measure with which to explore the extent of the shift in the production base of European farming from productivist agriculture to rural development-based SFSC activities.

The results make clear that SFSCs have developed substantially in all countries, although large differences occur. In terms of the number of farms involved, SFSCs are most developed in Mediterranean countries like Italy, France and Spain, but also in Germany. Activities of direct selling and quality production especially are widely developed there, sometimes reaching shares of 20–30 per cent of the total number of farms. These figures increase again when we take farms with a minimum economic size of two ESU as the reference point. SFSCs are much less developed in the UK and the Netherlands, and Ireland is clearly lagging behind, with very small numbers of farms involved in SFSC development: in the first two, SFSCs have sometimes reached shares of 5–10 per cent, while in Ireland figures never surpass 1 per cent. In terms of the number of farms, organic farming is generally much less developed than are other SFSCs, with the highest shares in Italy and France (1–2 per cent). However, we need to keep in mind that since 1998 the number of organic farms in some countries has increased rapidly.

There are striking differences in the specific types of SFSC that are most developed within the various countries. In Italy, Spain and France, SFSC development appears to a large extent to build on activities of regional quality production and direct selling with long-lasting traditions. National and EU legislation for the juridical protection of quality production (e.g. PDO and PGI) here appears to have served as an appropriate institutional stimulus for the consolidation (if not revival) of these activities. The difference lies with the UK, The Netherlands and Ireland, where PDO–PGI products have hardly been developed. In The Netherlands, the UK and, to a certain extent, also Germany, SFSC development more often is based on 'modern' quality definitions stressing, for example, environmental sustainability or animal welfare, while new and innovative forms of marketing (e.g. farm shop groups, box schemes, farmers markets) also more often play a critical role in SFSC development. The fact that in these countries the productivist agricultural model developed more strongly, threatening the survival of traditional production and marketing systems, plays an important role. For organic farming, less striking differences between countries occur. In several, such as

Table 6.1 Estimated incidence of Sass in seven European countries (1998)

	Netherlands	England & Wales	Germany	Italy	Spain	Ireland	France
Organic farming	962 certified farms	1,125 certified farms	9,200 certified farms	43,698 certified farms	7,392 certified farms	900 certified farms	8,140 certified farms
Quality production (i.e. s+p+ extended supply chains)	1,600 farms with quality beef label; 850 farms with free range eggs; 150 farms with free range meat; 690 on-farm dairy processing; 90 on-farm goat or sheep milk processing; 30 farmer groups with regional products (400–500 farms); 1,500–2,000 small scale food producers	700 farms with speciality products, including meat (203), cheese (98), yoghurt (70), ice-cream (77), wine (63), fruit juice-cider (77), pickles-preserves (56), water (7), bakery products (42), and beer (21); 1,100 farms with (regional) quality beef label; 550 farms with (regional) quality sheep label	190 on-farm dairy processing; 21,000 farm distilleries; 1,000 fruit processing; 11,000 farms with quality vine; 130 farms with free range eggs; 150 cooperative quality projects (7,500 farms); 60–80 projects regional quality meat (3,500 farms); 50 projects regional quality crops	30 PDO cheeses (40,000 farms); 24 PDO-PGI meat products (6,000 farms); 24 PDO-PGI olive oils (2,000 farms); 443 DOC-DOCG-IGT wines (154,000 farms); 25 PDO-PGI fruits, vegetables and cereals (1,800 farms); 6 other PDO-PGI products (1,000 farms)	113 Designated PDO-PGI product, including wines (156,000 farms), olive oil (27,000), cheeses, fresh meats, vegetables (c. 2,000), fruits (c. 11,000), legumes (320), honey, raisin (4,100), rice (6,700) and tubers (750) various other regional labels of autonomous communities	30 farms with farm-house cheese; 130 farms with other farmshouse-cottage foods (breads and cakes, jams and preserves, meat products)	Over-all 182,500 farms (census 2001), covering: 543 AOC–AOP labels 8,000 farms and 4,500 processors AOC–AOP cheese and beef; 59,400 farms with quality wine of which 33,000 AOP 630 other labels e.g. Label Rouge and IGP (51,000 farms)
Total Farms	5,880	2,350	44,370	204,800	207,870	160	102,500

Direct selling (specifically face-to-face chains)						
4,715 farms with on-farm sales (roadside sales, farm shops) 33 organic farmers markets (100 farms) 100 farms with box schemes 120 farms with home deliveries 500–1,000 farms with washing, cutting, pre-packing	2,850 farms shops 250 farmers markets (5,000 farms) 1,450 pick your own 3,450 farms with farm gate–roadside sales	24,000 farms with direct sales 110 cooperative farm shops 240 regional marketing projects (7,200 farms) 200 farmer markets (1,600 farms) 1,100 farms with meat packets 500 farms with home deliveries–box schemes 2,000 pick your own	800,000 farms, of which: wine (185,000 farms) cheese (c. 125,000) olive oil (280,000) vegetables and potatoes (85,000) fruits (49,000) meat (c. 300,000) eggs (175,000) honey (10,000)	153,000 farms, including farmers markets door-to-door selling farm gate sales 21 producer–consumer associations of organic products	650 farms with markets stalls 80 farms with box schemes 56 farms with roadside sales	102,000 farms (census 2000), of which c. 40,000 farms with farm gate sales (no production c. 60,000 farms with on-farm processing for direct sales
Total Farms 5,935	12,750	36,510	800,000	153,000	786	102,500

Table 6.2 Socio-economic impact levels (in millions of Euros) of SFSCs in seven European countries (1998)

	Netherlands	UK	Germany	Italy	Spain	Ireland	France
Organic farming							
Δ NVA (Euros)	23m	25m	845m	214m	42m	2.1m	31m
% of total NVA	0.3	0.2	0.8	1.1	0.2	0.1	0.1
N	962	1,472	9,200	43,698	7,392	900	8,140
% of total N	0.9	0.6	0.6	1.9	0.6	0.6	1.2
% of N over 2 ESU	0.9	0.8	2.1	3.5	1.0	0.7	0.7
Quality production							
Δ NVA (Euros)	85m	54m	209m	865m	142m	16m	887m
% of total NVA	1.3	0.5	2.0	4.3	0.8	0.6	3.5
N	3,000	3,200	40,000	143,000	224,000	160	182,500
% of total N	2.8	1.4	7.5	6.2	18.5	0.1	26.8
% of N over 2 ESU	2.8	1.7	9.3	11.5	28.8	0.1	32.7
Direct selling							
Δ NVA (Euros)	68m	318m	678m	328m	262m	17m	840m
% of total NVA	1.0	3.0	6.4	1.6	1.5	0.1	3.3
N	6,000	14,700	35,000	800,000	153,500	790	102,000
% of total N	5.6	6.3	6.5	34.6	12.7	0.5	15.0
% of N over 2 ESU	5.6	7.9	8.1	64.4	19.8	0.6	18.3

The Netherlands, UK, Ireland and Spain, organics continue to be relatively weakly developed. The lack of sufficient domestic demand, but also the restricted state and institutional support, are important factors. Only in Italy and Germany does the organic sector appear to have left behind its initial low development base.

With regard to the socio-economic impact of SFSCs, as expressed in the ΔNVA[3] compared to conventional agriculture, again very different stages of development occur. Germany, Italy and France are the countries where SFSCs have reached the highest socio-economic impact levels: we can estimate here that organic farming, quality production and direct selling add some 6–10 per cent to the total NVA realised in agriculture. The Netherlands, the UK and Spain obtain an intermediate position with c. 2–4 per cent, while in Ireland less than 1 per cent is added to total NVA by the development of SFSCs. These figures at first sight may seem low, but it needs to be stressed that they refer only to the ΔNVA generated by SFSC activities. Data referring to the total NVA associated with SFSC activities are unfortunately unavailable for most countries. However, for Italy it is known that the total NVA (including primary production) of organic farming, quality production and direct selling amounts to 5,395 million Euro, or 29 per cent of the total NVA of the agricultural sector as a whole, suggesting a significant share for SFSC developments.

Evolutionary dynamics and potentials of short supply chains

SFSCs, with their focus on consumers' needs and relatively extensive modes of production, may hold some of the keys to future developments in European farming in a context where existing support measures are increasingly under debate in the present WTO round, and given the enlargement of the EU and the current mid-term review of the CAP. However, a major question remains whether this represents a long-lasting counter-movement or a more short-term set of aborted initiatives.

As I show, this is associated not just with their particular internal economic and social strengths or vulnerabilities: it is bound up with their economic and institutional competitive relations to the conventional (and more corporate-controlled) sector. If SFSCs are able to play a significant role in the process of rural development, it is important to identify and analyse the evolutionary patterns and obstacles in their development, considering their long-term impact and future potential. This requires much more in-depth and longitudinal micro-analysis of case studies, as well as the necessary broader typological and comparative analysis attempted here. In particular, more attention is needed on the temporal, spatial and market evolutionary dynamics involved in SFSCs, so as to gauge whether they are economically, socially and environmentally more sustainable over the long term (see Marsden et al. 2000a). The analysis thus far suggests that sustaining rural development through the evolution of these more diverse supply chains must be based on both *institutional support* and new types of *associational development* involving a range of actors operating within the chains and their surrounding networks. Quality supply chains need new and innovative forms of institutional and associational regulation to protect their competitive position. Furthermore, these relationships must alter and reconfigure over time and space. Here, concerning these interactions between the farm, the institutions and the associational realm, there is no one dominant model of development. Such findings have important theoretical as well as policy-relevant implications. Are we witnessing the development of new rural economic relations emerging from the deepening crisis of industrial agriculture? If we are, it would seem that new institutional practices and interventions will be needed both to stimulate and to foster these diverse trends.

Such theoretical and conceptual questions surrounding the evolutionary dynamics of SFSCs need to incorporate the role of retailer-led governance. This is particularly the case in the UK where, I argue, the restricted quality prism of SFSCs is related in part, to the continued institutional and regulatory dominance of retailer-led food governance.

Case study: retailer-led food governance in the UK – keeping competitive control of quality

Unlike SFSCs, retailer-led or conventional chains are characterised by significantly higher levels of standardisation of product which are usually dictated by the retailer and national government agencies rather than by groups of producers or food processors. In addition, these chains are distinctive, not only in the sense that they are 'longer' or more complex; what marks them out as analytically distinct is rather their organisational and operation of supply chain power. This involves both a standardisation of product and a hyper-restrictive and bureaucratic framework within which production, supply and manufacture and packaging are organised. In these contexts quality becomes defined in more commercial (rather than regional or ecological) terms. And, in relation to the growing concerns over food quality since BSE and related food health scares, it increasingly also has to take on board sets of hygienic quality conventions (such as the stripping away of fats, offal, poorer quality meat cuts, etc.) so that a 'cleaner', more reliable, consumer-oriented supply system can be assured.

It is necessary at this juncture to provide some background on the mechanisms by which the corporate retailers have maintained their 'quality-constructed' market dominance over recent years, given the significant growth in consumer concern associated with food scares, and the growing media and political concern about retail power. Since we completed our decade of work on corporate retailer power in the 1990's (culminating in the text *Consuming Interests*, Marsden et al. 2000b), it is clear that the aforementioned development of SFSCs activated by those who are tacitly or explicitly attempting to short-circuit the conventional chains represents a more profound challenge to the retailers. Moreover, the setting up of the

FSA (in the UK) and similar organisations in other member states, as well as the new EFSA for the EU as a whole (Flynn et al. 2003), suggests a more complex publicly regulated quality framework for food which could potentially pose a significant threat to such retail power.

However, our most recent evidence suggests that this is far from being the case. Moreover, it would seem that it is the mutating nature of corporate retailer power itself, coupled as it is with its continued authority over conventional supply chains and consumption, which is the abiding characteristic of this most recent phase of food regulation. If this thesis is correct, and our emerging evidence suggests that it is, at least for the UK, it raises questions (and possibly a series of answers) over how these relationships impinge on the uneven development of the short supply chains outlined above. Is the maintenance and market dominance of corporate retail power (together with a supportive state), and the private-interest quality food regulations that go with it, a major reason for the thus far fledgling development of alternatives in the UK? How are the corporate retail chains reacting to the development of SFSCs which are based more on local and regional, rather than national and international, sets of market and regulatory arrangements? What do these competitive conditions tell us about the potential economic durability and evolution of the alternatives in the medium to long term? How significant is state policy in setting the rules for these competitive relationships?

In order to attempt to understand these competitive dynamics, I begin to address these questions by examining the role of corporate retailers in the UK with respect to the livestock crisis associated with BSE and beef and lamb prices, and farm incomes, which ensued between 1997 and 2001.

Background: the devalorisation of red meat production in the conventional sector

The Welsh Affairs Select Committee (WASC) of the House of Commons in the UK led an investigation into the role of the retailers in the livestock farming crisis during 1997–98 (HOC 1998). This followed a considerable amount of direct action on the part of livestock farmers, involving the forced dumping into the Irish Sea of retailers' shipments of beef from Ireland, and the broader protest about the widening price disparities between retail and farm gate prices (price spreads). To the livestock farmers and their unions it seemed that the all-powerful retailers were profiting from a crisis. WASC concluded that the 'producer had borne the brunt of the reduction in returns' (para. 19) and that there

> is a very strong case, we believe, for an independent study of the retailing pricing of meat products, perhaps as part of a wider examination by the Office of Fair Trading, to establish what level of wholesale and retail costs are now being passed on to the producer by the supermarkets. Research commissioned by the retailers, however impartial, is unlikely to convince. (para. 20)

After a considerable amount of political lobbying and a growing media concern about the relatively high retail prices, a Competition Commission (CC) enquiry was established, running from April 1999 until July 2000 (Competition Commission 2000). The terms of reference were multifaceted, but concentrated on three areas where there were allegations of unfair competitive practices being employed as a result of retailers' powerful market position:

- the public perception that the price of groceries in the UK tended to be higher than in other comparable EC countries and the USA;
- an 'apparent disparity between farm gate and retail prices, which was seen as evidence by some that grocery multiples were profiting from the crisis in the farming industry';
- continuing concern that the large out-of-town supermarkets were contributing to the 'decay of the high street in many towns' (p. 3).

For the purposes of this analysis I concentrate on the second of these areas. The CC's report did not suggest any curtailment or serious intervention by government into retail buyer or selling power, other than the need to establish a more consistent code of practice between the large retailers and their suppliers. This decision was taken despite evidence that 'the existence of buyer power among some of the main parties has meant that the burden of cost increases in the supply chain has fallen disproportionately heavily on the small suppliers' (p. 4). Moreover:

> There appeared to us to be a climate of apprehension among many suppliers in their relationship with the main parties. We put a list of fifty-two alleged practices to the main parties . . . we found that a majority of these practices were carried out by the main parties. They included requiring or requesting from some of their suppliers various non-cost-related payments and discounts, sometimes retrospectively; imposing charges and making changes to contractual arrangements without adequate notice; and unreasonably transferring risks from the main party to the supplier. We believed that, where a request came from a main party with buyer power, it amounted to the same thing as a requirement. (p. 6)

Furthermore:

> These practices, when carried on by any of the major buyers, adversely affect the competitiveness of some of their suppliers with the result that the suppliers are likely to invest less and spend less on the new product development and innovation, leading to lower quality and less consumer choice. This is likely to result in fewer new entrants to the supplier market than otherwise. Certain of the practices give the major buyers substantial advantages over the smaller retailers, whose competitiveness is likely to suffer as a result, again leading to a reduction in consumer choice. (p. 7)

Despite these findings it was concluded that 'taking all the above matters into consideration, we are satisfied that the industry is currently broadly competitive and that, overall, excessive prices are not being charged, nor excessive profits earned' (p. 7).

By the year 2000, then, the existence and operation of retail buyer power in conventional supply chains, during a period of heightened concern over food quality and food consumption, as well as declining farm gate prices, was not seen by the CC as a necessary justification for imposing any further regulation on the corporate retailing sector. The power of the retailers' arguments concerning the already burdensome regulation on the corporate retail sector effectively won the day.

It then took the Government eighteen months to produce the outline details for the Code of Good Practice between Supermarkets and Suppliers (DTI 2001), which is still under review (following the *Report of the Policy Commission on the Future of Farming and Food*, published in January 2002) and is creating considerable concern among producers. Meanwhile, the onset of foot-and-mouth disease (FMD) and the closure of livestock export markets dealt another blow to the conventional primary producer sector, while retail profits and prices spreads between the farm gate and the retail outlet continued to increase.

Regulating competition and the farm crisis in the conventional sector

By the end of 2001, following the CC's findings, the crisis of conventional livestock farm incomes had significantly deepened. It is important to recognise that despite the efforts of many producers and processors to create short supply chains, and a rise in local and regional quality food chains (as outlined above), these have still remained marginal in the British case. Corporate retailers have become more concerted in their efforts to develop green and quality food labels themselves, but these have been established under nationally and internationally organised principles. The construction of food quality has become more embedded into the competitive market relations which exist between conventional and alternative chains. Indeed, the role of national government, and its particular interpretation of European competition policy, becomes an important vehicle in continuing to marginalise, or 'damp down', alternative supply chain initiatives.

Overall, the evidence examined in our recent research, and that of a review of the more recent situation with regard to government committee enquiries (see HOC 2002) suggests that the conclusions reached by WASC in 1997 are still applicable and that, if anything, the position in the supply chains of conventional producers has *weakened* in relation to the corporate retailers. Perversely, this has the effect of continuing to 'lock in' the majority of producers to conventional support mechanisms (such as Hill and Livestock Compensation Allowances – HLCA – payments) rather than trying or attempting to adopt an alternative strategy.

Meat and Livestock Commission (MLC) data for 2000 and 2001 show an increase in the price spreads for lamb and beef, with increases in the retail prices and profits, and reductions in producer prices. Moreover, there are at least allegations by farmers and union leaders that the retailers profiteered from the onset of foot-and-mouth disease, given their price-setting behaviour during and after the outbreaks. Three major points can be made in assessing the current retailer–farmer relationships.

- The CC's report, while seemingly comprehensive and thorough, raises questions about the degree to which it *adequately* addressed both consumer and producer concerns. Its terms of reference did not take account of the overall supply chain relationships; and the timing of the inquiry excluded the data more recently presented by the MLC on price spreads. From the point of view of WASC's findings in 1997, the CC's report's brief was set *both* too narrowly, in terms of its exclusion of a full investigation of supply chain relationships and the supermarkets, *and* too broadly, in the sense that it did not adequately focus on meat supply chains, as recommended in WASC's report (HOC 1998).
- Price spreads have increased and little has changed in relation to the conclusion reached in WASC's report that 'the producer has borne the brunt of the reduction in returns' (para. 19). Moreover, it is clear that the CC's report found considerable evidence of 'unfair practices' operating between retailers and suppliers, as well as examples of individual retail buyer power, even though they did not represent wholesale 'cartel' activity. The CC looked in some considerable detail at retail margins in lamb and milk, finding variable degrees of increased and some reduced margins over the period. It did not study beef, finding that lamb margins had dropped on average by 35 per cent over the study's period. Milk margins had risen very strongly. The study finished at the end of 1999 showing strong growth in retailer margins in milk, some in lamb, but without information on beef.
- There are four interrelated reasons given for the growth in meat price spreads: retailer profiteering; the growth in costs in the chain related to dealing with the BSE crisis; the reduced amounts of meat materials that actually have a market price, or have a deflated market price (e.g. hides, skins, skin materials, poorer cuts); and the change in the balance of cuts – with the moves of supermarkets focusing on the higher quality cuts. It is important to recognise that whichever of these four factors is paramount, the burden of costs tends to fall *disproportionately* on the producer and the independent processor sector – in particular, the smaller producers and processors who are least able to absorb these increases in costs. Retailers, on the other hand, have a stronger 'power of selection' in opting for quality supplies and in 'burying the costs of crises' in the meat supply chains. Moreover, it should also be noted that under conditions of a strong pound retailers are free to import more cheaply while producers are disadvantaged in export markets. Through the operation of all four of these factors (rather than just one of them), the tendency is for both the price spreads and the market power to widen between retailers and their suppliers.

These tendencies have continued the downward pressure on conventional farm gate prices as well as discouraging moves towards many of the alternatives suggested in the first part of the chapter. (By 2000, there were 1,200 fewer dairy holdings in Wales than there had been in 1996, just before the first inquiry began.) What evidence is there, then, to suggest that these actions and processes on the part of retailers and government tend to continue to marginalise alternative food networks and chains in the UK?

The evidence does suggest at least that more could be done by UK Government, which is far from uninfluential in marginalising alternatives, however much it promotes market-based solutions to the problems of the agro-food sector. This covers several areas, and it represents an important factor in ensuring that local producers and processors can compete more openly and evenly both across the UK and across Europe. Some key issues are relevant here.

First, a more concerted attempt to progress PGI–PDO status for selected UK products is required. The delays and problems here (in comparison with other member states) is stark, and there is also confusion and ambiguity (even on the part of the CC) concerning the compatibility, or otherwise, of the operations of European, other member states' and the UK's competition policies. The milk producer groups suggest, for instance, that competition policy is being applied unevenly not only across the UK supply chain but across Europe as a whole, to the detriment of producer and processor organisations. As they argue:

> The competition commission's report into Milk Marque recommended its subdivision into three regional co-ops. This artificial structure is proving over-restrictive and may be unsustainable. Farmers would prefer larger co-ops with processing capability. However, there is considerable uncertainty whether this would be permitted by the competition authorities. The question this raises is why shouldn't such a structure be permitted given the degree of consolidation in both the processing sector and the retail sector?' (HOC 2002)

This is leading to import penetration in the UK at the same time as producers are unable to protect products through PDO–PGI designations. At the very least it would seem that the full benefits of the privatisation of milk marketing (since 1994) have not been fully realised. This has tended to increase the market power of the more concentrated retailer and corporate milk processing sectors.

Second, the competition authorities and government agencies (not least DEFRA) have not thus far examined closely how competition rules could *facilitate* rather than obstruct producer and processor innovation and (SFSC) business development. How could producer and processor organisations empower themselves in supply chains (e.g. through vertical integration activities) without contravening European and national competition policies? DEFRA's report *Strategy for Sustainable Farming and Food* (2002: 22) recognises the obstacles of competition policy in relation to cooperative developments, arguing that 'there are other potential obstacles to the development of cooperatives – for example, the £20,000 maximum share-holding . . . a recent review has suggested that this limit be removed'.

Third, government actions concerning food safety and quality regulation, associated with BSE and FMD, have also increased the financial and regulatory burdens on the upstream sectors in a disproportionate manner as compared to those on the retailers; yet the 'cost-compliance' justification for not extending regulation (used, e.g., by the CC) associated with any new forms of regulation seems to apply only to the retailers. It is increasingly clear that if this situation continues government policies will increasingly compromise local and regional producers and suppliers, and make the economic, social and environmental goals of rural development and sustainability more difficult to achieve. More emphasis and encouragement from government could be given to 'power-sharing' and collaboration across food supply chains, thereby stimulating short-supply chain developments. Many of the initiatives established over the period since 1997–98 have been resourced and based largely on producer and processor subscriptions.

Unless some of these issues are addressed by the UK Government it is likely that

- existing and further government funding in the agricultural sector will continue to be less than optimum in public accountability terms;
- the innovative and collaborative initiatives that have been established thus far in short supply chain developments will not spread more widely across the independent farmer and food processor population.

The CC's exercise was large and expensive, though it has yet to demonstrate the greater accountability and transparency promised with regard to the retailers in their supply chain relationships. More government interaction with the retailers could encourage them to take greater responsibility for contributing to the achievement of wider UK agricultural, food and sustainability policy goals, as well as the more specific supply chain cost and benefits.

Conclusions: quality competition and the competitive evolution of governmental retailer-led suppliers and SFSCs

This analysis indicates the complex ways in which governmental authorities, corporate retailers and producers are currently engaged in the competitive supply chain controversies surrounding 'quality' food production. Recent official reports support the development of small local–regional products; and more funding is being invested in quality and organic supply chains. In addition, we can see a growth in the activity and experience associated with concerted and collaborative activities by producers and processors in attempting to capture increased economic value in the upstream parts of the chains. The complexity and diversity of the SFSC sector are likely to increase, as can be seen from its depiction in figure 6.3.

However, as demonstrated by this UK case study concerning the competition authorities and retailers, we need to recognise that corporate retailers are not inactive 'bystanders' in this process. As the leaders, they communicate effectively with government authorities in maintaining a competitive and inflation-secure environment for the consumer, as well as providing a certain level of quality assurance. Recent experience demonstrates that with government assistance they have managed to expand the dominance of their supply chains during a period of crisis in the sector as a whole *and* maintain consumer confidence and governmental legitimacy.

Some of this legitimacy is based on justifications reflected in a recent British Retail Consortium statement:

> The price on the shelf reflects the intricacy of the food chain as consumer needs and safety requirements are met. Value is added in various ways by those involved in the haulage, processing, packing, product testing, storage, whole-saling, distribution and marketing industries. British consumers choose to spend 43 per cent of the £133 billion they spend annually in nine multiple retailers, 28 per cent on eating out and 29 per cent in other outlets. With more than 60,000 food-retailing businesses and over 35,000 restaurants, bars and cafés, we have one of the most competitive food chains in the world. Compare this to Sweden, where the top three retailers account for 95 per cent of consumer spending on food, or Norway, where the figure is 86 per cent, or even France, where the figure is 66 per cent. A viable and competitive food and drink industry is a key component of Britain's economy. In 1950 the average household spent one third of its income on food and non-alcoholic drinks. By 2000 this had fallen to one sixth. The ability of the modern British food chain to deliver increased choice at reducing real prices has therefore been a significant contributor to improvements in living standards. Any backwards step holds huge dangers for our economy and people's quality of life. (Ali 2003)

What becomes apparent here, then, are at least three areas of contestation and competitive boundary-making between government, retailer-led and alternative food suppliers (see table 6.3). Competition policy, on the one hand, tends to reinforce the distribution of costs in the supply chain, while, on the other, the UK's FSA leaves largely intact the private-sector systems of quality regulation implemented by the retailers. Government authorities thus restrict themselves to baseline food safety through the operation of the FSA; the corporate retailers are left to develop highly competitive and sophisticated food quality hierarchies above that baseline; and alternative short supply chains begin, as I have argued in the first part of this chapter, to develop a whole host of new quality conventions and certification systems in defiance of – in many ways in opposition to – the former two.

Understanding how these dynamic competitive arrangements play themselves out lies at the root of the question of whether alternatives – defined partly in terms of the attempt to capture value at the producer's end of the chain – will develop and be self-sustaining; and/or whether they will continue to be marginalised by the 'legitimate authority' over food quality and relatively cheap food prices garnered by current government and corporate actions. In the meantime, the onset of a growing concern over food quality in the UK seems only to have reinforced a system of retailer-led governance, albeit within a more competitive and contingent state. The competitive battlefield of quality, regulation and consumption continues, and the 'legitimate authorities' which result from this will continue to restructure both rural

Table 6.3 Hierarchies in the regulation of food quality

Level of governance	Quality criteria
Local, regional and extended	SFSC conventions based on regional–artisanal and organic–ecological criteria
National and global	Retailer-led quality criteria implemented through supply chain regulation; private-interest regulation
National–EU-based	Baseline state–public regulated safety standards implemented by environmental health officers and the FSA (UK)

production spaces and (largely) urban consumption spaces. However, the quality battleground is now more complex and contingent given the arrival of a diverse short food supply sector.

Notes

1 This represents the first stage of research work associated with the Flagship project of Food, Regulation and Retailing which has begun under the auspices of the ESRC Research Centre for Business Relationships, Accountability, Sustainability and Society (BRASS). The author also acted as Special Advisor on agricultural and rural affairs for the House of Commons Welsh Affairs Select Committee 1997–2002.

2 The IMPACT project was an EU Fourth Framework FAIR programme project. The full title was 'The socio-economic impact of rural development policies: realities and potentials' (CT-4288) (1999–2002). The analysis on which this part of the paper is based is associated with that collaboration, and the author wishes to acknowledge in particular the assistance of Henk Renting and Jo Banks who were members of the team.

3 In order to explore the national economic importance of SFSC's their socio-economic impact was also expressed in terms of the additional net value generated (NVA, see table 6.2). Given severe problems of availability of good data on impacts this was seen to be the most appropriate measure for socio-economic impact, because it covers both family labour and employed labour renumerated by the activity, expressing rural development benefits, at both the farm and regional level. The additional net value-added generated on top of conventional agricultural production was used as a measure to express the rural development gains in comparison to conventional farming activities. The data were elaborated on the basis of farm economic studies, representative sets of farm accounts and expert opinions. They are therefore very much estimations.

References

Ali, R. (2003), 'Supermarkets' powers', *The Times*, 20 January, letter, p. 25.

Allaire, G. and Sylvander, B. (1995), 'Qualité, innovation et territoire: séminaire qualification des produits et des territoires', paper presented at INRA Toulouse, 2–3 October.

Alonso Mielgo, A. M., Sevilla Guzmán, E., Jiménez Romera, M. and Guzmán Casado, G. (2001), 'Rural development and ecological management of endogenous resources: the case of mountain olive groves in Los Pedroches *comarca* (Spain)', *Journal of Environmental Policy & Planning*, 3(2), pp. 163–75.

Banks, J. (2001), 'Short food supply chains in the Marches', IMPACT Working Paper UK2, Cardiff, University of Wales.

Beck, U. (1992), *Risk Society: Towards a New Modernity*, London, Sage.

Broekhuizen, R., Klep, L. van, Oostindie, H. and Ploeg, J. D. van der (1997), *Renewing the Countryside: An Atlas with Two Hundred Examples from Dutch Rural Society*, Doetinchem, Misset.

Brunori, G. and Rossi, A. (2000), 'Synergy and coherence through collective action: some insights from wine routes in Tuscany', *Sociologia Ruralis*, 40(4), pp. 409–24.

Cochrane, W. (1979), *The Development of Industrial Agriculture: A Historical Analysis*, Minneapolis, University of Minnesota Press.

Competition Commission (2000), *Supermarkets: A Report on the Supply of Groceries from Multiple Stores in the United Kingdom*, Cm 4842, London, HMSO.

Council for Rural Areas (1998), *Trust and Care: Food Production in the 21st Century*, Amersfoort, Council for Rural Areas.

Department for Environment, Food and Rural Affairs (DEFRA) (2002), *Developing a Strategy for Sustainable Farming and Food*, London, HMSO.

Department of Trade and Industry (2001), 'Hewitt backs good behaviour code for supermarkets and suppliers', news release P/2001/606, 31 October, London, DTI.

Goodman, D. (1999), 'Agro-food studies in the "age of ecology": nature, corporeality, bio-politics' *Sociologia Ruralis*, 39(1), pp. 17–38.

Goodman, D. (2002), 'Rethinking food production–consumption: integrative perspectives', *Sociologia Ruralis*, 42(4), pp. 271–7.

House of Commons (HOC) Select Committee on Welsh Affairs (1998), *Second Report: The Present Crisis in the Livestock Industry*, HC 447, London, HMSO.

House of Commons Select Committee on Welsh Affairs (2002), Minutes of Evidence for Tuesday 4 December 2001 and Tuesday 11 December 2001: Farming and Food Policy in Wales, HC 427, London, Stationery Office.

Ilbery, B. and Bowler, I. (1998), 'From agricultural productivism to post-productivism', in Ilbery, B. (ed.), *The Geography of Rural Change*, London, Longman.

Ilbery, B. and Kneafsey, M. (1999), 'Niche markets and regional speciality food products in Europe: towards a research agenda', *Environment and Planning A*, 31(12), pp. 2207–22.

Institute of Agriculture and Trade Policy (1998), *Marketing Sustainable Agriculture: Case Studies and Analysis from Europe*, Minneapolis, MN, Institute for Agriculture and Trade Policy.

Knickel, K. and Renting, H. (2000), 'Methodological and conceptual issues in the study of multifunctionality and rural development', *Sociologia Ruralis*, 40(4), pp. 512–28.

Lash, S. and Urry, J. (1994), *Economies of Signs and Spaces: After Organised Capitalism*, London, Sage.

LEADER (2000), 'Marketing local products: short and long distribution channels', Rural Innovation: Dossier 7, LEADER Observatory, available: http://europa.eu.int/comm/archives/leader2/rural-en/biblio/circuits/contents.htm.

Long, N., Ploeg, J. D. van der and Curtin, C. (1988), *The Commoditization Debate: Labour Process, Strategy and Social Networks*, Pudoc, Wageningen, Wageningen Agricultural University.

Marsden, T. K. (1998), 'New rural territories: regulating the differentiated rural spaces', *Journal of Rural Studies*, 14(1), pp. 107–17.

Marsden, T. K. (2003), *The Condition of Rural Sustainability*, Assen, The Netherlands, Van Gorcum.

Marsden, T. K. and Arce, A. (1995) 'Constructing quality: emerging food networks in the rural transition', *Environment & Planning A*, 27(8), 1261–79.

Marsden, T. K., Banks, J. and Bristow, G. (2000a) 'Food supply chain approaches: exploring their role in rural development', *Sociologia Ruralis* 40(4), pp. 424–38.

Marsden, T. K., Flynn, A. and Harrison, M. (2000b) *Consuming Interests: The Social Provision of Foods*, London, UCL Press.

Marsden, T. K., Renting, H., Banks, J. and Ploeg, J. D. van der (2001), 'The road towards sustainable agricultural and rural development: issues of theory, policy and research practice', *Journal of Environmental Policy & Planning*, 3(2), pp. 75–83.

Mormont, M. and Van Huylenbroeck, G. (2001), *A la Recherche de la Qualité: Analyses Socioéconomiques sur les Nouvelles Filières Agro-Alimentaires*, Liège, Editions de l'Université de Liège.

Murdoch, J., Marsden, T. K. and Banks, J. (2000), 'Quality, nature and embeddedness: some theoretical considerations in the context of the food sector', *Economic Geography*, 76(2), pp. 107–25.

Nygard, B. and Storstad, O. (1998), 'De-globalisation of food markets? Consumer perceptions of safe food: the case of Norway', *Sociologia Ruralis*, 38(1), pp. 35–53.

Organisation for Economic Cooperation and Development (1995), *Niche Markets as a Rural Development Strategy*, Paris, OECD.

Ploeg, J. D. van der and Frouws, J. (1999), 'On power and weakness, capacity and impotence: rigidity and flexibility in food chains', *International Planning Studies*, 4(3), pp. 333–47.

Ploeg, J. D. van der, Long, J. and Banks, A. (eds) (2002), *Living Countrysides: Rural Development Processes in Europe. The State-of-the-Art*, Doetinchem, Elseviers.

Ploeg, J. D. van der, Renting, H., Brunori, G., Knickel, K., Mannion, J., Roest, K. de, Sevilla-Guzmán, E. and Ventura, F. (2000), 'Rural development: from practices and policies towards theory', *Sociologia Ruralis*, 40(4), pp. 391–408.

Policy Commission on the Future of Farming and Food (2002), *Farming and Food: A Sustainable Future*, available: www.cabinet-office.gov.uk/farming/pdf/PC%20Report2.pdf.

Renting, H. and Ploeg, J. D. van der (2001), 'Reconnecting nature, farming and society: Environmental cooperatives in The Netherlands as institutional arrangements for creating coherence', *Journal of Environmental Policy & Planning*, 3(2), pp. 85–101.

Renting, H., Roep, D. and Knickel, K. (2002), 'An RD toolbox: methodological and conceptual issues in the study of rural development', IMPACT Working Paper, Pudoc, Wageningen, Wageningen Agricultural University–Institut für Landliche Strukturforschung.

Roep, D. (2001), 'The Waddengroup Foundation: the added value of quality and region', IMPACT Working Paper, NL2, Pudoc, Wageningen, Wageningen Agricultural University.

Roest, K. de, and Menghi, A. (2000), 'Reconsidering "traditional food": the case of Parmigiano-Reggiano cheese', *Sociologia Ruralis*, 40(4), pp. 439–51.

Schucksmith, M. (1993), 'Farm household behaviour and the transition to post-productivism', *Journal of Agricultural Economics*, 44(3), pp. 466–78.

Shapiro, C. (1983), 'Premiums for high quality products as returns to reputation', *Quarterly Journal of Economics*, 98(4), pp. 659–80.

Smith, E. and Marsden, T. K. (forthcoming), 'Exploring the limits to growth in UK organics', *Journal of Rural Studies*.

Stassart, P. and Engelen, G. (eds) (1999), *Van de Grond tot in Je Mond: 101 Pistes voor een Kwaliteitsvoeding*, Leuven, Vredeseilanden-Coopibo.

Storper, M. (1997), *The Regional World*, London, Guildford Press.

Ventura, F. and Meulen, H. S. van der (1994), 'Transformation and consumption of high-quality meat: the case of Chianina meat in Umbria, Italy', in Ploeg, J. D. van der and Long, A. (eds), *Born from Within: Practice and Perspective of Endogenous Rural Development*, Assen, Van Gorcum.

Ward, N. (1993), 'The agricultural treadmill and the rural environment in the post-productivist era', *Sociologia Ruralis*, 23(3–4), pp. 348–64.

Whatmore, S. and Thorne, L. (1997), 'Nourishing networks: alternative geographies of food', in Goodman, D. and Watts, M. (eds), *Postindustrial Natures: Culture, Economy and Consumption of Food*, London, Routledge.

7

A new aesthetic of food? Relational reflexivity in the 'alternative' food movement

Jonathan Murdoch and Mara Miele

Introduction

In recent times, an apparent contradiction between high levels of output and improved food quality has arisen within the food sector. The development of mass food markets, alongside 'Fordist' methods of production and their associated economies of scale, has generated unprecedented abundance (Montanari 1994). Yet, at the same time, industrialisation processes have resulted, seemingly, in greater and greater product standardisation, so that differing foods are rendered more alike in terms of their manufactured content. This process of standardisation affects not just production, processing and retailing, but eating itself, so that meals now carry their industrial properties into the stomachs of modern consumers.[1]

Critics of the industrial approach to food provisioning argue that food quality is compromised both by the growing homogenisation of foodstuffs and by the increased health risks that emerge from *within* overly industrialised food production processes. The ensuing food scares provoke increased consumer concern about the conditions of food production (Griffiths and Wallace 1998) and, as a consequence, a sizeable and growing minority of consumers turn to alternative food sources. Fernandez-Armesto summarises this trend, at the end of his recent history of food (2001: 250), when he says that

> an artisanal reaction is already underway. Local revulsion from pressure to accept the products of standardised taste has stimulated revivals of traditional cuisines . . . In prosperous markets the emphasis is shifting from cheapness to quality, rarity and esteem for artisanal methods . . . The future will be much more like the past than the pundits of futurology have foretold.

This 'artisanal reaction' comprises a turn towards products that are apparently delivered by simpler and more *natural* processes of production and preparation than is usually the case in mass markets. Local foods, organic foods, traditional foods, GM-free foods, and the like, have become popular in recent years as consumers look for enhanced security through some re-engagement with natural qualities (Nygard and Storstad 1998; Murdoch and Miele 1999). Such products frequently carry claims that their processes of production are 'traceable', and these claims aim to provide reassurance in a world where industrialised foods are seen as 'placeless' in origin (Miele 2001a).[2] While the rapid expansion of markets for these so-called 'niche' products can be attributed to a number of factors,[3] it is clear that the consumer response to food scares plays a key role.

By differentiating those parts of the food system that are dominated by economic conventions from those that prioritise a wider range of qualities it is possible to show that patterns of development in food consumption are now diverse and multiple rather than singular and uniform (Miele and Murdoch 2003). That is, the food sector is not headed towards ever-greater standardisation but rather towards growing divergence in the kinds of products available. Yet, while the contemporary food market may be able to accommodate (at least temporarily) the various commodities emerging from differing parts of the food sector (Ritzer 2001), it is likely that contradictions between the production of, on the one hand, large volumes and, on the other, distinctive and high-value foods will become more pronounced (see, e.g., Spencer 2002). For instance, industrialised foods challenge the conventional notions of quality that have long been established around traditional and natural methods of production, while the reassertion of alternative foods implies a turning away from industrial technologies and a rediscovering of more typical or authentic production processes. Thus, differing parts of the food sector appear to be heading off on opposing trajectories of development, some towards a more refined or intensive application of science and technology (e.g. GM foods), others towards a re-engagement with natural or traditional production methods (e.g. organic and traditional foods). As this struggle unfolds, so differing conceptions of 'quality' come to be ranged against one another (Wilkinson 1997).

In this chapter we wish to consider one part of this complex picture by examining some contemporary understandings of quality prevalent within *alternative* food markets and networks.[4] In particular, we aim to assess these alternative conceptions of quality from the perspective of *aesthetics*. Within food sector studies, the aesthetic value of food has been a rather neglected area, with aesthetic aspects often seen as secondary to economic concerns (although a notable exception is Gronow 1997). Yet the aesthetic dimension of quality is clearly important, if for no other reason than that food consumption is ultimately a deeply sensual experience. According to Parasecoli (2001: 69), all the senses are involved in some way in the appreciation of food quality:

> Smell . . . allows us to perceive the different ingredients and stimulates us to excrete substances like saliva that precede digestion . . . Appreciation related to touch is based on differences in texture and temperature . . . The sense that is least involved in eating is beyond doubt hearing, which is employed only in the case of crunchy textures and slurping sounds. [But] eating (in a cultural sense) is impossible without taste . . . [there are] primary tastes (sweet, salty, acid, bitter) and nuances (tart, astringent, spicy, balsamic – for which there does no yet exist a satisfactory categorisation) [and an] appreciation of harmony between elements which is primarily intellectual.

As Parasecoli goes on to say (p. 71), beyond those elements 'there is something more to food', something connected to experience, cultural belonging and the way foods are ordered within our cultural worlds. It is this 'something more' that perhaps comprises the aesthetics of food production, preparation and consumption.

We take this observation as a starting-point for the claim that the narrative of 'aestheticisation' might yield an alternative to the 'economisation' repertoire that has so often dominated the production and consumption of food and which seems to throw up many problems in the world of food consumption (Fine 1996; Miele and Murdoch 2002a).

In order to study the aesthetic dimension more closely we begin by considering the relationship between economic and aesthetic discourses in the food sector. We identify a process of 'market aestheticisation' in which economic concerns configure the quality of given foodstuffs so that the aesthetic becomes merely a means of disguising industrial processes of food delivery. We then go on to speculate that concerns around food safety are provoking the emergence of a new food aesthetic, one based on 'relationalism' and 'embeddedness'. Our hypothesis here is that as food scares reveal the sheer complexity of underlying production relations in the conventional food sector, so consumers seek out foods that enshrine potentially 'traceable' social and natural connections. In so doing, consumers act on the belief that those relations are more 'trustworthy' than are industrialised relations. We speculate that consumers are subsequently involved in a new engagement with food, one that embraces 'embedded relations'. We argue that the concern for *embeddedness* brings 'relational reflexivity' to the fore among consumers and that this requires a new aesthetic of food to be put in place. Next, we turn to examine the role of new social movements in heightening awareness of the economic, social and environmental relationships that surround foodstuffs. We argue that the market for *quality* foods is strongly configured by the activities of those social and political groupings that aim to alert consumers to the significance of food as a cultural, social and environmental 'good'. In other words, new social movements promote a form of 'relational reflexivity', which encourages consumers to appreciate a broad range of quality characteristics when selecting food items.

We focus on three main characteristics of food:

- its *local* provenance;
- its *environmental* qualities;
- its *social* significance.

We choose three networks that promote each of these quality characteristics. First, in the arena of local foods, we outline the activities of the Slow Food Movement, a group that works to link a gastronomic aesthetic to local and traditional foods. Second, by considering the activities of the Soil Association, an organic food network, we illustrate how environmental qualities can be promoted. Third, we outline how socio-economic considerations are brought to bear in the Fair Trade Movement. We argue that these three examples serve to illustrate how social movements mobilise a new sensibility towards particular aspects of *quality* in consumption practices. We conclude that the mobilising of this sensibility requires also the mobilising of a new relational aesthetic.

The aestheticising of food

Before turning to examine the role of aesthetics in differing food cultures we clarify our general approach to the notion of *quality*. At a minimum it is obvious that all food, in order to qualify *as* food, must hold quality attributes. Further, these attributes are likely to be both *intrinsic* and *extrinsic* to the foodstuff. As Callon et al. (2002) explain, the intrinsic qualities of goods derive from material composition, edibility, taste and appearance, while extrinsic qualities refer to judgements and evaluations brought to bear by human actors. In practice, the quality of a food product emerges from an interaction between these two dimensions. As a consequence of this interaction, quality can vary markedly from one actor or food culture to another as differing evaluations and judgements are made.

Any foodstuff will therefore comprise a bundle of characteristics and properties – in short, quali*ties* – which are revealed through processes of 'qualification' that serve to define the nature of the good (Wilkinson 1997; Murdoch et al. 2000). As Callon et al. (2002: 199) put it: 'All quality is obtained at the end of a long process of qualification, and all qualification aims to establish a constellation of characteristics, stabilised at least for a while, which are attached to the product and transform it temporarily into a tradable good in the market.' Quality is not, then, a *fixed* characteristic; rather, it is fluid and malleable, and tends to shift as a good passes from one social context to another. Each actor in the food supply chain will aim to evaluate the quality of that good and each evaluation will be made on slightly differing terms. Thus, the good is a 'variable', one that can be manipulated by the different actors involved in its production and sale (2002: 200).

One key means of manipulation derives from marketing and communication strategies. In general terms, the role of such strategies is to distinguish the food product from other comparable products so that it stands out from the crowd and easily comes to the attention of consumers. With increasing industrialisation in the sector it is arguable that products are becoming more standardised; thus, packaging and presentation come to the fore in order to draw consumers towards particular brands. At its most superficial level, then, marketing manipulation of the food product aims simply to provide an aesthetic *veneer* of quality. In line with this view, one commentator has recently claimed that

> the 'variety' you can see on entering a supermarket is only *apparent*, since the basic components are often the same. The only difference is in packaging and in the addition of flavouring and colouring. Fresh fruit and vegetables are of

standard size and colour, and the varieties on sale are very limited in number.
(Boge 2001: 15, emphasis added)

Following Welsch (1996: 3), this aesthetic veneer might be referred to as a
form of 'market aestheticisation' in which commodities are given a 'sugar
coating' of 'aesthetic flair'.

Some commentators believe this market aesthetic has become increasingly
significant over the course of the industrialisation process. As the distance
between producer and consumer has grown, some means of reconnecting
consumer and product (within relatively impersonal markets) has been
required. Slater (1997: 31) believes the reconnection can be achieved if the
product is somehow 'personified' so that 'the producer must create an image
of use value in which potential buyers can recognise themselves'. In certain
instances, Best and Kellner (2001: 4) argue, this process of 'personification'
is so well-advanced that it is the 'appearance of the commodity that is more
decisive than its actual "use value"'.

As is now well known, the food sector has become increasingly globalised
and production–consumption relations have been continually stretched
(Goodman and Watts 1997). It is therefore to be expected that food commodities have been subject to varying degrees of 'personification'. The
process is perhaps most evident in the arena of fast food. Here, increasing
standardisation (well described by Ritzer 1996) has been overlaid by relent-
less waves of branding (well described by Klein 1999). In his recent book *Fast
Food Nation*, Eric Schlosser (2001: 4) claims that McDonald's 'spends more
money on advertising and marketing than any other brand. As a result it has
replaced Coca-Cola as the world's most famous brand.' Kroker et al. (1989:
119), in reflecting on McDonald's marketing of its products, argue:

> Hamburgers . . . have been aestheticised to such a point of frenzy and hysteria that
> the McDonald's hamburger has actually vanished into its own sign. Just watch the
> TV commercials. Hamburgers as *party time* for the kids . . . as *nostalgia* time for
> our senior citizens . . . as *community time* for small town America; and, as always,
> hamburgers under the media sign of *friendship time* for America's teenagers
> (Quoted Smart 1999: 13)

These advertising and marketing efforts raise the profile of fast foods to such an
extent that the food itself seems almost residual to the McDonald's experience.[5]

Yet, while the process of market aestheticisation is undoubtedly well-
advanced in the food sector, recent events seem to indicate that the commodity has not disappeared quite as completely as Kroker et al. and others assume.
In particular, a whole range of food scares has forced the product back into
view. In the wake of these scares, eating a burger has become, in psychologist
Paul Rozin's words, 'fraught with danger' (quoted in Nemeroff and Davis
2001: 116). Thus, as consumers become aware of the potential dangers of
BSE and other diseases so they are forced to rediscover the product 'behind
the sign'. In this sense, the increased food risks appear to limit the degree to
which a market aesthetic can overwhelm food commodities.

It seems, moreover, that consumers can no longer rely on the aesthetic veneer in evaluating the quality of some industrialised food goods because, as Beck (2001: 273) puts it, 'many things that were once considered universally certain and safe and vouched for by every conceivable authority [e.g. beef] turn . . . out to be deadly. Applying that knowledge to the present and the future devalues the certainties of today.' Beck suggests that, in this uncertain consumption context, many consumers become more 'reflexive' in their relationships with food and other commodities: goods that were once taken for granted are now subject to a critical distancing in which some form of judgement (perhaps based on information stemming from government, media or new social movements – see below) is brought to bear. Halkier (2001: 208) thus believes that, in making their food consumption choices, individuals are 'pulled between an increased insecurity about knowing what to do and an increased awareness of possessing agency, the capacity to do something'.

One means of resolving this tension is through the conscious assessment of *quality*; and, in order to make such an assessment, consumers appear to require an awareness of the economic, social and ecological relations that underpin food production processes. Enhanced reflexivity around product quality may therefore prompt the emergence of a deeper understanding of the complex set of associations that surround both the production and the consumption of food.

In the view of some commentators, there are good reasons for believing that such an understanding may be emerging among growing numbers of consumers. For instance, David Goodman (1999) has recently suggested that the food sector has entered an 'age of ecology' wherein the complex 'metabolic reciprocities' that link production and consumption have come more fully into view (see also FitzSimmons and Goodman 1998). This 'age of ecology' can be discerned, Goodman suggests, in the popularity of organic foods, which are held to retain key natural qualities, and in the consumption of typical and traditional foods, which are believed to carry cultural qualities associated with long-established cuisines. In their different ways, he argues, these food types challenge the instrumental rationalities of the industrialised food sector and require more relationally embedded forms of production and consumption.

Goodman's account seems to indicate that consumers, in assembling food preferences, choices and tastes, are entering into a changed relationship with the objects of those preferences, choices and tastes. And in this changed relationship, they not only 'reflect' on the qualities of food goods but express a desire to genuinely immerse themselves in natural and socio-cultural relations. Thus, organic foods promise some reconnection with a nature that is being increasingly lost to industrial foods, while traditional or typical foods promise a reconnection with social and cultural formations that were previously distant in space or time. By consuming such goods, consumers seem to hope that a greater sense of connectedness can be achieved and that this connectedness will keep at bay the risks associated with industrialised foods (Nygard and Storstad 1998).

In assessing these two aspects of 'embedded consumption' – 'reflection' on the one hand, and 'immersion' on the other – we might follow Lash (1998) in proposing that consumers will somehow need to balance 'experience' and 'judgement': that is, they will need to apply an instrumental rationality (concerned, for instance, with risk or economic calculation) at the same time as they attempt to deal with indeterminacy and uncertainty in both the knowledge systems that underpin this rationality and in the goods themselves. Lash argues that the need to combine these two aspects of consumption practice will lead consumers to rely on a new form of 'aesthetic judgement', one that involves intellectual reflection (in order to establish a rule, something to guide the act of consumption) and imagination, understanding and feeling (in order to establish an aesthetic relationship with the commodity).

The notion of 'aesthetic judgement', proposed by Lash, has something in common with Crang's 1996 notion of 'aesthetic reflexivity'. Crang suggests that such reflexivity involves tracing the emergence of food commodities as they move through spaces of production, processing and consumption. In Crang's view, this approach involves 'roughing up the surfaces' of normally 'smooth' and 'unblemished' commodities to reveal the webs of connection and association that necessarily compose foods (see also Bell and Valentine 1997, especially chapter 8). An illustration of such aesthetic reflexivity is provided by Probyn (2000: 14) when she writes that a reflection on eating

> can be a mundane exposition of the visceral nature of our connectedness and distance from each other, and from our social environment . . . [It allows us to consider] what and who we are, to ourselves and to others, and can reveal new ways of thinking about those relations . . . In eating, the diverse nature of where and how different parts of ourselves attach to different aspects of the social comes to the fore and becomes the stuff of reflection.

Probyn's discussion of McDonald's, vegetarianism, eating disorders and other aspects of the consumption process can be read as an attempt to reflect on *connectedness*. It might therefore be seen as an attempt to utilise the notion of aesthetic judgement outlined by Lash and by Crang. In Probyn's account, this aesthetic appears to impose a dual requirement. On the one hand, consumers must assess risks and other aspects of the product in reflexive terms. This process requires that a *critical distance* is established between subject and object of consumption so that a reflexive evaluation can be carried out. On the other hand, it requires a new aesthetic relationship of some kind so that a sensual connection, something that lies outside of formal systems of calculation, can be established. By combining these two aspects, we can suggest that a 'relational aesthetic' is required as consumers attempt to assess the various quality foods that confront them.

Relational reflexivity in the new food movements

Gronow and Warde (2001: 219) have recently proposed the term 'ordinary consumption' to describe routine consumption activities such as the purchasing of food. In their view, ordinary consumption implies that consumer choices are made in line with 'taken-for-granted' assumptions generated within particular social worlds (associated with varied forms of social belonging). From that perspective, it seems likely that conventional mass food markets have developed on the back of ordinary consumption activities. However, ordinary consumption depends on consumer trust in conventional products. As we have shown, there are now reasons for believing that this trust has begun to break down: recent trends suggest that many consumers – as they attempt to come to terms with the implications of food scares – are engaged in a requalifying of foodstuffs. This requalification process requires new assessments and judgements to be made that can dislodge or replace the many taken-for-granted assumptions about food quality that have prevailed in the post-war era. We have argued above that requalification requires consumers to *distance* themselves from food goods in order that they might *reconnect* in new ways.

One striking feature of such distancing and reconnecting processes is that they are led, in the main, not by governments or producers' associations but by new social movements, notably environmental groupings and consumer associations. These actors have long pointed to the problems associated with industrialised and globalised production processes, and have gone on to assert alternative modes of production and consumption. Thus, new social movements frequently play a key role in adjudicating over notions of quality. They attempt to broaden out quality criteria in order to incorporate the environmental, social and cultural impacts of production and consumption.

In what follows we illustrate how the new social movements attempt to complicate notions of quality; in doing so we use a number of short case studies, based on the assertion of local, natural and social quality criteria. These studies highlight how concerns over culture and tradition, the environment and the social impacts of production and consumption are brought to bear in the construction of 'alternative' food markets. We consider whether these concerns work to orchestrate relational reflexivity in the food sector and whether they might come to comprise a new aesthetic of food.

Local connections: the Slow Food Movement

We begin with a group which has made the improvement of food quality its main area of concern – the Slow Food Movement which emerged out of the regional cultures of food that predominate in Italy. The organisation was established in 1986 in Bra, a small town in the Piedmont region, by a number of food writers and chefs. Their immediate motivation came from an anxiety about the potential impact of McDonald's on local food cultures (Resca and Gianola 1998). The movement's founders were concerned that the arrival of McDonald's would threaten not the up-market restaurants frequented by the middle- and upper-class urbanites, but the local *osterie* and *trattorie*, the places serving local dishes which have traditionally been frequented by people of all classes. Because, in the Italian context, traditional eateries retain a close connection to local food production systems, Slow Food argued that their protection requires the general promotion of local food cultures. Slow Food thus proposed that resistance to 'McDonaldisation' requires the expansion of markets for local and typical foods (Miele and Murdoch 2002b).

In keeping with that objective, Slow Food established a local structure, to be coordinated by a central headquarters in Bra. Initially the local branches were confined to Italy, though in 1989 Slow Food was formally launched as an international movement. The international manifesto indicates that within the organisation gastronomic issues were to the fore. It says that Slow Food is committed to 'a firm defence of quiet material pleasure' and claims its aim is 'to rediscover the richness and aromas of local cuisines to fight the standardisation of Fast Food'. In keeping with a gastronomic sensibility, it goes on to say, 'our defence should begin at the table with Slow Food. Let us rediscover the flavours and savours of regional cooking and banish the degrading effects of Fast Food . . . That is what real culture is all about: developing taste rather than demeaning it' (www.slowfood.com). The movement thus began to establish itself outside Italy and at the time of writing, convivia exist in 50 countries and the movement has around 70,000 members.[6]

In articulating a response to the spread of McDonald's, Slow Food has effectively become a clearing-house for gastronomic information about local foods, initially in Italy but, latterly, across the globe. The main means by which knowledge of local and typical cuisines is disseminated is the movement's publishing company, established in 1990. It publishes a range of guides in order to lead consumers to the food products available in local cuisine areas. These publications have developed a highly aestheticised approach to local and traditional foods, displaying such foods in lavish settings, using extensive artwork and photography. Typical foods are shown to be simultaneously authentic *and* sophisticated. Colours are rich and warm, shapes are elegant and evocative, settings are sophisticated and stimulating. Thus, Slow Food presents traditional and typical foods as visually luscious; it enhances their optical qualities so that these food products appeal to the sophisticated visual sensibilities of modern consumers (thereby, hopefully, expanding traditional markets).

However, Slow Food also tries to draw consumers beyond the aesthetic veneer. For instance, it concentrates a great deal of attention on what it calls 'taste education', by which it means ensuring that people retain the ability to appreciate the varied physical ('intrinsic') qualities of local foods.[7] In the main, this educative process takes place through the activities of local members and groups. Every Slow Food group is encouraged to organise theme dinners, food-and-wine tours, tasting courses, local food conventions, and so on. Likewise, the central headquarters puts a great deal of emphasis on national and international taste events as a means of keeping 'alive forgotten flavours'.[8]

Such activities seek to expand the markets for traditional foods by bringing them to the attention of both local and cosmopolitan consumers. Slow Food thus articulates an alternative set of quality concerns for those consumers suspicious of the industrial approach to food provisioning. In so doing, it voices implicit and explicit criticisms of the 'massification of taste', criticisms it articulates in the main *aesthetically*. Slow Food sees food as an important feature of the quality of life, the pleasure it gives is therefore its most important characteristic. As the Slow Food manifesto puts it, the aim is to promulgate a new 'philosophy of taste', the guiding principle of which is 'conviviality and the right to taste and pleasure'. The pleasurability of food derives from the aesthetic aspects of production, processing and consumption. All such activities are considered 'artful': they require skill and care, and they evolve by building on the knowledges of the past to meet the new social needs of contemporary consumers.

In sum, Slow Food aims to challenge the diffusion of a fast-food culture by asserting an alternative aesthetics of food production, preparation and consumption. Starting from the acknowledgement that food is imbued with symbolic meanings, and that patterns of food consumption have evolved over time according to the gradual acquisition of specific tastes, Slow Food promotes the values of typical products and regional cuisines because they reflect long-established cultural 'arts of living'. As leading Slow Food activist Alberto Capatti (1999: 4) has put it, 'food is a cultural heritage and should be consumed as such'. Thus, for Slow Food an aesthetic appreciation of food requires an appreciation of the temporal flow of food from the past into the present: 'Slow food is profoundly linked to the values of the past. The preservation of typical products, the protection of species . . . the cultivation of memory and taste education – these are all aspects of this passion of ours for time' (1999: 5).

Ecological connections: the Soil Association (SA)

The SA was formed in the UK in 1946. It campaigns to increase the amount of organic food produced and consumed within the UK and acts to certify organic standards on farms and in food-processing enterprises. Its logo provides an assurance that the food has been produced and processed according to high organic standards. Currently the SA has around 20,000 members (its highest ever figure), and is involved in food qualification at all stages of the food chain – production, processing, retailing and consumption. In short, the SA is a key regulator of organic quality in the UK.[9]

The catalyst for the SA's formation was the publication in 1943 of Lady Eve Balfour's *The Living Soil*. In it Balfour identified the importance of soil restoration and improvement and argued for an 'organic' approach to farming the land – that is, an approach with soil fertility at its heart. The book identified a number of problems with contemporary farming practice and alerted a group of influential scientists and activists to the need for improved standards of land management. Three years later these activists came together to form the SA. Its avowed aim was nothing less than the renewal of British agriculture.

During its early years the SA focused on investigating the scientific principles that underpin environmentally integrated agricultural systems, with particular attention paid to soil management and animal husbandry. As Matless (1998:106) explains, 'English tradition was to be supplemented by scientific experiment. A dissident ecological science was seen as confirming the virtues of traditional practice as opposed to contemporary "progressive" orthodoxy.' Using scientific research farms, the SA developed a rigorous set of methods for the management of more 'ecologically friendly' agricultural systems. Having over a number of years derived a set of organic principles from in-depth research it then felt able to incorporate them into organic standards that could be applied in a variety of production locations. Through the dissemination of information and advice on organic farming the SA could push forward the renewal of agriculture for which Eve Balfour had earlier called.

The need for renewal became starkly evident during the 1960s following the publication of Rachel Carson's *Silent Spring* (1962). In a context where the problems with scientific, or industrial, agriculture were being widely discussed, the SA's standards gained new legitimacy – a legitimacy that was further enhanced by the emergence of the environmental movement in the late 1960s and early 1970s. Now the organic 'greening' of agriculture could be set alongside the more general 'greening' of industrial society.

Yet, despite growing support for the organic approach, the SA remained somewhat distant from the environmental movement (Clunies-Ross and Cox 1995). In part, this distance reflected tensions within the organisation over its role and objectives. On the one side, a group of traditionalists (including the founding members) believed that the SA should continue to concentrate on scientific research; on the other, a younger group argued that the SA should campaign more aggressively against industrial food production and seek to influence consumers so that the market for organics could be expanded. According to Reed (2000a) these tensions came to a head at the SA's 1982 AGM when both groups put forward their views in a heated and, at times, acrimonious debate. The view of the traditionalists was summarised by Eric Clarke in the *Soil Association Quarterly Review* for 1982:

> I do not believe . . . that the Soil Association should take as a major activity a policy to persuade consumers to buy the products produced by some of our members. There may well be a useful place for such a campaign, but it should be carried out by those organisations specifically orientated to those interests. (Clarke 1982: 22)

The alternative view was summarised by another member, Francis Blake, in the *Soil Association Quarterly Review* for 1983: 'It is our duty, and our opportunity, to take our organic message to the consumer, to educate them, to safeguard them and to provide the meeting point between them and producers' (Blake 1983: 24).

Ultimately, the latter view prevailed and the younger, more radical, grouping took control of the SA. It now began to campaign more vigorously on consumption issues, as illustrated by its new campaign – 'Eat Organic'. The new approach stemmed from the belief that

> without an increase in public demand wholefood shops will drift away from sell-ing organic food: without a strongly growing demand from such outlets there will be no increase in acreage under organic cultivation. It is not possible to achieve or create this demand without a process of education. (Soil Association 1982: 2)

In other words, the SA would teach consumers to think 'organically'.

A further fillip to the consumer awareness campaign came with the BSE crisis in the late 1980s. Now the concerns about industrial agriculture expressed by Eve Balfour, Rachel Carson and others were seemingly being borne out by the emergence of a mysterious new disease. Moreover, it soon became clear that BSE was associated with the intensive production systems that had come to dominate the livestock sector in the UK; and on that basis it seemed likely that organic farms would remain disease-free. As a result the SA launched the 'Safe Meat' campaign in 1989, alerting consumers to the virtues of organic meat products. This theme endured throughout the 1990s and organic sales began to increase, especially after the Government admit-ted the link between animal and human forms of CJD in 1996. As Reed (2000b: 21) explains:

> Throughout the 1980s and 1990s, [organic agriculture] had shown itself free from the disease, so side-stepping the gradual erosion of confidence otherwise experienced by the food industry. This was the disease opportunity structure; freedom from disease gave not only market share but also cultural ascendancy and political advantage. The industrial order had become pathological; the observational order of organic was healthy.

With the growth of the market for organic products in the wake of the BSE crisis, the SA increased its membership along with the income generated from certification processes.[10] It now administers certification standards on behalf of the UK government and has extended its certification schemes into nineteen countries around the world. Moreover, the increased resources available to the organisation have allowed it to diversify its activities. In particular, it has begun to focus on local food linkages around the organic food supply chain. In a recent joint-venture with the Countryside Agency, the 'Eat Organic – Buy Local' campaign, it aims to set up local partnerships and networks in order to support local producers, link production and con-sumption, and ensure that organic products find their way into local public institutions such as schools and hospitals. It is also assisting with the devel-opment of box schemes (i.e. direct sales of organic products), community-supported agriculture and farmers' markets. All these initiatives are aimed at strengthening the local capacity of the organic system.

Over the course of its history the SA has moved a long way from its early scientific origins. It now operates as a campaign group, as a certification body, as a research organisation and as a consumer information service. In its engagement with almost all aspects of organic production and consumption the SA must balance a number of competing demands on its time and resources. However, it is clear that attention to the concerns of consumers has grown significantly in recent years. As the SA's website (www.soilassociation. org) admits: 'Raising awareness will be instrumental in elevating the commitment of the British public to organic food.' This awareness-raising aspect of the SA's activities perhaps accords most closely with the notion of relational reflexivity discussed above. In provoking consumers to think about the relationship between the ecologies of production and the safety of food products, the SA is seeking to draw consumers towards its reassuring logo in the expectation that this aesthetic mark will provide a robust connection to safe and healthful environments.

Social connections: 'fair trade'

While Slow Food works to protect and promote local food products, and the SA aims to enhance the 'sustainability' of food through the dissemination of organic principles and practices, fair trade (FT) focuses on the economic and social dimensions of food production. In particular, it aims to challenge conventional terms of trade so that poorer producers might benefit (Raynolds 2000). Its goal, according to its website (www.fairtrade.org.uk) is to 'change international commercial relations in such a way that disadvantaged producers can increase their control over their own future, have a fair and just return for their work, [have] continuity of income, and decent working conditions' (Quoted Raynolds 2003: 60). The FT network acts to link producers to consumers through a labelling scheme, which provides a means of identifying FT products. The scheme is backed up by systems of certification undertaken by the various FT organisations. These systems work to register producers and license importers (importantly, the certification process is paid for by the importers of the products; see Raynolds 2003). Once producers are incorporated into a scheme they receive the international product price plus a premium that ensures reinvestment at the local level of production. Importantly, they also benefit from favourable trading arrangements, as Rice (2001: 48) explains:

> According to the fair trade rules of operation, grower associations may request up to 60 [per cent] of their payments as pre-payment for promised deliveries, essentially obtaining credit from these buyers. For importers handling, say a container of coffee. . .such advances mean substantial outlays of capital prior to receiving the product. The credit often comes at times when grower groups are most in need of resources in preparing their farms for the upcoming harvest.

At present, around 70 per cent of FT goods are from the food sector, mainly coffee, cocoa, bananas and sugar, and around 400 producer organisations in 45 countries engage in some form of FT. In Europe, FT products are sold through approximately 65,000 retail outlets and the annual aggregate retail value of the market is calculated to be around 260 million Euros (EFTA 2002).

The European Fair Trade Association (EFTA) began in the early 1960s when Oxfam UK decided to create an alternative trading channel through which products from deprived regions in southern hemisphere countries could be marketed in ways that were of primary benefit to the producers. Parallel initiatives were established in other European countries, so that by the 1980s there was a profusion of competing schemes. Products were sold within the alternative channels through accredited retailers, mail order catalogues and local market outlets. From the mid-1980s onwards, however, FT products began to appear in more mainstream stores. This extension of the market was facilitated by the use of FT labels on all certified products. The labelling organisations offered commercial importers 'a register of monitored producer groups, a set of criteria as to how to do Fair Trade business, and a label that distinguished Fair Trade products from others' (EFTA 2002: 23).

This formalisation of 'fair trade' required a rationalising of the competing networks. In 1990 twelve European organisations came together to form EFTA, a coordinating body that serves to disseminate information to the various FT networks. The number of differing labels was also reduced by the founding in 1997 of the Fairtrade Labelling Organisation (FLO), which incorporated EFTA's groups as well as similar networks in the USA, Canada and Japan. According to Renard (2003: 90), the FLO is responsible 'for securing certification of all labelled products as well as granting licences for the use of the label to manufacturers and/or importers who comply with the conditions of Fair Trade'. It has established certification procedures for coffee, bananas, cocoa, tea, sugar, honey, orange juice, rice and wine. These procedures aim to ensure:

- direct linkages between producers and importers;
- the payment of premium prices for FT goods;
- the provision of producer credit;
- democratic accountability among producer groups;
- the application of international labour standards;
- environmental best practice (Raynolds 2003).

As the FT network has achieved greater cohesiveness, so the FT label has gained in significance. FT goods are now sold in a host of locations, from organic wholefood shops through to Starbucks. Whatever the retail location, the label carries a guarantee that the proceeds from the product's sale will go directly from consumer to producer. Thus, as Raynolds (2002: 415) puts it, 'Fair Trade labels address . . . global ethical concerns, assuring consumers that, as the Fairtrade mark reads, buying these products "guarantees a better deal for Third World producers"'. In this sense, FT 'humanises' the trade process: it makes the 'producer–consumer chain as short as possible so that consumers become aware of the culture, identity, and conditions in which producers live' (EFTA 1998, quoted Raynolds 2003: 61).

Evaluation

These three 'alternative' food movements present consumers with differing quality considerations. First, Slow Food responds to the crisis of trust in the food sector by highlighting the 'quiet material pleasure' (as the Slow Food manifesto puts it) that comes from an immersion in local and regional cuisines. This 'quiet pleasure' requires the gastronomic appreciation of typical tastes and a reflexive appreciation of quality, where quality stems from the consumer's understanding of both the intrinsic properties of food and the way these properties derive from cultural connections. Second, the SA emphasises the environmental problems that spill out of the conventional food sector. It claims that a 'cheap food policy' has delivered 'dramatic declines in farmland wildlife, greenhouse gas emissions, soil degradation, a decline in food nutrient content, pesticide residues, food scares, rapidly increasing incidence of food allergies and intolerance, and a loss of consumer confidence' (Soil Association 2001: 2). The SA claims that these 'externalities' can be effectively incorporated back into the food chain only if organic principles and practices are brought to bear. Thus, the SA charter mark allows consumers to connect to the 'environments of production' in order to promote 'best organic practice'. Lastly, FT seeks to establish direct and unmediated relations between producers and consumers so that increased value can be fed back down the supply chain to the sites of production. Again, certification procedures are used in order to tie both producers and retailers into a 'fair trade' regime. The FT logo allows consumers to *buy into* this regime in the expectation that a significant part of the value generated will find its way back to the social contexts of production.

These three movements highlight the varied nature of quality criteria in the 'alternative' food sector. They show that 'quality' can be interpreted in different ways and that it can be used to throw light on diverse aspects of production and consumption. While the intrinsic properties of the goods are important (notably for Slow Food and the SA), the socio-economic evaluations made by both producers and consumers are also emphasised (notably by Slow Food and FT). The three groups aim to regulate and monitor alternative food chains while simultaneously attracting consumers to their 'quality' food products.

Moreover, all three networks utilise aesthetic criteria in their efforts to draw consumers towards the goods. Such criteria are used to provide assurance that these 'alternatives' can be genuinely differentiated from conventional product ranges; that is, they aim to go beyond the market aesthetic by showing that the aesthetic veneer of the product is closely aligned with its substantive and intrinsic qualities. Thus, charter marks and logos are employed to draw consumers into a new relationship with the environments of production. In short, the marks and logos *fold* complex sets of relations into the food products in ways that permit easy consumer appreciation. They therefore promote a new aesthetic of food, one based on *connectedness* to those natural and social conditions that are thought to ultimately determine the quality of food.

Conclusion

In the preceding pages we have argued that new notions of quality are being brought to bear within new food chains and movements. We have suggested that these new notions derive in part from a growing dissatisfaction with conventional food supply chains. This dissatisfaction has concentrated around food scares and the apparent quality problems that follow from the industrialisation of the food sector. Standardised and mechanised processes of production yield homogeneous products that are thought to vary little in their quality attributes. Thus, consumers turn to 'alternatives', to products that are thought to carry environmental, cultural and social qualities into the consumption experience. These alternative products come in many shapes and sizes, but all hold the promise that their relations of production are ultimately traceable in some way.

We have further argued that this shift in perception requires both a disconnection from foodstuffs – so that some form of re-evaluation can be made – and a reconnection – so that some new pattern of consumption can be established. We have termed this double movement 'relational reflexivity', a notion that indicates how consumers distance themselves from conventional food products before establishing revised relations with the alternatives. We have suggested that this relational perspective requires a new aesthetic appreciation of food, one that is grounded in the multiple connections that run through and around food supply chains. We have also proposed that new social movements are instrumental in promoting this 'relational aesthetic'. In seeking to alter food consumption patterns in line with a heightened awareness of cultural, social and environmental criteria, the new food movements simultaneously alert consumers to problems in the conventional food sector and to the virtues of 'quality' food products in the local, organic and FT arenas. New social movements thus play a key role in orchestrating relational reflexivity.

In conclusion, we wish (following Browne et al. 2000) to enter a caveat to the rather broad distinction between conventional and alternative food chains utilised in this chapter. We have attempted to argue here that differing notions of quality are being employed in the two spheres. Yet, on close inspection it is clear that there are many similarities between the two: on the one hand, supermarkets and other key players in the conventional chain point to increasing safety, nutrition, taste, and so on, in the goods they produce and sell; on the other hand, the SA and the FT groups tailor their products so they can be sold through conventional outlets to conventional consumers. The result is that goods designated 'conventional' or 'alternative' begin to shade into one another so that their clear separation seems almost impossible (see Winter 2003).

It is for this reason that we have focused our attention here on the aesthetic dimension; we have suggested that the sensibility towards quality being promoted by the new food movements leads to a 'relational aesthetic' and that this differs markedly from the 'market aesthetic' found in conventional chains. While the two approaches often use the same tools, their objectives are entirely different: the market aesthetic aims to cement a *disconnection* between the producers and the consumers of food by disguising food's industrial origins; the relational aesthetic aims to cement a *connection* between the two by highlighting the social and natural environments in which food is made. In this respect, the 'alternative' food sector can be seen as giving rise to a new appreciation of food, one that sees food quality as intrinsically bound into the rich and varied contexts of production.

Notes

1 Consider the following description of McDonaldised fast food: 'the entire fast food meal is composed of separable, modular interchangeable elements. The inner structure of the burger itself can easily be separated into further components, all open for inspection. The assembly of each hamburger has a clearly mechanical nature. Even the look of the different parts alludes to various technological processes, rather than having the conventional appearance of cooked food' (Boym 2001: 7).

2 It is, however, evident that supermarkets are seeking to put traceability systems in place for a wide range of food markets. Consumers are being asked to trust the product by trusting the supermarket.

3 Miller (1995: 7) identifies the following as significant factors: 'the ability of shops to use new information technology exactly to match supply and demand; the market niching of stores now carefully differentiated by segments defined by marketing research and recognized by designers; the dynamic forms of customisation with flexible automation; [and] the degree of subcontracting'.

4 We put 'alternative' into quotation marks because we recognise the elusive nature of what the term is used to describe. We use it here to identify overt attempts to counter standardisation and globalisation in the food sector – notably those associated with local, traditional and organic products. As some authors (e.g. Winter 2003) have pointed out, there are problems with the notion of the 'alternative food sector' as the grounds for allocating production processes to either the conventional or the alternative sector are frequently unclear. We have elsewhere (Murdoch and Miele 1999) accepted this point and have sought to show how conventional and alternative products might be allocated to the differing domains.

5 Ray Kroc is famously quoted (by Love 1995: 303) as saying of McDonald's: '"We're not in the hamburger business; we're in show business."'

6 According to its founder, Carlo Petrini (2001a: xii), Slow Food now comprises 'a vast global network of men and women capable of generating ideas and programs to defend taste and the right to a responsible, knowing form of pleasure; one that is respectful of cultural and material diversity, and one which is open to all'.

7 As Carlo Petrini (2001b: 5) puts it, 'much knowledge is to be gained through the taste buds and the mucous membrane in the nose, and attaining such knowledge is an experience that is closely related to pleasure'.

8 The following are perhaps the most noteworthy: 'Excellentia', a three-day meeting involving 5,000 people from all over Italy in twice-yearly blind tastings of

international and Italian wines; 'Taste Week' (*La Settimana del Gusto*), which sets out to familiarise young people with quality catering; and the 'Hall of Taste', a food fair held every two years in Turin, a large, prestigious event that in 1998 recorded over 120,000 visitors.

9 It claims to inspect around 70 per cent of the organic food grown in the UK and its logo is perhaps the best known of all the organic trademarks. It claims that its organic standards are among the highest and that these laid the basis for the official UK organic standards regime when it was introduced in 1987.

10 For instance, the demand for organic food in the UK is calculated by the SA to be increasing at an annual rate of around 40 per cent (see Soil Association 2002).

References

Balfour, Lady Eve B. (1943), *The Living Soil and the Haughley Experiment*, London, Faber & Faber.

Beck, U. (2001), Ulrich Beck in interview with the editors (George Ritzer and Don Slater), *Journal of Consumer Culture*, 1, pp. 261–77.

Bell, D. and Valentine, G. (1997), *Consuming Geographies: We Are Where We Eat*, London, Routledge.

Best, S. and Kellner, D. (2001), 'Debord, cybersituations, and the interactive spectacle', *Illuminations Online*, available: www.uta.edu/huma/illuminations/best6.htm.

Blake, P. (1983), 'Letter', *Soil Association Quarterly Review* (winter), p. 24.

Boge, S. (2001), 'Insidious distance', in Petrini, C. and Watson, B. (eds), *Slow Food: Collected Thoughts on Taste, Tradition, and the Honest Pleasures of Food*, White River, VT, Chelsea Green Publishing.

Boym, C. (2001), 'My McDonald's'. *Gastronomica*, 1(1), pp. 6–8.

Browne, A., Harris, P., Hofny-Collins, A., Pasiecznik, N. and Wallace, R. (2000), 'Organic production and ethical trade: definition, practice and links', *Food Policy*, 25(1), pp. 69–89.

Callon, M., Meadel, C. and Rabeharisoa, V. (2002), 'The economy of qualities', *Economy & Society*, 31(2), pp. 194–217.

Capatti, A. (1999), 'The traces left by time', *Slow*, 17, pp. 4–6.

Carson, Rachel (1962), *Silent Spring*, Boston, MA, Houghton Mifflin.

Clarke, P. (1982), 'Letter', *Soil Association Quarterly Review* (winter), p. 22.

Clunies-Ross, T. and Cox, G. (1995), 'Challenging the productivist paradigm: organic farming and the politics of agricultural change', in Lowe, P., Marsden, T. and Whatmore, S. (eds), *Regulating Agriculture*, London, Fulton.

Crang, P. (1996), 'Displacement, consumption and identity', *Environment & Planning A*, 28(1), pp. 47–67.

European Fair Trade Association (1998), *Fair Trade Yearbook: Towards 2000*, EFTA, Druk in de Weer, Brussels.

European Fair Trade Association (2002), *EFTA Yearbook*, Maastricht, EFTA.

Fernandez-Armesto, F. (2001), *Food: A History*, London, Macmillan.

Fine, G. (1996), *Kitchens*, Berkeley, University of California Press.

FitzSimmons, M. and Goodman, D. (1998), 'Incorporating nature: environmental narratives and the reproduction of food', in Braun, B. and Castree, N. (eds), *Remaking Reality: Nature at the Millennium*, London, Routledge.

Goodman, D. (1999), 'Agro-food studies in the "age of ecology": nature, corporeality, bio-politics', *Sociologia Ruralis*, 39(1), pp. 17–38.

Goodman, D. and Watts, M. (eds) (1997), *Globalising Food*, London, Routledge.

Griffiths, S. and Wallace, J. (1998), *Consuming Passions: Food in the Age of Anxiety*, London, Mandolin.

Gronow, J. (1997), *The Sociology of Taste*, London, Routledge.

Gronow, J. and Warde, A. (2001), 'Epilogue: conventional consumption', in Gronow, J. and Warde, A. (eds), *Ordinary Consumption*, London, Routledge.

Halkier, B. (2001), 'Consuming ambivalences: consumer handling of environmentally related risks in food', *Journal of Consumer Culture*, 1(2), pp. 205–24.

Klein, N. (1999), *No Logo*, London, Flamingo.

Kroker, A., Kroker, M. and Cook, D. (eds) (1998), *Panic Encyclopedia: The Definitive Guide to the Postmodern Scene*, London, Macmillan.

Lash, S. (1998), *Another Modernity/A Different Rationality*, Oxford, Blackwell.

Love, J. (1995) *McDonald's: Behind the Arches*, New York, Bantam.

Matless, D. (1998), *Landscape and Englishness*, London, Reaktion.

Miele, M. (2001a), 'Changing passions for food in Europe', in Buller, H. and Hoggart, K. (eds), *Agricultural Transformation, Food and the Environment*, Basingstoke, Ashgate.

Miele, M. (2001b), *Creating Sustainability: The Social Construction of the Market for Organic Products*, The Netherlands, University of Wageningen, Circle for Rural European Studies.

Miele, M. and Murdoch, J. (2002a), 'The practical aesthetics of traditional cuisines: Slow Food in Tuscany', *Sociologia Ruralis*, 42(4), pp. 412–18.

Miele, M. and Murdoch, J. (2002b), 'Slow Food', in Ritzer, G. (ed.), *McDonaldization: The Reader*, Thousand Oaks, CA, Sage.

Miele, M. and Murdoch, J. (2003), 'Fast food/Slow Food: differentiating and standardising cultures of food', in Almas, R. and Lawrence, G. (eds), *Globalization, Localization and Sustainable Livelihoods*, Basingstoke, Ashgate.

Miller, D. (1995), 'Consumption as the vanguard as history', in Miller, D. (ed.), *Acknowledging Consumption: A Review of New Studies*, London, Routledge.

Montanari, M. (1994), *The Culture of Food*, Oxford, Blackwell.

Murdoch, J., Marsden, T. and Banks, J. (2000), 'Quality, nature and embeddedness: some theoretical considerations in the context of the food sector', *Economic Geography*, 76(2), pp. 107–25.

Murdoch, J. and Miele, M. (1999), '"Back to nature": changing worlds of production in the food system', *Sociologia Ruralis*, 39(3), pp. 465–84.

Nemeroff, C. and Davis, M. (2001), 'Puritanical proscriptions', in Petrini, C. and Watson, B. (eds), *Slow Food: Collected Thoughts on Taste, Tradition, and the Honest Pleasures of Food*, White River, VT, Chelsea Green Publishing.

Nygard, B. and Storstad, O. (1998), 'De-globalisation of food markets? Consumer perceptions of safe food: the case of Norway', *Sociologia Ruralis*, 38(1), pp. 35–53.

Parasecoli, F. (2001), 'Deconstructing soup: Ferran Adria's culinary challenges', *Gastronomica*, 1(1), pp. 60–73.

Petrini, C. (2001a), 'Preface', in Petrini, C. and Watson, B. (eds), *Slow Food: Collected Thoughts on Taste, Tradition, and the Honest Pleasures of Food*, White River, VT, Chelsea Green Publishing.

Petrini, C. (2001b), 'Building the Ark', in Petrini, C. and Watson, B. (eds), *Slow Food: Collected Thoughts on Taste, Tradition, and the Honest Pleasures of Food*, White River, VT, Chelsea Green Publishing.

Probyn, E. (2000), *Carnal Appetites*, London, Routledge.

Raynolds, L. (2000), 'Re-embedding global agriculture: the international organic and fair trade movements', *Agriculture & Human Values*, 17(3), pp. 297–309.

Raynolds, L. (2002), 'Consumer–producer links in fair trade coffee networks' *Sociologia Ruralis*, 42(4), pp. 404–24.

Raynolds, L. (2003), 'Forging new local/global links through fair trade agro-food networks', in Almas, R. and Lawrence, G. (eds), *Globalization, Localization and Sustainable Livelihoods*, Basingstoke, Ashgate.

Reed, M. (2000a), 'Governing and constructing the organic sector: the vital powers of the Soil Association', unpublished paper, University of the West of England.

Reed, M. (2000b), 'The uses of Zoonoses: how animal disease has been used by the Soil Association to advance organic agriculture in the UK', paper presented at the World Congress of Rural Sociology, Rio de Janeiro, July.

Renard, M. C. (2003), 'Fair trade: quality, market and conventions', *Journal of Rural Studies*, 19(1), pp. 87–96.

Resca, M. and Gianola, R. (1998), *McDonald's: Una Storia Italiana*, Varese, Italy, Baldini & Castoldi.

Rice, R. (2001), 'Noble goals and challenging terrain: organic and fair trade coffee movements in the global marketplace', *Journal of Agricultural & Environmental Ethics*, 14(1), pp. 39–66.

Ritzer, G. (1996), *The McDonaldisation of Society*, 2nd edn, London, Sage.

Ritzer, G. (2001), *Explorations in the Sociology of Consumption*, London, Sage.

Schlosser, E. (2001), *Fast Food Nation: The Dark Side of the All-American Meal*, New York, Houghton Mifflin.

Slater, D. (1997), *Consumer Culture and Modernity*, Cambridge, Polity.

Slow Food (2000), *The Ark of Taste and Presidia*, Bra, Italy, Slow Food Editore.

Smart, B. (1999), 'Resisting McDonaldisation: theory, process and critique', in Smart, B. (ed.), *Resisting McDonaldisation*, London, Sage.

Soil Association (1983), 'Eat organic', *Soil Association Quarterly Review* (winter), p. 2.

Soil Association (2001), *The Soil Association Response to the Curry Report*, Bristol, Soil Association.

Soil Association (2002), *Organic Food and Farming*, Bristol, Soil Association.

Spencer, C. (2002), *British Food: An Extraordinary Thousand Years of History*, London, Grub Street.

Welsch, W. (1996), 'Aestheticization processes: phenomena, distinctions, prospects', *Theory, Culture & Society*, 13, pp. 1–24.

Wilkinson, J. (1997), 'A new paradigm for economic analysis?' *Economy & Society*, 26(3), pp. 305–39.

Winter, M. (2003), 'Embeddedness, the new food economy, and defensive localism', *Journal of Rural Studies*, 19(1), pp. 23–32.

8

The political morality of food: discourses, contestation and alternative consumption

Roberta Sassatelli

Anthropology and sociology have been keen to show that consumption is a social and moral field, and that consumer practices are part of an ongoing process of negotiation of social classifications and hierarchies. Food consumption in particular has been associated with symbolically mediated notions of order (Douglas and Isherwood 1979). We know that particular foods are identified with annual festivities, set apart for specific categories of people, deployed to indicate indulgence or self-restraint, to declare one's own beliefs and to signify one's place in the community. While there may be no essential *national* food, food consumption has been implicated in the construction of national communities of taste (Douglas 1996; Bell and Valentine 1997). The private cooking routines of everyday life have contributed to the 'us and them' logic of community-building, setting local produce against far-away crops or the national against the foreign, and mapping these distinctions on the fundamental opposition between what is appropriate and what is corrupting. Food consumption has a long history of moral and political problematisation. The continual flow of gastronomic works which appeared across Europe from (at least) the nineteenth century, for example, responded to articulated political agendas, including the education of the public, the consolidation of senses of national identity and superiority, and even the marketing of national heritages.

Discourses surrounding the consumption of food, in particular, are doubly interesting. On the one hand, they are coextensive with practices that are, so to speak, necessary; in other words, they involve, in different ways, all social actors. On the other hand, and also because of its necessary character, food consumption is a contested moral field and one that is *discursively problematised* as such: it raises issues of fairness both within and without the human community, and is imbued with a set of crucial binaries such as immediate versus delayed gratification, nature versus culture, necessity versus luxury, body versus mind, etc. These ethical issues do not arise after the fact, as justifications; they are also part of the way food is consumed. They are, for example, used more or less implicitly in the qualification of food and food consumption in everyday life – witness the pressure parents routinely exercise on their children to finish what they have on their plate by recalling the sufferings of Third World children.

In this view, food consumption is an important, if often forgotten, aspect of a consideration of the political morality of contemporary consumer practices and culture. In more than one way food is indeed crucial to how we negotiate consumption as a specific and meaningful set of activities. This is both because of the position of food in all societies we know – the role it plays in the different forms of cohabitation, for example – and because of its special features in contemporary societies. Food consumption is now a very dynamic field, with changes and innovations which are, to some extent, jeopardising its workings as a taken-for-granted route to people's sense of identity and belonging (Warde 1997). In general terms, food consumption is both imbued with morality and constitutes a territory for the practical translation of moral and political visions. Indeed, when we look at the ways consumer culture is being criticised in contemporary society, we see that food consumption is one way in which people start to imagine a different world.

Moral criticism, moral rhetorics and reflexivity

When it comes to consumer culture, feminists and critical theorists alike have played largely similar tunes (Marcuse 1964; Galbraith 1969; Bell 1976; Ewen 1976; Bordo 1993). This might be aptly summarised by saying that consumer culture is the antithesis and the enemy of culture: within consumer culture

> individual choice and desire triumph over abiding social values and obligations; the whims of the present take precedence over the truth embodied in history, tradition and continuity; needs, values and goods are manufactured and calculated in relation to profit rather than arising from authentic individual or communal life. (Slater 1997: 63)

In recent times, such criticisms have been rendered through anti-globalisation rhetoric. George Ritzer's popular critique *The McDonaldization of Society* (1993), for example, considers consumer culture to have a dehumanising effect due to the rationalisation process which it embodies. McDonald's is taken as the paradigm case of a relatively new type of business which relies on the practical articulation of four principles:

- efficiency – an emphasis on saving time;
- calculability – an emphasis on quantification;
- predictability – an emphasis on replicability and standardisation;
- control – substitution of non-human for human technology.

The shopping mall, catalogue shopping, drive-through windows and fast-food restaurants appear as efficient means to a given end; and they entail a focus on quantity to the detriment of quality, relying on bureaucratic principles, standardisation and technological controls which should enable people to know what to expect at all times and in all places. The result is a world of consumption which 'offers no surprises' (Ritzer 1993: 99), a world which is monotonous and morally empty.

These views seem to inherit as well as adjust a well-established moral criticism (Horowitz 1985; Porter 1993), one which in the twentieth century has been most famously developed by the 'Frankfurt school', that considers all consumption as potentially dangerous and corrupting. While this very stance has been for some time a dominating force throughout the academy, the renewed interest in consumption studies of the 1980s may be understood, at least to a degree, as an attempt to *de-moralise* the academic reflection on consumption and to treat it as just another social practice (Douglas and Isherwood 1979; Miller 1987). Daniel Miller (2001: 226) well exemplifies this view in a recent article in which he laments that the

> discrepancy between the quantity and the quality of research is largely the result of the central role taken by morality within consumption research which has led to this branch of studies becoming largely a site where academics can demonstrate their stance towards the world, rather than a place were the world stands as a potential empirical critique of our assumptions about it.

He goes on to illustrate the poverty of a moral critique of consumption which forgets that human development may, and often does, go hand in hand with increases in material wealth. Such moral criticism typically holds a deeply ethnocentric (American) view, an ascetic and conservative vision of consumer culture, and the pessimistic, yet elitist, theory of consumer identity whereby the 'deluded, superficial persona who has become the mere mannequin to commodity culture is always someone other than ourselves' (Miller 2001: 229).

While Miller's observations are timely and important, we do have quite a lot to learn both from the rich symbolic structure which is embodied in contemporary material culture and from moral discourses from all quarters about consumption. Moral criticism of consumption is and should be an important object of study for those who want to understand consumer practices and culture. Indeed, in this chapter I contend that the study of the arguments and discourses deployed to criticise or otherwise qualify consumption is important to the political morality of consumption. When considering consumer practices as a moral field where social order is constantly produced, reproduced and modified, we should acknowledge discourses about consumption as an important part of that field. This obviously raises a number of theoretical and epistemological questions about the character and nature of *discourses,* issues requiring much more space than is allowed here. Still, it is useful to stress that a methodological attention to the discursive is compatible with a grounded, contextualised and, even, *materialistic* approach, if discourses are understood themselves as socially and institutionally located practices. In this view, discourses about consumption are best taken as a set of diverse practices which are assembled in specific contexts and reflect, more or less directly, the consumer practices they describe and/or the moral and social order they take for granted, promote or otherwise qualify. While considering consumers' experience as ordered and patterned, and material culture as a means by which to fix the categories of culture (Douglas and Isherwood 1979) or to objectify people's values (Miller 1987), the sociology and anthropology of consumption have not been keen to pursue the study of the discursive in this way. Still, in a culture like ours, where the discursive has grown and is entrenched in various and ever-more compelling ways, we need to make more space for its analysis.

Thus, rather than take at face value what Miller considers is today's task for consumption studies – the attempt 'to rescue the humanity of the consumer from being reduced to a rhetorical trope in the critique of capitalism' (Miller 2001: 234) – we should consider that this rhetoric is itself part of a grammar, or a discourse, which is articulated in the world of consumption in specific ways and contributes to changes in consumer practices themselves. Social moralisation – in the form of moral rhetorics which accompany the use and deployment of goods – is an important process both because those rhetorics contribute to the classification and qualification of the goods to which they refer and because they help to define visions of social and personal order. If moral criticism should be left to philosophers we, as social scientists, nevertheless can – indeed should – consider closely the ways in which consumer goods and practices are moralised.

To proceed in this direction and strike the right balance between a due consideration of the discursive and an oblivious parody of the semiotic fallacy, we need further examination of the discursive as a practice. This might be done by further exploring the suggestion that accounts are themselves a practice, reflexively linked to the practices they describe. In recent social theory we often hear about reflexivity in conjunction with the idea of reflexive selves. This adumbrates the idea that modern individuals are caught up in the necessity of managing the fragmentation and complexity of everyday life, and through this they become reflexive (i.e. calculating) risk managers who choose different identities and lifestyles (Giddens 1991; Beck 1992).

'Reflexivity', though, has another meaning when it is applied to explanations, very much in line with its use in the ethnomethodological tradition. Harold Garfinkel (1985: 55) famously argued for the 'reflexive' or 'embodied' character of accounts, emphasising that 'the procedures used by members to make accountable' actions and situations are 'identical' to the activities through which members produce and manage such situations. In other words, actions and accounts are mutually constitutive: accounts construe and support the reality of those situations on which they comment, while they themselves are reflexively linked – so far as their intelligibility is concerned – to the socially organised occasions of their use.

Within this framework discourses about consumption are important objects of study as they can tell us something about the practical ways in which people make sense of the world, qualify it and their own practices, and act accordingly. However, they should not be treated at face value as the symbolic manifestation of a commonsensical 'collective consciousness', as if they were one homogeneous, equivalent and straightforward source of analysis. Not all of the criticism aimed at ethnomethodology for its collaborative vision of the taken-for-granted and for the absence of a historical–institutional perspective is misguided. It is important both to give priority to the 'study of the methods through which we reach mutual understanding' (Garfinkel 1985: 84) and to consider how differently people from distinct institutional positions may act and, especially, how certain themes and evaluation criteria get entrenched and become hegemonic over time, that is, how power and history shape the conditions for mutual understanding. Discourses are different: they are pronounced by individuals (whose class, status, gender, etc., differ), in distinct contexts (more or less formal, institutional, etc.), and they are materialised in different ways (in manuals, magazines, etc.). Above all, discourses are visible in so far as they take a stand *for* or *against* something. They thus contribute through a continuing battle over how best to judge and justify something as worthwhile and right or as meaningless and corrupting.

In this view, moral discourses can be conceptualised as drawing on repertoires of evaluation, or 'orders of worth', which pre-date the individual and are available across situations even if they are realised, made salient and transformed by individuals in particular settings and circumstances (Boltanski and Thévenot 1991; see also Lamont and Thévenot 2000; and, for a critical discussion, Wilkinson 1997 and Wagner 2001). These repertoires become emphasised especially in moments or episodes of contestation that can up-end or overturn conventional and well-established discourses and frames of justification, by shifting to new forms of evaluation. Whether successful or not, contestation makes explicit what in normal circumstances is tacit and taken-for-granted.

Contestation may thus be seen as a multilevel phenomenon which involves distinct categorisation processes, of which some are identified as practical and others as discursive. In other words, leaving aside the important issue of their efficacy, these processes of categorisation can be more-or-less overt as well as more-or-less aware of their status as forms of protest. Like the reproduction of order, contestation happens first and foremost through a processes of routine categorisation. In everyday life distinctions are obviously made between types of consumer and consumer practice, and the notion that we are all consumers is as important as the notion that we all consume differently. The social regulation of consumption – with its levels of entrenchment ranging from implicit routines to institutionally enforced manners, highly formalised rules and the implementation of social policy – is based now, as it was in the past, on the classification of different goods, different spaces of consumption and different types of consumer. The literature on consumer practices is full of examples of the way in which consumers use goods to place moral weight onto their actions and relationships (see Bourdieu 1979; De Certeau 1984). Consumers as well as goods can be deemed normal or deviant, fair or unjust, innocent or corrupting, articulating hegemonic views of consumption, choice and selfhood to negotiate their practices (Sassatelli 2001).

Similar classifications may be implicitly or explicitly directed against contemporary consumer culture, people expressing through their choices the fear of materialism which is so clearly epitomised by critical theories about consumption. Home-making or the socialisation of children as consumers are clear examples of this: when organising their houses, people try to take some measure to counter the anti-social potential of their material culture (Wilk 1989), as much as parents, when allowing children to use money, deploy clues which, although varying according to parental style, clearly work as ways of moralising consumption (Carlson and Grossbart 1988). Miller himself indeed reckons that consumption is an important means by which ordinary people confront, day by day, their sense of being in a world that is often oppressive, to the point that 'far from expressing capitalism, consumption is most commonly used by people to negate it' (2001: 234). Thus, while not all academics today find it either important or appropriate to moralise about consumption, non-academics routinely engage in such moralising. Overall, people's moralistic insistence on consumption signifies that it can be singled out as a weapon with which to attack large dehumanising processes such as commodification, globalisation, bureaucratisation, etc. This might be because, paradoxically, other spheres of action are less open to criticism or simply appear as beyond individual reach.

Here, I wish to pursue and develop Miller's belief (1987) that it is through consumption that people recreate the identity as labourers they feel they have lost, and thus use mass goods to counter the homogenisation of capitalist production. New forms of consumption, such as ethical and critical consumption, the adoption of a frugal lifestyle or the preference for fair trade goods are cases in point. In general, the discourses which surround these practices are important indicators of the extent to which the terrain of consumption is contested. More to the point, these discourses allow for an examination of the problematising of consumption as an ingredient crucial to the (often unconscious) pursuit of one's own moral superiority. They tell us something of a world envisaged by diverse actors as fair and just as opposed to what they perceive to be dominant and commonplace.

Alternative consumption and public denunciation

My concern here is with the set of discourses surrounding what appears to be an important feature of food consumption in contemporary western societies, discourses that I collect beneath the banner of 'alternative consumption'. Alternative consumption may be taken to identify a bunch of heterogeneous practices and discourses, stretching across the developed world. These consumer practices and consumption discourses herald a critique of (some forms of) consumption and propose alternative lifestyles. Their supporters may be right in saying that we can take them as indicators of a quiet, slow cultural revolution which has to do with the fears about capitalist industrial methods of food production. Certainly, alternative food consumption is an important locus for conceptualising how certain materials are classified as good to eat, stressing that *goodness* is intimately associated with the attribution of a moral quality to food. This is so because the various alternative forms of food consumption and their discourses rarely deal with food alone: they rather place food practices in the context of broader issues and are implicated with notions such as justice, propriety, nature, health, etc., which work as codes for the practical justification of action.

The growth of self-professed *alternative* forms of consumption – as manifested in the rising demand for organic food across Europe and the USA or in the ever-growing variety of Fair Trade (FT) products available – is often taken as an example of what is widely portrayed as a bottom–up cultural revolution. Of course, alternative consumption cannot be considered as a purely demand-side phenomenon. The switch to green consumption, FT and sustainable production is, for example, supported also by Co-op retailers around the world – witness the strong statement released in 2000 by Aliza Gravitz, Co-op America's executive director or the recent ethical consumption campaign promoted in Italy by Co-op Italia. From this point of view, green consumption may appear as a marketing strategy for product diversification (or even niche marketing) by relatively disadvantaged business in the face of growing concentration.

Nevertheless, alternative consumption seems to involve a shift in the way food is classified as 'good to eat'. Alternative consumer practices and discourses often up-end conventional and well-established discourses of use and recommendation. For example, Ethical Consumer – a major association for ethical and responsible purchases in the UK – offers its constituency a magazine (of the same name) which professes to be a guide to 'progressive products', helping to avoid unethical companies and products, and providing a list of 'ethical best-buy' options (www.ethicalconsumer.org; Gabriel and Lang 1995). Best-buys are indeed defined through a variety of ethical criteria, i.e. criteria which go beyond the short-term instrumental interest of the individual consumer shopping around to embrace long-term effects on a range of third parties. They include the impact on the environment (through pollution, nuclear power), on animals (animal testing, factory farming), on humans (oppressive regimes, workers' rights, irresponsible marketing) and 'extras', which involve more than one party, such as the use of GMOs. The particularistic, self-interested and instrumental logic of classical comparative tests – witness the ' value for money' approach of successful magazines such as *Which?* in the UK or *Altroconsumo* in Italy – is lacking here, though it is exposed. Furthermore, issues most conventionally related to food quality, such as safety and taste, are marginal even in an *Ethical Consumer* special report that extensively discusses a particular food. In a report on bananas, for example, consumers are invited to buy organic produce and encourage FT.

The report highlights primarily the wages and working conditions of banana workers employed by the major multinational companies, and the banana varieties which produce high yields but are more susceptible to pests, thereby harming the workers and the ecosystem. Only at the very end of the report is there a passing reference to *taste*, when it is pointed out that that FT bananas are 'distinctively smaller and sweeter' (Atkinson 1999). Overall, *Ethical Consumer* seems to propose a particular vision of the notion of quality: good for eating is first and foremost good for public values, such as the environment or human rights. Apparently safety, health and taste, or refined aesthetic pleasure, are not primary concerns.

Similar discourses about quality and food are typically articulated by a number of publications dealing with ethical shopping. The set of discourses which surround ethical shopping have to do with one of the themes which has been expunged from conventional consumer defence, i.e. the redistribution of resources and the role therein of demand. The conditions of labour in general and child labour in particular, as well as the south–north divide are the main codes marshalled to frame this issue. A recent guide to ethical shopping, for example, construes its readership as comprised of 'consumers concerned about the working conditions under which the products they buy are produced in developing countries' (Young and Welford 2002: ix). Consumers are said to be 'raising consciousness' and 'becoming aware' of a new dimension of consumption: the production–consumption equation is not a natural one, is not, that is, a morally neutral mechanism which every consumer has to exploit, it is exposed as a political and ethical relation. As free trade and globalisation are said to have removed the protecting influence of the nation states and the local communities, it is only consumers themselves who are seen as having the potential – and the duty – to safeguard both fair distribution and the environment. Indeed, the realisation that what the western world consumes is 'subsidised by the poor' in the form of unsafe and underpaid labour, and the exploitation of natural resources means that consumers can and must pressurise retailers, producers and governments to change their practices and bring about an equitable world trading system.

Food quality as a health and safety issue is never directly addressed in similar guides. These guides are typically concerned with offering a set of ethical criteria for the evaluation of a host of producers. When at all present, the currently hegemonic call for a healthful lifestyle is integrated with or, better, subordinated to concerns for the health of the community, the planet and the human species. Thus we hear that 'in many parts of the world consumers eat so much that their health deteriorates, when at the same time millions of people in poor countries do not have enough to eat' (Young and Welford 2002: x). Similar discourses are articulated by a number of environmental organisations. In the Worldwatch Institute press release which accompanies the report *Vital Signs 2001* (2001), for example, we find that the all-you-can-eat economy is making the world sick. We're eating more meat, drinking more coffee, popping more pills, driving further and getting fatter . . . We're finding more and more evidence that the developed world's consumption-filled lifestyle choices are often as unhealthy for ourselves as for the planet we inhabit. (24 May 2001)

The underlying assumption here seems to be that healthful eating will be the natural result of a fairer, more sustainable, system of production and trade.

Conventional issues of health and safety are still relevant, though, as they offer alternative themes opportunities to reverberate in larger social circles by clinging on to widespread motives. The most important contestation episodes and narratives are indeed themselves often related, and they refer to episodes of breach of trust in the market brought about by health risks associated with industrial food production and globalisation. Eric Schlosser's best-selling *Fast Food Nation* (2002), a powerful attack against industrialised food production and servicing, points to both environmental and labour issues, and to threats to human health such as E.coli and BSE which are prompted by the minimisation of costs logic of the fast-food industry. The BSE crisis in particular has indeed been incorporated into the wider campaign against McDonald's. In Italy, for example, there was a 'Boycott Day' following the discovery of a case of BSE among cattle raised by McDonald's itself. To broaden its reach and penetrate new sections of the public, the campaign's organisers can therefore count on a most sensational theme. This is then articulated through the usual environmentalist arguments, such as that meat production entails an inefficient use of resources, as well as criticism of aggressive advertising, and fears of globalisation and homogenisation.

In recent times there have been a host of *ad hoc* consumer boycotts and campaigns which have helped consolidate the field of alternative consumption. Some campaigns, such as that against McDonald's, have placed the emphasis on safety and the environment. Others have concentrated on the conditions of labour, e.g. campaigns against Nike. Still others have stressed environmental and humanitarian issues, as did campaigns against Nestlé's distribution of artificial baby-milk in Africa or the wider movement against GMOs. The anti-McDonald's campaign and similar focused initiatives show that, besides entailing a sombre shift in everyday purchases, alternative consumption may be sponsored on special occasions that take the shape of specific campaigns or boycotts. These are best understood as episodes of contestation. Following Luc Boltanski and Laurent Thévenot (1991), we might focus on the production of agreement in a case of public denunciation, a route which may make more visible the taken-for-granted criteria marshalled for justification. From a social-theoretical point of view, these situations help us consider that individuals are constantly required to interpret their situations, with structure–culture being at the same time a resource for agency and the product of interaction. From a more empirical point of view, these are episodes where new and distinctive forms and rhetorics for the classification of food and consumption may get entrenched and obtain wider attention.

From 'fair trade' to community barter

It is not easy to draw an inclusive map of the issues which are comprised within the boundaries of alternative consumption. Many forms of alternative consumption share some kind of interest in environmental values (Goodman 1999; Murdoch and Miele 1999). For this reason Mary Douglas (1996) has branded them as instances of a 'movement of renunciation', or 'non-consumption', akin to that of early Christianity or of Ghandi, which puts public or collective goods before one's own individual desires or involves 'a rejection of the world as we know it'.

There are, however, some difficulties with this view. For one thing, it is difficult to consider all the instances of alternative consumption as comprising a cohesive movement, at least in the absence of a relatively abstract definition. This might be provided if we look at the minimum common denominator of the many voices that come together in a major event which aims specifically to critically address western consumer culture – the so-called 'Buying Nothing Day' (www.buyingnothingday.co.uk; see also www.adbusters.org). This is a day of public denunciation and protest in the form of boycotts and other events which is now celebrated in several European countries as well as the USA and Canada. People are invited to 'switch off' from shopping for one day and to consider that 'over-consumption' is 'the root of global disasters' such as climate change. What seems, at a first glance, an invitation to turn away from the excesses of consumption is indeed a melting-pot for the amalgam and distillation of many forms of alternative consumption. Environmental, humanitarian, ethical and political motives, for example, are all present in the discourses that accompany the Canadian web resources:

> the rich Western countries, only twenty per cent of the world population, are consuming eighty per cent of the earth's natural resources, causing a disproportionate level of environmental damage and unfair distribution of wealth. As consumers we need to question the products we buy and challenge the companies who produce them. (BND-UK press release, 23 November 2001)

Most of the themes deployed in the initiative are only superficially close to an ascetic rhetoric of renunciation. While there are attempts to expose 'shopaholicism' as a condition that is reaching epidemic proportions, it is very clear that it is not *shopping* in itself that is harmful, but rather that people typically shop without considering issues such as the environment and poverty in Third World countries.

Most of the themes articulated by the campaigners in this 'anti-consumerist' syndicate are related to food – from the negotiation of the notion of *necessity* with respect to the north–south divide, to environment and sustainable agriculture, to new patterns of consumption relying on self-production. The separation of consumption and production is exposed and various ways of re-embedding consumer practices in the local natural environment, in communal–social relationships and in the production process are advocated. Consumers are invited to take action by considering alternative combinations and recombinations of production and consumption. Contrary to the classical free-market rhetoric, only more integrated forms of economic life – localised and community based – can give consumers more control over their choices. This is mirrored by the idea that product labelling, as advocated by traditional consumerist campaigns, is not enough and that 'ethical consumers' ought to know the 'sustainability cost' of their choices – i.e. how much pollution has been created and how many non-renewable resources have been spent in the manufacture and the distribution of any given product. Here, consumer sovereignty is something other than consumer choice as predicated on the variables singled out by neo-classical economics and free-market ideologies alike (i.e. price and quantity). The logic of value-for-money does not hold when the target is both individual satisfaction and a set of public goods. Consumer sovereignty itself is predicated not on hedonistic premises but on responsibility. All in all, this may suggest that in many forms of alternative consumption there is – to varying degrees – an attempt to re-establish a direct relation to food (and goods in general). This attempt appears to be aimed at countering *risk* as the perception that one is no longer controlling one's material world, a perception which accompanies the growth of material culture and the separation between the spheres of production and consumption (Sassatelli and Scott 2001).

While we may consider that the boundaries of alternative food consumption themselves are defined by the tension involved in establishing a different relation to food, and even when a variety of alternative consumption issues come together in an overtly *anti-consumerist* initiative like the 'Buying Nothing Day', it is still possible to identify distinct and, at times, contrasting issues. As I have suggested, not all of the alternative forms of consumption are characterised by environmental concerns in the same way – nor only by those concerns. Each form of alternative consumption is, furthermore, internally complex. Work on vegetarianism (e.g. Twigg 1983; Beardsworth and Keil 1992), green consumption (James 1993) alternative green consumption (Belasco 1993) and organic food (Miele and Pinducciu 2001), for example, indicates that distinct themes and issues typically contribute to each specific form of alternative consumption and that they are far from being internally coherent. For example, the demand for organically grown vegetables comes from diverse sources, from a large vegetarian movement as well as health-conscious *and* gourmand carnivores; meanwhile practices and issues may be synergistic or not – just as green consumers may or may not sympathise with the redistributive concerns which inspire FT initiatives. Such contradictions might be acknowledged, yet they are not tackled easily by activists themselves. For example, *Enough!*, a magazine published by the Centre for a New American Dream (www.newdream.org) which campaigns for a more healthful and sustainable lifestyle, celebrates the rise of organic food consumption and the fact that major multinationals are getting into organic business, while recognising that organic food is still too expensive for many consumers.

While it is important to acknowledge their variability and internal complexity, precisely because different instances of alternative consumption are strongly linked – sometimes in contradictory ways – it remains important to consider them together as a specific domain. To that end, and in order to draw an inclusive space while considering its internal complexity, it is useful to portray some of the main characteristics of the most significant forms of alternative consumption. In fact, alternative consumption practices vary according to their overt *target* – the consumer herself or himself, the community or nature – and their declared *scope* – challenging contemporary capitalism, or offering an expressive investment, or, finally, providing alternative forms of integration in contemporary capitalist culture.

Working in this typological fashion allows a map of the domain of alternative consumption (figure 8.1) to be drawn that helps to identify its diversity. Initiatives such as community bartering are meant to subvert the functioning of the capitalist economy and can thus be contrasted with frugal consumption movements which push for a rearrangement of individual consumption–production practices in order that the individual may adjust to adverse capitalist conditions. More precisely, community bartering is an oppositional, expressive and community-centred phenomena – the most famous instance of which is Ithaca Hour, a system for the local exchange of goods and labour based on barter. Frugal consumption is characterised mainly as a non-subversive, instrumental and self-centred way of consuming, concerned with ways of saving money on basic or frivolous consumption so as to invest in meaningful, durable goods. Vegetarianism, when it is not merely a personal health choice, is an expressive phenomenon which addresses the boundaries of the edible, negotiating a different relation with nature whereby the human and the animal are reallocated. While organic production may be considered to negotiate food quality in relation to a renewed relation to land, sustainability and traditional farming, the FT initiatives negotiate food consumption with reference to a renewed attention to local communities and a clear opposition to globalisation and economic concentration.

While still partial, this map helps to qualify some of Douglas's remarks on green consumption. Discussing environmentalism, risk and blame allocation Douglas (1996: 161) wrote that 'though there is a movement of renunciation,

	Self	Nature	Community
Subversive			Community bartering
		Fair trade	
Expressive	Organics, vegetarianism		
Integrated	Frugal consumption		

Figure 8.1 The domain of alternative consumption

the main criticism is not against the consumer, but against authority'. Yet, if we look at the discourses which are produced in the context of the forms of alternative consumption illustrated above, only those instances of consumption which are strictly self-oriented might be said to fulfil this specification. Mainly, it does not appear that what Douglas considered typical of alternative consumption in early 1990 holds in the same way today: blame is not just externalised – placed on companies and authorities – but is internalised – placed on the individual as a consumer.

The emphasis on the consumer as a political and moral actor is probably the main shift to have happened in the last decade, shaping the contemporary landscape of alternative consumption. Historically, we may trace this shift to the coming together of traditional consumerist issues (relying on possessive individuality as much as the market ideology which is confronted) and environmental issues (which shift attention to the communal dimension of consumption, emphasising public as against private satisfaction; see Sassatelli 2003). Their synergy is probably to be related to how globalisation has been perceived. Globalisation is often perceived to be fuelling an explosion of consumerism that poses serious threats to the natural world. In this context, as *Enough* points out, it appears 'absolutely vital' that 'products and commodities be produced and harvested differently – with a long-term focus on resource conservation, labour and community impacts, and limiting waste production' (Taylor 2000: 11).

In general terms, we may say that the consumer is thus considered both increasingly 'active' and increasingly 'public'. As a consequence, the dominant attitude is not that of renunciation of consumption, but rather that of a re-evaluation of what it is to consume. *Oneworld*, a US based organisation, brings together a wide number of associations, NGOs and foundations which describe themselves as working for social justice, and deals with, among other things, ethical consumption. It accepts the fact of consumption while scrutinising how it is carried out in western countries.

> Almost any consumption – we find it in the self-presentation of *Oneworld* – uses up resources. But since one can't live without some consumption . . . how could I live just as satisfyingly with less? People are increasingly experimenting with living simply but more fulfillingly. (www.oneworld.net)

Oneworld thus promotes 'elegant sufficiency', which, we discover, is a mixture of environmentalism (e.g. opting for sustainable wood furniture instead of mahogany) and detachment from mass-fashion. Its emphasis is on *choice* as a political and ethical process – indeed, that it is only as such that we can speak of choice. We are invited to consider that 'to buy is to vote' and that 'we vote "Yes" with every purchase we make – a pound of bananas, a tank of diesel fuel – and we vote "No"' with every purchase we turn down, forcing the companies to diversify into products we prefer'.

These themes can be further explored by looking at *Ethical Consumer*, the UK-based consumer organisation which proclaims itself as the only truly 'alternative' one. This organisation considers that individuals are helpless only if they decide to be so: through their consumption they can encourage 'sustainable businesses' that do not exploit or pollute. Ethical consumerism is thus said to offer a 'powerful additional tool' to traditional political action (i.e. joining a party or supporting campaign groups) that is considered on utilitarian grounds to be 'both practical and accessible'. As an alternative consumer association *Ethical Consumer* insists on 'convenience' as a plus of ethical buying:

> after all, everyone needs to go shopping or to consume resources in one way or another. As an ethical consumer every time you buy something you can make a difference . . . send[ing] support directly to progressive companies working to improve the status quo, while at the same time depriving others that abuse for profit. (www.ethicalconsumer.org)

The core of ethical consumerism is thus practical, ordinary and mundane: we are urged to check our own daily purchases: 'buy things that are made ethically by companies that act ethically', i.e. 'without harm to or exploitation of humans, animals or the environment'. This can be achieved through a combination of different types of action, from positive buying (favouring ethical products, be they FT, organic or cruelty-free goods), to negative purchasing (avoiding products you disapprove such as battery eggs or cars with polluting fuel systems), to company-based purchasing which targets one business as a whole (e.g. the boycott against Nestlé). Consumer choices become *actions* in the strong sense, i.e. those capable of making a difference – consequential actions. Choice as expressive of power, and therefore of *duty*, is also a key theme in discourses surrounding other forms of alternative consumption, including fair trade initiatives: we can 'make a difference with every cup' of coffee, says a well-known book on FT coffee (Waridel 2002). It might be too early to say whether this prefigures a shift in the notion of choice itself. Yet, it accents choice as a public, other-related and therefore moral action, rather than a self-interested, private and therefore amoral affair.

Conclusion

This chapter has developed the idea that consumption is a moral field and that we must study its political morality as an ongoing process of negotiation of the social order. Moral discourses surrounding consumer practices are crucial to that process and should be studied as an important indicator of what it is to consume. Different moral rhetorics and orders of justification become visible and are stressed especially in moments or episodes of contestation. These episodes often overturn conventional and well-established discourses of quality, use and recommendation. Contestation itself is related to a breach of trust in the market, the effects of which will vary along with specific political, cultural and organisational features. This general framework has here been applied to the specific field of food consumption.

Looking at discourses surrounding different forms of alternative food consumption, from FT to organic produce, from vegetarianism and frugal consumption to community bartering, one could say that they vary as to their target – be it the individual consumer, the community or our relation to the natural – and their scope – subversive, expressive or integrative. While acknowledging the differences within these forms of alternative food consumption, this analysis has offered an initial map indicating how diverse moral qualities are attributed to food. Food quality is both shaped by technological processes and continually negotiated via the (contested) attribution of moral value. While the scope of alternative consumption is still to be ascertained, the discourses which surround it indicate a shift in the definition and evaluation of consumer choice. Individual choice is charged with political power and appears to be defined less in terms of *rights* than of *duties*.

References

Atkinson, J. (1999), 'Banana drama', *Ethical Consumer* (October), available: www.ethicalconsumer.org).

Beardsworth, A. and Keil, T. (1992), 'The vegetarian option: varieties, conversions, motives and careers', *Sociological Review*, 40(2), pp. 253–93.

Beck, Ulrich. (1992), *Risk Society: Towards a New Modernity*, London, Sage.

Belasco, W. (1993), *Appetite for Change*, Ithaca, NY, Cornell University Press.

Bell, D. (1976), *The Cultural Contradictions of Capitalism*, Heinemann, London.

Bell, D. and Valentine, G. (1997), *Consuming Geographies*, London, Routledge.

Boltanski, L. and Thévenot, L. (1991), *De la Justification*, Paris, Minuit.

Bordo, S. (1993) *Unbearable Weight: Feminism, Western Culture and the Body*, Berkeley, University of California Press.

Bourdieu, P. (1979), *La Distinction: Critique Sociale du Jugement*, Paris, Minuit.

Carlson, L. and Grossbart, S. (1988) 'Parental style and consumer socialization', *Journal of Consumer Research*, 15, pp. 77–94.

De Certeau, M. (1984), *The Practice of Everyday Life*, Berkeley, University of California Press.

Douglas, M. (1996), *Thought Styles*, London, Sage.

Douglas M. and Isherwood, B. (1979), *The World of Goods: Towards an Anthropology of Consumption*, New York, Basic Books.

Ewen, S. (1976), *Captain of Consciousness: Advertising and the Social Root of Consumer Culture*, New York, McGraw-Hill.

Ewen, S. (1988), *All Consuming Images: The Politics of Style in Contemporary Culture*, New York, Basic Books.

Gabriel, Yiannis and Lang, Tim (1995), *The Unmanageable Consumer: Contemporary Consumption and its Fragmentation*, London, Sage.

Galbraith, J. K. (1969 [1958]), *The Affluent Society*, 2nd edn, London, André Deutsch.

Garfinkel, H. (1985 [1967]), *Studies in Ethnomethodology*, Cambridge, Polity.

Giddens, A. (1991), *Modernity and Self-Identity*, Cambridge, Polity.

Goodman, D. (1999), 'Agro-food studies in the "age of ecology": nature, corporeality, bio-politics', *Sociologia Ruralis*, 39(1), pp. 17–38.

Horowitz, D. (1985), *The Morality of Spending: Attitudes toward the Consumer Society in America, 1875–1940*, Baltimore, MD, Johns Hopkins University Press.

James, A. (1993), 'Eating green(s): discourses of organic food', in K. Milton (ed.), *Environmentalism*, London, Routledge.

Lamont, M. and Thévenot, L. (eds) (2000), *Rethinking Comparative Cultural Sociology*, Cambridge, Cambridge University Press.

Marcuse, H. (1964), *One-Dimensional Man*, Boston, MA, Beacon Press.

Miele, M. and Pinducciu, D. (2001), 'A market for nature: linking the production and consumption of organics in Tuscany', *Journal of Environmental Policy & Planning*, 3(2), pp. 149–62.

Miller, D. (1987), *Material Culture and Mass Consumption*, Oxford, Basil Blackwell.

Miller, D. (2001), 'The poverty of morality', *Journal of Consumer Culture*, 1(2), pp. 225–44.

Murdoch, J. and Miele, M. (1999), '"Back to nature": changing "worlds of production" in the food sector', *Sociologia Ruralis*, 39(4), pp. 465–83.

Ritzer, G. (1993), *The McDonaldization of Society*, Newbury Park, CA, Pine Forge Press.

Sassatelli, R. (2001) 'Tamed hedonism: choice, desires and deviant pleasures', in Warde, A. and Gronow, J. (eds), *Ordinary Consumption*, London, Routledge.

Sassatelli, R. (2003), 'La politicizzazione del consumo e l'evoluzione del movimento dei consumatori', in Capuzzo, P. (ed.), *Genere, Generazione e Consumi*, Rome, Carrocci.

Sassatelli, R. and Scott, A. (2001), 'Trust regimes, wider markets, novel foods', *European Societies*, 3(2), pp. 211–42.

Schlosser, E. (2002), *Fast Food Nation*, London, Penguin.

Slater, D. (1997), *Consumer Culture and Modernity*, Cambridge, Polity Press.

Taylor, B. (2000), 'Buy different: building consumer demand for sustainable goods', *Enough!*, 12 (summer), available: www.newdream.org/newsletter/buydifferent.pdf, pp. 1–2, 11.

Twigg, J. (1983), 'Vegetarianism and the meaning of meat', in Murcott, A. (ed.), *The Sociology of Food and Eating*, Aldershot, Gower.

Wagner, Peter (2001), *A History and Theory of the Social Sciences*, London, Sage.

Warde, A. (1997), *Consumption, Food and Taste*, London, Sage.

Waridel, L. (2002), *Coffee with Pleasure: Just Java and World Trade*, London, Black Rose Books.

Wilk, R. (1989), 'Houses as consumer goods', in Rutz, H. and Orlove, B. (eds), *The Social Economy of Consumption*, Lanham, MD, University Press of America.

Wilkinson, J. (1997), 'A new paradigm for economic analysis?', *Economy & Society*, 26(3), pp. 305–39.

Worldwatch Institute (2001), *Vital Signs 2001*, Washington, DC, Worldwatch Institute.

Young, W. and Welford, R. (2002), *Ethical Shopping*, London, Fusion Press.

Conclusion: quality and processes of qualification

Mark Harvey, Andrew McMeekin and Alan Warde

A book about quality is inevitably about controversy over standards, and the foregoing chapters display a set of diverse and detailed observations and analyses of what it is to make a claim that something is of *better* quality than something else. This has been a central issue of wider social scientific and cultural discussion for a couple of decades, a result of the development of postmodernist thought. Who shall decide what is good, and how might such goodness be established in a non-arbitrary and non-self-interested way? Claims to quality, like claims to value or good taste, become highly problematical in the face of such questions. Several of the chapters contribute very useful clarifications of some of the issues involved, particularly because they are addressing substantive items in the social realm rather than dealing with them at a purely abstract epistemic level.

Between them, the authors make a very sound case for the existence of many relevant qualities, or different dimensions of 'quality', reminding anyone who would want to use the term that it is not a unified one-dimensional concept. Nor is it one that can easily be defined and delimited. Genevieve Teil and Antoine Hennion are perhaps the most radical in their insistence that, as regards quality in food, several criteria pertain, none of which has priority. They observe that academic disciplines, which have themselves in the past taken on the role of arbiters of quality, tend to view the matter narrowly in the light of the presuppositions of their own specialisms and theoretical preoccupations. Yet, when looked at from even a short distance beyond the boundaries of sociology or sensory physiology, it becomes very difficult not to agree that there are multiple criteria, none of which can be dismissed as irrelevant. As these authors demonstrate (p. 25), quality cannot be considered to be inherent to the product; nor is it simply a matter of some conventional agreement. It is not independent of context, and it cannot be separated from some sense of processing through the individual heart and body: 'Different people in different situations bring into play a collective knowledge, of which taste is a result. In other words, taste is a way of building relationships, with things and with people; it is not simply a property of goods, nor is it a competence of people.'

This view of quality as a multidimensional concept is further strengthened by considering the variety of different attributes considered in this book. Quality is variously understood as being constituted by religious, moral and aesthetic dimensions, and the several chapters that focus on provenance as an attribute draw attention to geographical, organisational and institutional factors. A book aimed at providing an exhaustive review of different quality attributes could also have included contributions from sensory studies, biology, toxicology, psychology and others.

Thus we are forced to question the idea of a privileged observer role for social scientists, or any other disciplinary specialist, and allow the possibility that 'amateurs', or enthusiasts, have a better (because quasi-interdisciplinary) appreciation of the several grounds on which judgements might be founded. What Teil and Hennion then advocate methodologically is the observation and analysis in detail of the ways in which, in practical everyday contexts, people go about making judgements. They emphasise the process of determining quality – *how* quality is established – as indeed, in different ways, do all our authors. If there is one lesson to be learned here it is that determining quality is a *social process*.

In a variety of ways, emanating from the distinct methodological approaches taken, all of the authors share the view that quality comes to be attributed in the process of qualification. There is a describable social process whereby products come to be understood to have particular properties which are valued or, equally, come to be despised. It is not the products in themselves, nor is it simply the social characteristics of the persons pronouncing judgement, that determine how an item is evaluated. Rather there is a complex of social and economic processes, and a set of competing discourses, out of which emerges an (always contestable and therefore always provisional) approximate consensus about value. Approaches differ markedly between, say, amateur tasting, social worlds, and SFSCs, but it is commonly accepted that quality is the outcome of processes of qualification. All treat quality as something made, not given; and all turn their analyses to different understandings of ways of *quality*-making, for which we have adopted (from Allaire) *qualification* as the general term.

The authors identify mechanisms occurring at different stages in the process of establishing a claim to quality. It is not just, as Roos observed during the CRIC international workshop, that different conceptions of quality pertain in different parts of the food chain. Rather, in addition, the modes of activity involved operate in accordance with different logics. Thus Gronow describes the internal operation of social worlds, Murdoch and Miele call on the logic of social movements to understand the phenomenon of Slow Food, while Teil and Hennion emphasise the role of reflexivity as integral to the appreciation of things. The extent to which these are complementary rather than competing ways of understanding the process we lay to one side for the moment. What all of the authors show, however, is that the process is far less a matter of personal opinion than it is a collective determination of quality. Individual judgement is developed in ongoing interaction and dialogue with other people who suggest and confirm personal views. That a judgement is collective, however, does not mean that it is indisputable. Indeed, establishing value is accomplished through controversies which, though often conducted in an entirely friendly and cooperative manner, are not therefore without profound impact on commercial competition or consequence for social distinction.

None of this answers the question of what kinds of actors are most able to make their claims about quality stick. Who has the authority to pass judgement, and of what kind is that authority? These were fundamental issues posed by postmodern thought; does anyone, and should anyone, have that authority? There are several responses presented here. Murdoch and Miele identify new forms of expertise emerging from social movements, challenging old authorities in the name of consumers. Teil and Hennion argue for the superior value of claims made by amateurs, or lay-persons, as against those of experts. For them, the amateur is the only true expert. The judgements of *practitioners*, engaged in their everyday activities, are the only properly grounded ones. Practitioners, thus, have much to teach theorists. But not all of the contributors are satisfied with this. Gronow, in searching for an objective element to aesthetics, is clearly looking for some condition beyond individuals within particular social circles achieving consensus. Conventional standards have foundations other than current local opinion.

The chapters of this book illustrate some of the ways in which the duty of interpretation may be conducted, suggesting a number of different ways to handle the quandaries of judgement. They do not suggest any single solution to the perennial problem of validating judgements of taste or quality. But they provide a set of investigative techniques, or methodological protocols, for addressing that most intriguing of social science questions: how do people come to think that some things are better than others – in this case, that some foods are of finer quality than others. As Teil and Hennion indicate, it is very hard to imagine that either the intrinsic attributes of the product or the authority of some judge is a sufficient basis for a sound answer. They, like most of the book's authors, proceed instead to examine how judgements actually are formed in practical contexts. They try to answer the question: what are the processes that make possible the framing of a recommendation which ensues from the qualities of an item?

The methodological protocols are varied. Several authors make use of conventions theory, which is particularly useful because it focuses attention on the conduct of potential and actual controversies which occur when actors insist on comparing incommensurable qualities. The central idea that in the course of arguments disputants shift the grounds of debate between different 'orders of worth' – between, for example, aesthetic, economic and ethical registers – captures some of the dynamics of the process whereby claims to quality are advanced and interrogated.

Ultimately, this approach views quality as entirely contingent, specific to time and space. For others, this is to ignore questions of who has greatest capability to make themselves heard and who is the greatest authority to determine outcomes. That implies taking wider cognisance of the power relations between key actors in the field, examining the priorities of each and seeing whether those priorities are imposed on others. Institutional approaches to processes of regulation, as exemplified by Barling in chapter 5, offer a way in which to evaluate claims to quality. A third approach concentrates on describing the processes by which particular judgements are made, in concrete circumstances, leaving largely in abeyance the question of whether some are inherently more worthy – or, indeed, practically more persuasive – than others. Accounts like those of Teil and Hennion and Murdoch and Miele represent quality as an *outcome* of a process of continual negotiation, fluid and unstable, a matter constantly subject to revision according to circumstances. Gronow also accepts that judgements are constantly subject to challenge and alteration, but is more concerned to analyse the general preconditions which operate to establish consensus among groups of practitioners or members of social worlds. Outcomes are, then, not so unpredictable, the range of plausible judgments not so wide, the degree of individual discretion not so great. Even in aesthetic matters, the organisation of social worlds ensures at least some quasi-objective standards whereby judgements must be made. A final investigative framework might be described as one based on 'thick description' of social processes which lead to the common acceptance of that complex *mélange* of definitive intrinsic attributes and relevant positive valuations which comprise elements sufficient to ascribe satisfactory quality to product, as with halal meat in Bergeaud-Blackler's account.

Taken together, these do not yet suggest a single coherent solution, but they surely preclude simple acceptance of the orthodox view that the problem of European food is guaranteeing its safety, thereby reestablishing consumer trust, and reject the idea that there is some common single metric or analytic process of judgement (or set of criteria) with which to establish that some food is quality food.

It is reassuring that our contributors do not simply equate quality with safety, or attribute uncertainties and worries to perceptions of risk and problems of information. It is indeed unfortunate that so much of the analysis of contemporary food controversies has been filtered through the lens of the 'risk society' thesis. While there is something compelling about the claim that our current anxieties revolve around invisible dangers created by modern science – BSE and fears about GMOs are prototypical examples – the thesis has numerous flaws. Questions arising from the shifting significance of 'Bordeaux', 'fair trade' or 'religious' quality, or the aesthetics of tasting are just some of the quality issues that escape reduction to a risk analysis of quality and its crises. The limitations of risk reductionism are revealed by viewing the controversy over quality within *alternative* conceptual frameworks, as has been done in this book. Here the single overarching description of the problem as inestimable risk is replaced by framings which capture the complexity of the processes by which judgements come to be made.

All of our contributors agree that the processes leading to claims to quality are to an extent a rhetorical manoeuvre. Actors seek to attach to their products, their practices and their preferences the 'quality' tag. Often this is a means of emphasising a particular attribute which is in the interests, or is a main concern, of those who enunciate the claim. Products have, for instance, many distinct qualities that appeal differentially to potential customers. Familiarity, innovativeness, renown, consistency, technical virtuosity, religious acceptability and ethical legitimacy – all are qualities that in certain circumstances will recommend a product to a purchaser. No wonder that those engaged in commercial competition operate, in part, by emphasising some qualities rather than others, and by talking up those qualities – for instance, through advertising – which are calculated to have greatest effect. Promotion, as the culturally savvy populations familiar with mass media codes know very well, is an exercise in rhetoric, and audiences are suitably sceptical in their reception of such messages. But no author in this book is entirely happy with the view that we should understand quality as simply and solely victory in a rhetorical context, notwithstanding that effective rhetorical promotion is consequential. Quality cannot be reduced to, or rather the analysis of quality cannot be abandoned by, presuming that the most effective rhetorical performances determine the outcomes of contests over judgements. That would imply, for one thing, that the distribution of resources and power had no effect in establishing conventions of judgement.

Quality is contextual and, in important senses, fluid. The claim to quality needs to be made continually, and it is clear that claims accepted in some quarters will be rejected in others. The sense in which there is continual dialogue, competition and controversy is one clear lesson. The social procedures by means of which people come to make judgements, and make them stick, are very complex, and we still have no satisfactory answer as to what makes some qualities adhere to particular products. Convention theory has no answer – it is contingent, and there is probably insufficient consideration of the operation of power in the process of qualification. The social worlds account probably attributes little power to consumers either, but does identify the role of enthusiasts and their supporters in shaping understandings and evaluations. There is here an identification of agents and some explanation of how influence operates to establish value, even if only temporarily. Such enthusiasm might be seen as a related aspect of contemporary commercial consumer culture. Teil and Hennion see the process as equally contingent and in some ways highly temporary and transitory, though again they stress the importance of engagement and a certain type of reflexivity in establishing standards. For them, standards are informally established, never able to be subjected to formalised and authorised guarantee.

The nature of the relationship between power and opinion is not simple. Sociologists have always recognised that the content of much communication is influenced by the interests of the actors delivering a message, and that those with most power are likely to be persuasive. Power and truth are often at odds with one another. But it is often difficult to prove who has power, and there is no simple causal link between power and consensus. Moreover, there are important asymmetries of power between retailers, manufacturers and farmers, and between consumers and each of the former. Indeed, Marsden argues that quality is inherently contested in power conflicts between these different actors endowed with different forms of power. The question of the dominance, or hegemony, of a particular 'logic of quality' becomes a historical and comparative matter – one of 'when and in what circumstances?'.

One might argue that there are now rather more agencies involved in the process of qualification than in the past. More departments of state take an interest in the various attributes of food system – nutrition, safety, economic competitiveness, national interest. The EC presents an additional level of regulatory activity: new agencies, like the FSA in the UK, have come into being, taxed with an impartial advisory role and speaking especially as the voice of consumers who are now supposed to be consulted through organisational channels and not merely through the offerings of the market. Then there are the market actors themselves which, in the UK especially the supermarkets, exercise both industrial strength and officially devolved regulatory powers. All these actors tend to bring with them their own preferred criteria for judging quality. Their competing concerns provoke aggravation. The scope for controversy expands.

As Marsden points out 'quality reallocates power and constructs consumer interests'. The effect of successful ascriptions of quality alters the relations between the actors. In this book we have directed comparatively little attention up-stream. Marsden is an exception, in that he explores how quality is associated among producers in Wales with expensive local niche produce. Academics sometime succumb to the same temptation to consider quality as that which is not mass produced, to forget that consistency and low cost are attributes which appeal positively to a large section of the population. But in terms of producers appealing to niche markets – a practice which can only increase within Europe as barriers to international trade are soon to be further dismantled – quality is associated with the local, the knowable, the specialised and the exclusive. Allaire discussed the process of producers and states protecting markets by getting products linked to place or *terroir*, through the use of various labels of product origins, as a means both of establishing distinction, authenticity and perfection and of obtaining commercial advantage. One way that such advantage can be achieved is through emphasising the scarcity attribute. A food product containing rare ingredients, such as caviar or truffle, would often be perceived as of higher quality than one based on more widely available ingredients. The former will usually be able to command a higher price than the latter. But firms and governments can create scarcity by controlling the availability of products and by instituting place-of-origin quality labels, as Allaire explains.

Marsden points out that regulation in the field of food – increasingly a hybrid function of public and private governance – is a lens through which one can estimate inequalities of power as one traces the procedures through which relations between actors are channelled. The exploration of the adding of value along the chain is a similar means of inference in understanding the relative power of actors in the market stages of the food system. In addition, many of the grounds for recognising some foods as of high quality are precisely a consequence of their formal recognition and regulation, through systems like Appelation Contrôllé, DOC, not to mention claims made by marketing organisations, for Scottish beef for instance. By such regulations states are able to continue to protect small and diverse producer organisations in the face of economic globalisation. The scant attention paid in the book to the up-stream stages in establishing quality is intentional: our primary focus of attention are comparatively neglected aspects of consumption, a realm where quality arises as contentious in a particularly illuminating way.

To inquire into quality requires that attention is paid also to ethics and aesthetics. Aesthetics has eclipsed ethics. New concerns associated with the aestheticising of culture add a further dimension. Though not an issue for states and not a subject of regulation, the spread of gourmet considerations has added another dimension to judgement. For some people, and arguably for some countries, 'quality' refers less to properties of safety, which could be regulated, than to some intrinsic attributes of pleasure to be derived from eating. Having sufficient food is no longer a major consideration for much of the population of Europe, but aesthetic criteria are strongly present – manifested in the creation of gourmet-club cultures, national culinary identity, regional authenticity, etc. In terms of conventions theory, which is used very effectively, if mostly in passing, by several of our authors, industrial and market orders of worth are not central to much of the public and media discussion of food, whereas attention is paid more to other orders of worth – renown (including brands and DOC), civics (in ethical food) and domestic (familiarity and local proximity). Probably this is a feature of a middle-class protest voice. We do not much doubt that science, large corporate producers and multiple retailers have sufficient power to defeat and/or incorporate such opposition. There is nevertheless vocal opposition, couched partly in ethical, partly in aesthetic, terms – from social movements to lifestyle consultants – which is playing a full part in controversy over food and challenging powerful vested interests.

Perhaps aesthetic considerations are just insignificant play at the edges of the dominant understanding of quality and price pedalled by hegemonic economics? There are many who would say that price remains the principal concern of the majority of consumers, and there is much in the commercial world that would suggest price consciousness is paramount. One could see this historical conjuncture as an achievement – security of supply, lack of contaminants and alleviation of monotony would have been more important than quality in the past. But, equally, the USA, as the largest (in all senses) food nation in the world, might be seen to currently face a quantity rather than quality crisis. Kraft, one of the biggest global food producers, is now engaged in a new moral rhetoric of moderation. The message is not even the Leninist one of better less but better, but simply better less of the same.

In terms of conceptual advance, perhaps the most promising substantive conceptual notion contained in this collection is that of processes of 'qualification'. We do not yet have enough of the axioms and principles which would constitute a synthetic theory of the processes of 'qualification', but several ideas have been thematised which might contribute to moving that intellectual process forward. Equally engaging has been the range of views concerning judgement of quality (and how that relates to the processes of qualification). Less consolidation, more fuel for further debate, this most persistent of social science issues, the basis on which hierarchies of judgement are established, is revealed to be highly contested, even *within* the social sciences: quality as highly contingent or quality as objective attribute.

Broadening the food quality question

The book has collected together a number of contrasting approaches to quality of food. In adopting particular theoretical and methodological standpoints, of course, some avenues are opened up, while others are passed by. In this final section, we reflect on some major considerations about quality of food that might constitute significant and unexplored avenues. There are four main avenues, and they are broad: biology and ecology; history and cuisine; cooking and eating; innovation and competition. They join at a roundabout, around which circulate questions concerning the specificity of quality of food. Are the registers to quality in food different from those to quality in music, architecture, clothing and visual arts? And if so, why? For example, are there similar or different articulations between the outcomes of high gastronomic art and junk food, as there are between classical music and muzak? Why is there no comparable succession of quality style to food as renaissance, baroque, classical, etc, although there is nouvelle cuisine, a question concerning differences in historical constructions of quality? Can there be an equivalent in food quality to the revolutions in music arising from the well-tempered scale or from atonality, or the transforming potentiality of concrete in architecture? Has there been a growth of fashion in food quality, similar to that in clothing, where the periodicity of changing fashion is inherent to quality? In what different ways are food quality distinctions articulated with social, symbolic or cultural capital as compared to these other domains? Food manners and concert-going have both similarities and differences in the reproduction of distinction. Or, instead of these domains, should we be comparing food quality with quality of transport? In other words, what is it about food that involves particular articulations between the aesthetic and the utilitarian? Are food quality crises (e.g. obesity) similar to crises in road congestion or death-rates on the road, or to crises in modernist architecture? We have seen identified in the various chapters safety crises, ethical crises, aesthetic crises, environmental crises, but why do these quality crises combine in the ways they do in food particularly? The roundabout is a busy one, and there could be many more questions yet to come.

The first broad avenue feeding the roundabout is the specific role of *biology and ecology* in food quality. In advanced economies, people live longer and grow significantly taller than they did, even over the relatively short span of a couple of centuries. Not all of this can be attributed to food, of course, or to quality as opposed to quantity. There are well-established epidemiologies of food habits and a variety of human diseases. But toxicity, nutritional value, the physiology of taste, digestive processes – all register an impact on food quality. Hearing certain music can harm (cause hearing damage) or be aesthetically truly painful, but not poison the listener. So the theoretical questions generated by this first avenue concern the *interaction* between biological processes and socio-economic and cultural processes of qualification of food. In terms of the physiology of taste, it is true, different cultures educate people to be pleasured or disgusted by the same food, but they do so by and with the same biological sensual apparatus of taste, texture and smell. Excessive doses of arsenic and prions are fatal in any culture. Food allergies have biological symptoms. The role of the body in respect of food is different from its role in respect of music or of housing. Statements such as 'adult tasters of 6–n–propylthioracil (PROP) are more sensitive to bitter taste and fattiness in foods, and often show lower acceptance of foods that are high in these taste qualities' (Keller et al. 2002: 3) are becoming increasingly prominent in scientific journals, with significant advances in establishing genetic predispositions towards taste. Some of these studies have attempted to segment populations into 'supertasters', 'medium tasters' and 'non-tasters', according to the intensity with which each group is able to taste PROP, and have argued that there is a palpable genetic basis for such characterisation. This need not lead to a genetic reductionist view of taste. Rather, it suggests that the cultural and historical processes of qualification involve a particular relationship between organic matter and human physiology to make biologically good food, so that while there are enormous differences in the composition of diets, there is always a biological bottom line. So the question is how aesthetic or ethical dimensions, for example, are articulated with this biological bottom line to constitute the specificity of food quality.

That question, as raised by the chapters in this book, is most frequently posed in the negative, especially through the spectre of BSE, invoked variously as inevitable outcome of global industrial capitalist agriculture, the loss of connection between humans and nature, the lack of personal knowledge of the farmer and his organic cow Daisy, or the sinful treatment of animals as human fodder. But the spectre invoked rarely regards the outbreak of BSE on animal health and its consequent appearance as vCJD in humans as a biological process, related to the as yet relatively poorly understood nature of prions. The behaviour of prions in industrial fodder under certain treatment processes, their transference through reproduction or ingestion, and their subsequent behaviour in animal and human physiologies are what produced the epidemics. And prions are not a fabrication of industrialisation or globalisation. Nor do they belong, in terms of actor-network theory, to the same or an equivalent domain of actors. In that respect, foot-and-mouth, dioxin poisoning, Salmonella and E.coli poisoning are both biologically *and* socio-economically very different types of crisis. Although the 1918–19 influenza epidemic and the SARS outbreak may be characterised as, respectively, prototypically twentieth- and twenty-first-century diseases, no one suggests that mass urbanisation should be reversed or global travel suppressed, as if these were the *causes* of the diseases to which remedies had to be applied.[1] The question, therefore, is one of how biological factors interact and combine with socio-economic and cultural food causalities, rather than of explaining such a quality crisis in terms of one type of causality or another in either socio-reductionist or biological reductionist ways.

In a similar fashion, *ecology*, as the second carriageway of this avenue, generates distinctive questions about food quality, and again ecologies of food production and consumption are in interaction with socio-cultural differences, rather than reducible to them. Different ecologies clearly have a major impact on food provisioning systems, in terms of variety, aesthetic characteristics, nutritional value and content, in ways that need to be developed further than the perspectives offered by a 'grow local' or short supply chain approach. The available lexicon of ingredients for the construction of cuisines in semi-desert, sub-arctic, temperate sub-tropical or tropical ecologies is of considerable significance, and the cuisines are no more directly derivable from the lexicon than the ingredients are simply cultural constructs. But in listing these ecologies, a misleading emphasis may be drawn to suggest different cuisines in distinct natural environments, when, in most cases, including hunter–gatherer food provisioning systems, there is an intermediary nature between society and 'naturally occurring' nature, namely cultivated ecologies. Overwhelmingly, differences in food quality are derivatives of cultivated nature, and it is the diversity of cultivated ecologies that form the basis of interactions between environments and socio-economic and cultural processes. Wild almonds contain toxic levels of arsenic, and only as a result of long processes of hybridisation and cloning did almonds become safe to eat, a couple of millennia ago. Agricultural land and all food produce developed from it are both cultivated natural and socio-economic ecologies.

Whereas original local biodiversity in naturally occurring ecologies led to different trajectories of cultivation and consumption, for millennia, travel, trade and diffusion have resulted in the substantial restructuring of food and food quality, but only as a consequence of variation between different cultivated ecologies. Single, local ecology food, is a peculiarly twenty-first-century construct. Sugar, the potato, the tomato, maize and many other 'New World' foods transformed the range and scope of culinary expression, but in distinct and uneven ways in different European food provisioning and culinary systems (Mintz 1986; Zuckermann 1999; Harvey et al. 2003). The contrast in historical trajectories of the potato and the tomato in Europe, Ireland or Italy, France or England is evidence of the complexity of interactions between agricultures and food consumption. Transfers from one ecology to another involved both a cultivation and a consumption transformation, new agricultural processes and hybrids, as well as new cuisines and culinary hybrids. It is difficult to think of quality transformations in other domains that involve this kind of complex interaction with ecologies, and it is for this reason that ecology contributes to the specificities of food quality.

One of the key alterations in the relationship between cultivated ecologies and food provisioning and consumption, although prefigured by earlier developments, occurred with mass urbanisation. It is well known that industrial revolution was preceded and facilitated by agricultural revolution producing surpluses permitting population movement and a new qualitative structural separation of urban from rural society. The fundamental questions of global sustainability relate to this configuration of cultivated nature and socio-economies, where the ecosystem as a whole embraces both the urban conglomerations and diversely cultivated natures, within a periphery of non-cultivated natures (Green et al. 2003). This ecosystem is one in which the quality and sustainability of mass urban food has become the irreversibly dominant feature, and has generated issues of standardisation, aesthetics, nutrition, and hygiene that are quite specific to the quality of food. In this respect, it may be worth a brief contrast with mass urban architecture. Tower blocks replaced tenements and then were turned into detested monoliths of little boxes, a largely discarded (at least temporarily) quality standardisation. If deconcentration and the spread of housing into rural areas is clearly not an ecological solution, new forms of high-density housing quality for large urban populations are necessary, and in global terms will be increasingly so. That being the case, if there is to be an alternative to McDonaldisation (no close equivalent to tower blocks), then, likewise, there will have to be new forms of mass urban food quality. That is the quality, as well as eco-sustainability, challenge.

In order to progress, however, the second avenue, equally broad, of *history and culture* needs to be widened, and indeed has already unavoidably intruded into biological and ecological questions of the specificity of food quality. And, following the previous section, it may be remarked, first, that already there have been several major transformations of high-density urban food quality in many European and US food cultures. These transformations have been of the whole 'qualification process' from farm to fork, and passing through different intermediaries, with different ranges of interpreters and discursive frames, recasting the registers of quality.

With apologies for UK parochialism, the example of fish and chips represented a minor revolution in working-class food quality, and it went through several quality leaps; and in recent times it has witnessed further product and service differentiation, with new chains and outlets (Walton 1992). From becoming a major source of urban working-class takeaway meals for dual earner families in the period from the mid–late nineteenth century to the Second World War, quality (of cooking oils, vinegar, potatoes, fish), standardisation (price, portion size) and cooking processes were matters of great controversy. The 1907 Public Health Act attempted to control quality across several dimensions, describing fish and chips as 'an offensive trade', and legislative changes were made through to 1936. There were also many homilies about the quality of the food as undermining family cooking, encouraging laziness and debauchery – with the food being standard fare for 'falling out' time when the pubs shut. But there is little question that there has been an improvement in the quality of fish and chips, especially in the cooking oils used, partly as a result of increasing regulatory and market barriers to entry to unregulated and 'front-room' businesses. The story of the American hamburger, likewise, is one of major qualitative transformations and improvements through standardisation and quality competition from the emergence of the White Castle chain in the interwar period, squeezing out adulterated meat and establishing dedicated supply chains with traceability (Hogan 1997). This transformation represented most of all the emergence of a new form of food quality related to the newly mobile consumer: standardisation and reliability of quality across vast geographical spaces, so that a consumer could be assured of buying the same quality in Wichita or New York. These are just two examples of the need to look at historical transformation of quality in general, but also with respect particularly to mass urban food quality.

The second, and parallel, carriageway of this avenue is cuisine as a vehicle crucial to the articulation of food quality, its registers of evaluation, its raw materials and its process of provisioning. The meeting of the 'New' and 'Old' Worlds clearly was a major historical as well as ecological quality transformation, in both directions. But it also resulted in a major cuisine transformation, if one regards the European and Mediterranean cuisines prior to the tomato, the potato, maize, capsicum, chocolate, and many other now central components of many culinary vocabularies (Coe 1994; Santich 1995; Coe and Coe 1996). It has long been recognised that cuisines are 'good for thinking with' (Levi-Strauss 1970), but from the standpoint of an analysis of food quality, the key aspect of a cuisine is the construction of a repertoire of relationships between qualities, and hence a quality as an articulation of multiple evaluations and evaluative criteria. It is clearly important to go beyond an analysis of food quality in terms of separate items of an overall diet, tasting, production, and so on, to view cuisines as qualifying systems. Major national variations in these qualifying systems may underpin widely different conceptions of quality that might be missed by viewing, say, the quality of beef in a post-BSE food provisioning system. It has been argued that a major 'qualitative turn' occurred in post-Medieval Europe when control over excessive gluttony, or quantity, was transformed into control over quality, with the emergence of a bourgeois culture of gastronomy, and its strong and enduring contrasts as between France and England (Mennel 1985).

Cuisines as qualifying systems lead us easily into the third main avenue that opens out further questions concerning the specificities of food quality, namely *cooking* and *eating*. Many of the contributions to this volume considered quality as *purchased* quality, and the analysis of quality that came closest to eating was Teil and Hennion's account of the performativity of tasting. Allaire considered cooking tangentially in terms of the economist's view of a 'buy-in' as opposed to a 'cook' decision, whether to outsource cooking or to do it oneself in the home. However, any analysis of the qualification process for food that stops with the purchase of food misses a crucial specificity of food quality: the continuation of that process, to varying extents, by cooking and utilising skills available in the household as the main social institution of final food preparation. Indeed, cooking has been described as the 'first great revolution' of food (Fernandez-Armesto 2001). As an early example of the significance of cooking for quality, as distinct from quality as a property of a food ingredient, the Aztec practice of nixtamalisation (de-husking with lime and ash) transformed maize from a carbohydrate into a rich protein, so creating a food energy surplus that conferred comparative military advantage by enabling armies to march and fight with greater stamina (Coe 1994). Cooking thus changes not only physical quality, but the scales on which food may be evaluated and judged. Europeans adopted the food ingredient rather than the cooking technique, unaware of its virtues.

One can usefully question the relation between TV cookery programmes and actual domestic cooking, from none, where the function is pure entertainment, to significant, where the aim is primarily pedagogic. But, in both extremes these media-generated cultures of cooking, and then the social practices of cooking, take the quality of food beyond the act of purchase and beyond market provisioning systems into non-market areas of consumer routines and practices, the production and reproduction of cooking skills, and how these elaborate quality. In this area, the different and historically changing combinations in the *relations* between market and non-market processes of qualification become significant. It is clear that whatever separations or disconnections might exist between the consumer and the market's provision, there is a persistently significant social connection between domestic production and consumption. In questioning this quality aspect of food, contrasts might be drawn with music or architecture: the disappearance of families entertaining themselves by playing music and the growth of DIY and lifestyle domestic spaces.

This leads us to ponder the need to bring eating into the accounts of food quality. As a culminating phase of the process of qualification, the institution of the meal as a consumer practice, and its historical transformations and cultural differences, are clearly significant. The threat to commensality, moral homilies on 'grazing' or the TV dinner, are frequently presented as negative images in a qualitative evaluation of certain types of socially organised eating as constitutive of quality. Teil and Hennion note that the social context of tasting is part of the performativity of tasting for amateurs. In much more routine and generalised forms of practice, the different social organisation of eating, the structure of meals, the distinctions between the ceremonial and the everyday created by eating practices count among the many possible aspects to the process of food qualification to which eating contributes. The social organisation of food consumption is structurally different from other domains of consumption, and eating therefore forms a significant reason why food qualification differs from other qualification processes. One might say, inviting further derision from sociologists, that the eating of food matters.

The final avenue connects the 'roundabout of quality' to 'up-stream' economic processes concerning the *innovative* and *competitive* activities of firms. While the principal focus of this book has been to examine quality in the consumption sphere, several of the contributions have tacitly recognised links to commercial considerations. This avenue of commercial innovation and competition links the 'roundabout of quality' to the 'roundabout of provision'. Innovation in food qualities, emanating from the R&D and marketing departments of seed, agro-chemical, food-processing and retail firms, goes hand-in-hand with the competitive imperatives of market share and profit. In considering the discussion contained in this book, it is clear that innovation strategies can be directed towards both substantive and symbolic quality attributes. Some of this attention has focused on reducing the cost of the provision of food, potentially enhancing the relative position of those firms that have followed this route in a context of price competition. Considerable innovative effort has been directed towards increasing agricultural yields and enhancing the (cost-)efficiency of food processing. But this book has indicated that price is only one quality attribute and that, in reality, the importance of competition between goods of identical attributes over price has been greatly exaggerated in orthodox economics. A far more common tendency has been for innovative firms to strategically circumvent price competition in favour of product differentiation based on quality differentiation and this has involved the development of new technologies to achieve improvements in performance in one or more quality attributes. Indeed, particular quality attributes might be seen as heuristic devices for organising the direction of firms' innovation strategies. The increasing specialisation in particular quality domains has been accompanied by an increasing range of specialist economic agents and there are now firms that specialise in the provision of food additives, preservation technologies, distribution and logistical services, packaging and the preparation of ready-made meals representing a variety of the world's cuisines. Aesthetic and symbolic innovation are more likely to originate from the marketing departments of firms, drawing on the usual techniques of branding and advertising in persuading potential customers to purchase their food products. It is in this realm that the battle is fought, by firms, over which qualities are the more important and over the demonstration of superior performance for a given quality. Winning the rhetorical contest for quality has become a major strategic objective for many firms.

But this avenue is a two-way carriageway because consumers are also innovative and notoriously behave in ways that were not predicted by the firms selling to them. We have already discussed the importance of cooking and eating in establishing the importance of the social practices of qualification that occur beyond the point of purchase. It appears that the disjuncture between firms' expectations of what consumers do with products and the reality of what consumers do has become an increasingly important preoccupation among firms.

The rise in expenditure on market research by food-related companies during the twentieth century demonstrates the increasing pressure felt by competing firms to better understand the quality judgements made by consumers and the processes of qualification through which they arise. Initially, those efforts were directed mostly towards gathering intelligence to facilitate the marketing process, but increasingly similar techniques are being used to contribute to the development of new food products. In a striking cultural turnaround, ICI, the traditional smokestack chemicals firm, has reinvented itself as a provider of sensory experience. With foods as one major application area for their products, this change has brought about other significant shifts to the orientation of their innovation processes, with one key element now involving organised attempts to better understand how consumers make quality judgements on the basis of sensory experiences. With 400 different strawberry flavours, ICI regularly uses consumer trials to select which flavour product to use. To achieve this, consumer trials involve a combination of tasting exercises and focus group-style interviews, and the information generated is used in conjunction with genetic data regarding different predispositions to particular taste sensations. It would seem from this that ICI has gone some way towards learning the lessons of the amateur tasters as described by Teil and Hennion, by attempting to combine psychological, social, demographic, genetic and sensory approaches, while laying aside, for the sake of practical outcomes, any epistemic conflicts arising from the combination of those distinct approaches.

In reflecting on the varied dimensions of food quality and its specificity, it can be seen just how problematical the notion of quality is, but at the same time how questioning quality reinforces the obvious centrality of food in society, and brings to light the sometimes disruptive interactions between the biological, the ecological and the social. It is also clear that asking the quality question breaks down disciplinary boundaries, precisely because it asks us to look at the whole *process* of qualification, and hence the changing relationships between market and non-market spheres, the breakages, the linkages and the shifting boundaries between production and consumption. It involves the rhetoric and the social worlds of amateurs, intermediaries and experts of all sorts, prions and semiotics. Conflicts and power relations between different processes of qualification generate the contemporary controversies between alternative qualities. We hope that this collection of approaches to food quality provides insight to the breadth and depth of the contemporary food quality crisis, and why a food quality crisis is different.

Notes

1 Cholera, typhoid, and dyptheria, on the other hand, can be seen as directly related to quality of food, and, as water-borne diseases, can be addressed by ensuring clean water supply and good sewage systems.

References

Coe, S. (1994), *America's First Cuisines*, Austin, University of Texas Press.

Coe, S. D. and Coe, M. (1996), *The True History of Chocolate*, London, Thames & Hudson.

Fernandez-Armesto, F. (2001), *Food: A History*, London, Macmillan.

Green, K., Harvey, M. and McMeekin, A. (2003), 'Transformations in food consumption and production systems', *Journal of Environmental Policy & Planning*, 5(2), pp. 145–63.

Harvey, M., McMeekin, A., Randles, S., Southerton, D., Tether, B. and Warde, A. (2001), 'Between demand and consumption: a framework for research', CRIC Discussion Paper No. 40, Manchester, University of Manchester.

Harvey, M., Quilley, S. and Beynon, H. (2003), *Exploring the Tomato: Transformations of Nature, Economy and Society*, Cheltenham, Edward Elgar.

Hogan, D. G. (1997), *Selling 'em by the Sack: White Castle and the Creation of American Food*, New York, New York University Press.

Keller, K. L., Steinmann, L., Nurse, R. J. and Tepper, B. J. (2002), 'Genetic taste sensitivity to 6–n-propylthioracil influences food preference and reported intake in preschool children', *Appetite*, 38(1), pp. 3–12.

Lévi-Strauss, C. (1970), *Introduction to a Science of Mythology*, vol. 1: *The Raw and the Cooked*, London, Cape.

Mennell, S. (1985), *All Manners of Food: Eating and Taste in England and France from the Middle Ages to the Present*, Oxford, Blackwell.

Mintz, S. W. (1986), *Sweetness and Power: The Place of Sugar in Modern History*, London, Penguin.

Santich, B. (1995), *The Original Mediterranean Cuisine: Medieval Recipes for Today*, Kent Town, Australia, Wakefield Press.

Walton, J. K. (1992), *Fish and Chips and the British Working Class, 1870–1940*, Leicester, Leicester University Press.

Zuckerman, L. (1999), *The Potato*, London, Macmillan.

Index

abstraction principle of consumer demand, 42
accountability, 88, 150
accumulation principle of consumer demand, 42
actor-network theory, 10, 63, 82, 132, 201
advertising, 51–2, 115, 160, 196
Advertising Standards Authority, 118
aesthetic aspects of food, 62, 38–9, 45–7, 51, 56, 157–63, 170–2, 195, 198, 200
Agenda 2000, 86, 110–11, 120
Agreement on Agriculture (AoA), 110–11, 120, 125
Aïd el Adha, 101
Akerlof, A. G., 69, 73
alcohol consumption, 102–3
Alcoholics Anonymous, 55
alternative food sector, 157, 163, 170–2, 181–90
'amateur' food- and music-lovers, 8, 19–20, 25–35, 193–4, 205
American Soybean Association, 119
Anania, G., 73
animal welfare, 4, 116, 120, 136, 200–1
Appadurai, A., 86
Appelation Controle, 198
architecture, 202, 204
Atkins, P., 6
Australia, 124
Austrian economics, 76–8
autosuggestion, 42–3

Aztec civilisation, 21, 204

Balfour, Eve, 165–7
banana trade, 182–3
Barjolle, D., 73
Beck, U., 27, 161
Becker, G., 67–8
Becker, H., 34, 53–4
Benkheira, Mohammed, 102
Best, S., 160
biological processes, 200–1
Blair, Tony, 114, 119
Blake, Francis, 166
Boge, S., 159–60
Boltanski, Luc, 74, 184
Bordeaux region, 96
Bordeaux wines, 11, 73
Bourdieu, Pierre, 2, 21–2, 52–3, 103
Bowler, I., 6
boycotts, 184–5, 189
Bra, 163–4
branding, 134, 159–60, 198
Browne, A., 171
BSE, 3, 23, 56, 66, 81, 88, 99, 102, 108, 111, 115–21 *passim*, 130, 144–5, 148–9, 160, 167, 184, 195, 200–1
Burgess, A., 5
'Buying Nothing Day', 185–6
Byrne, David, 121, 123

Callon, Michel, 10, 15, 159
Capatti, Alberto, 165
cars, attributes of, 44, 67, 82

Carson, Rachel, 166–7
Centre for a New American Dream,
    186
certification processes, 74–5, 134,
    167–70
Chamberlin, E., 66–7
choices made by consumers, 10, 45,
    188
citizenship, 5–6
CJD, 167, 201
Clark, J., 112
Clarke, Eric, 166
Clifford, J., 27
Coca Cola, 44, 160
Codex Alimentarius, 102, 104
Cohen, L., 6
commodification, 23, 181
Common Agricultural Policy (CAP),
    64, 109–12, 114, 118–20, 124–5,
    143
community bartering, 187
Competition Commission (CC),
    145–50
conformism of consumers, 43
consumer attitudes, 4–6, 118
consumer culture, 176–8, 181, 196
consumer demand, principles of, 41–3
consumer technology, 44
Consumers' Association, 119
consumption theory, 6–7, 16–17,
    67–70, 78, 178–9; see also 'ordinary
    consumption'
conventions theory, 10, 15–17, 194,
    196, 198
cooking, 204
Co-op Italia, 182
cooperatives, development of, 149
correspondence principle of consumer
    demand, 42
Cosgel, M. M., 78–9
Countryside Agency, 167
Crang, P., 162
credence goods, 11, 70–6, 83–5
crises in food supply, 23, 64–6, 76, 88,
    99, 102, 108, 124, 145–8, 156, 158,
    160, 163, 171, 200
criteria of classification and judgement,
    10, 40, 182–3, 192–5
Csikzentmihalyi, M., 41

cuisine, transformations of, 203–4
cultural relativism, 38
Curry Commission, 108, 116, 118

Darby, M., 71
databases, use of, 85–6
Department for Environment, Food and
    Rural Affairs (DEFRA), 108–9, 111,
    116, 118–20, 125, 149
Department of Health (DH), 114–17
diet policy, 116–17, 122
dieting, 55
differentiation of food products, 21,
    62–7, 88, 135, 205
discourses on food, 180–5, 189–90
Ditton, R. B., 49
Douglas, Mary, 185, 187–8

'Eat Organic' campaign, 166–7
eating, social organisation of, 294–5
eating out, 63
E.coli, 114, 184, 201
ecology, 168, 200–2
economic theory, 10–12, 76–7
embedded consumption, 158, 162
Enough! magazine, 186, 188
entrepreneurs, 78–80, 83
environmental concerns, 4, 75, 119,
    135, 166, 170–1, 184–6
Erlebnissociety, 41, 44
ethical consumerism, 182–3, 189, 198,
    200
ethnomethodology, 7–8, 12, 25, 27,
    179–80
European Commission (EC), 4, 6, 13
European Fair Trade Association, 169
European Food Law Regulation, 123
European Food Safety Authority
    (EFSA), 108–9, 112–13, 120–5, 145
European Parliament, 121–2
European Union (EU), 86, 108–13,
    119–25, 139, 143, 197
evolutionary economics, 10, 76–7
experience goods, 70–1
expert knowledge, 71

Fair Trade (FT) movement, 16, 158–9,
    168–71, 181–3, 186–9
Faitrade Labelling Organisation, 169

Falk, Pasi, 41
fast food, 160, 164–5, 184
Fernandez-Armesto, F., 156, 204
fish and chips, 203
Food for Britain, 120
Food Chain Centre, 120
Food Safety Act (1990), 113
Food Standards Agency (FSA), 14,
    108–22, 125, 144–5, 151, 197
foodism, 69, 75
foot-and-mouth disease (FMD), 108,
    111, 130, 147, 149, 201
France, 31, 94–104, 122, 139, 143,
    151
Frankfurt school, 178
free-range products, 136
Frouws, J., 132

Galician veal, 73–4
Gans, H., 43
Garfinkel, Harold, 179–80
General Agreement on Tariffs and Trade
    (GATT), 110
genetically-modified organisms
    (GMOs), 64, 75, 86–7, 116, 119–21,
    136, 156, 182, 184, 195
Germany, 139, 143
globalisation, 3, 11, 16, 62–6 passim,
    73, 76, 81, 84, 87, 102, 160, 163,
    181–4, 187–8, 198
good manufacturing practice (GMP),
    113
Goodman, David, 63, 161
Gravitz, Aliza, 182
green consumption, 5, 64, 147, 166,
    182, 186–7

habitus, 22
halal meat, 12–13, 94–104, 195
Halkier, B., 161
Hassan, D., 74
Hatchuel, A., 84
Hayek, F., 77, 84
hazard analysis critical control point
    (HACCP) practices, 113
healthy eating, 183–4
Hennion, A., 51
hill and livestock compensation
    allowances, 147

Hirschman, A. O., 76
home authority principle, 114
homogeneity of consumption, 43

ICI, 206
identity networks, 86–7
IMPACT research programme, 132,
    138
'industrial' food production, 15–16,
    131, 156–66 passim, 171–2, 184
innovation, commercial, 205–6
Institute of Grocery Distribution, 120
institutionalist analysis, 111–12, 195
integrative capacity, 82–7
Ireland, 139, 143, 145
Islam, 94,–103 passim, 103
Italy, 139, 143, 163–4, 182, 184
Ithaca Hour system, 187

James, Phil, 114–16
Jones, A., 112

Karni, E., 71
Karpik, L., 64
Keller, K. L., 200
Kellner, D., 160
Kindleberger, C., 65
Klein, N., 160
Kraft, 199
Krebs, Sir John, 115–17, 119
Kroker, A., 160

labelling of food, 11, 14, 63, 70, 73–4,
    97, 103–4, 115, 123, 125, 134, 147,
    168–70, 186, 197
Labour Party, 114
Lancaster, K. J., 67–8, 72, 81
Langlois, R.N., 78–9
Lash, S., 62, 162
Lévi-Strauss, C., 203
Linux operating system, 50
Loureiro, M. L., 73

McCluskey, J. J., 73
'McDonaldisation', 164, 177, 184,
    202
McDonald's restaurants, 54, 160,
    162–3
McSharry reforms, 110

mad cow disease *see* BSE
Malaysia, 104
Marcus, G. E., 27
market research, 206
marketing of food products, 51–2, 56, 139, 160, 198; *see also* niche marketing
Matless, D., 166
maximum residue levels (MRLs), 113
Meacher, Michael, 119
Méadel, C., 51
Meat and Livestock Commission, 147–8
Merleau-Ponty, M., 24
Miele, M., 82
milk products, 39–40, 46, 57, 149
Miller, Daniel, 178–9, 181
Ministry of Agriculture, Fisheries and Food (MAFF), 108, 114–15, 117
Monier-Dilhan, S., 74
monopoly, 11, 66
morality of consumption, 189–90
multilevel governance, 109–11, 124–5
Murdoch, J., 82
music, appreciation of, 19, 28–35, 199–200, 204
Muslim communities, 94–104

needs, satisfaction of, 20–1, 41
Nelson, P., 70
Nelson, R. R., 83
Nestlé, 184, 189
Netherlands, the, 139, 143
networks *see* product networks
niche marketing, 157, 182, 197
Nike, 184
Nisticò, R., 73
Nonaka, I., 75
non-governmental organisations (NGOs), 13, 117, 188
Norway, 151
Nürnberg, 40
nutrition policy, 112–16, 120–2, 125

obesity, 4, 200
Office of Fair Trading, 145
Olympic Games, 50
Oneworld organisation, 188

'ordinary consumption', 162–3
organic farming and food, 64, 74–5, 86–8, 114–20 *passim*, 134–9 *passim*, 143, 150, 156, 161, 165–71, 182, 186
Orléan, A., 77
Oxfam, 169

Parasecoli, F., 157–8
Parsons, Talcott, 7
Pasqua, Charles, 97
path dependence, 14, 112
PDO labelling, 73–4, 139, 149
'personification' of food products, 160
PGI labelling, 73–4, 149
Ploeg, J. D. van der, 132
pork and pork products, 102–3
postmodern thought, 194
power relations, 15, 129–30, 195–8, 207
price of food, 145–8, 151
prions, 201
Probyn, E., 162
Prodi, Romano, 121
product networks, 10–12, 82–6
Proust, Marcel, 33
public attitudes to food, 3–4, 16–17, 108, 184
Public Health Act (1907), 203

qualification processes, 10–17, 62, 159, 163, 193, 197–206 *passim*
quality, concept of, 1–3, 10–12, 38, 57, 62, 157–9, 170–1, 192–3, 206
quality chains, 1, 3
quality definitions and conventions, 129–39, 144; *see also* standards of quality
'quality turn' in food studies, 63–5, 71, 88

Raynolds, L., 169
Reed, M., 166–7
reflexivity, 20, 24–7, 35, 161–3, 168, 171, 179, 193, 196–7
regulation of food supply, 13–14, 56–7, 64–5, 73, 113, 130, 149–50, 198
religious ideologies, 12–13, 94–5, 102–3

Renard, M. C., 169
reputation effects, 67–70, 76, 134
Retail Consortium, 151
retail margins, 148
Rice, R., 168
risk assessment and risk management,
    115–18, 122–4, 195–6
Ritzer, George, 160, 177–8
Rozin, Paul, 160
'rules of the game', 48, 50
Ruskin, John, 33

'Safe Meat' campaign, 167
safety of food, 3, 14, 108, 112–25,
    151, 195
salmonella, 108, 201
Santer, Jacques, 121
scarcity value, 197–8
Schlosser, Eric, 160, 184
Schulze, Gerhard, 9, 40–4, 50
Scottish beef, 198
search goods, 70
Searle, J. R., 65
segmentation of social worlds, 48–50
self-regulation by food suppliers,
    113
Simmel, Georg, 9, 38, 48, 52
Slater, D., 160, 177
Slow Food Movement, 16, 54–5, 158,
    163–5, 168, 170, 193
social movements, 55, 159, 163, 171,
    193–8 *passim*
social worlds theory, 9–10, 38–40,
    45–57, 196
sociological analysis, 31, 35, 197
Soil Association (SA), 16, 158,
    165–71
Sony, 87
sovereignty of consumers, 16, 186
Spain, 139, 143
sport, 32–3, 47, 50
standardisation of food, 156–60, 171,
    203
standards of quality, 65–6, 74–5, 88,
    114, 196–7
Starbucks, 169
Stigler, G., 66–8
Strauss, Anselm, 46–7, 49
subjectivity, 40–1

supply chains for food, 113, 119–24,
    169–71
  shortening of, 4, 14–15, 130–44,
    150–2
supply of products and services,
    principles of, 50–3
Sweden, 151
Sylvander, B., 73
symbolic interactionism, 9
symbolism of food consumption, 44,
    165, 176

taste, 2, 7–10, 19–20, 28–35, 38–9, 43,
    165, 192–3, 200
  as an activity, 24–5
  concept of, 20–4
technical change, 70; *see also* consumer
    technology
Thévenot, Laurent, 74, 76, 184
'thick description' of social processes,
    195
time allocation by individuals, 79
tourism, 53–4
trademarks, 85, 87
trust in food, 6, 14, 72, 117, 124, 132,
    158, 163, 170, 184, 189, 195

Unilever, 113
United Kingdom, 108–22, 124–5, 130,
    137, 139, 143–51 *passim*
United States, 5, 124, 199
Unruh, David R., 47–8, 54
Urry, J., 62, 82
Uruguay Round, 110

valuation of objects, 38–9
value-added, 138–9, 143, 198
variation principle of consumer
    demand, 42
vegetarianism, 186–7
'voice', 76

Wales, 15
Weber, Max, 45
Weight Watchers, 55
Welford, R., 183
Welsh Affairs Select Committee
    (WASC), 145, 147–8
Which? magazine, 182

White Castle chain, 203
wine, appreciation of, 28–35, 39,
    45–6
Winter, S. G., 83
Wolf, S., 84–5, 87

World Trade Organisation (WTO), 14,
    102, 111, 124, 143
Worldwatch Institute, 183–4

Young, W., 183

Lightning Source UK Ltd.
Milton Keynes UK
UKOW05f0115310813

216235UK00005B/111/P